Soldier-Artist of
the Great Reconnaissance

Soldier-Artist of the Great Reconnaissance

John C. Tidball and the 35th Parallel
Pacific Railroad Survey

Eugene C. Tidball

The University of Arizona Press
Tucson

The University of Arizona Press
© 2004 The Arizona Board of Regents
First printing
All rights reserved
Manufactured in the United States of America
09 08 07 06 05 04   6 5 4 3 2 1

Library of Congress Cataloging-in-Publication Data

Tidball, Eugene C., 1930–
Soldier-artist of the great reconnaissance : John C. Tidball and the 35th Parallel Pacific
Railroad Survey / Eugene C. Tidball.
p. cm.
Includes bibliographical references and index.
ISBN 0–8165–2253–7 (cloth : alk. paper)
1. Tidball, John C. (John Caldwell), 1825–1906. 2. Whipple, Amiel Weeks, 1817?–1863.
3. Southwest, New—Discovery and exploration. 4. Southwest, New—Description and
travel. 5. Overland journeys to the Pacific. 6. Indians of North America—Southwest,
New—History—19th century. 7. Surveying—Southwest, New—History—19th century.
8. Explorers—Southwest, New—Biography. 9. Soldiers—Southwest, New—Biography.
10. Artists—Southwest, New—Biography. I. Title.
F786.T53 2004
917.904′2′092—dc22   2004006005

A portion of this book was originally published in an earlier form in
the *Journal of Arizona History* 37 (Summer 1996).

To Ardie

Contents

Figures

Preface

One should write, Chekov said, so that the reader needs no explanation from the author. Yet it seems that we authors, especially those of us who write about history, find it necessary, in a preface or an introduction, to explicate the book that follows—to define the scope and boundaries of the subject to be examined.

The 35th parallel survey, led by Lieutenant Amiel Weeks Whipple, was one of five expeditions sent out to search for a Pacific railroad route. The results of the surveys were compiled in the *Reports of Explorations and Surveys to Ascertain the Most Practicable and Economical Route for a Railroad from the Mississippi River to the Pacific Ocean* (hereafter called *Pacific Railroad Reports*, or *Reports*), which were published between 1855 and 1861. The first published memoir of a participant in the expedition was Heinrich Balduin Möllhausen's *Diary of a Journey from the Mississippi to the Coasts of the Pacific*, a memoir written for publication shortly after the expedition concluded. It was not until 1941 that the first book-length study of the Whipple survey was written—Grant Foreman's *A Pathfinder in the Southwest*. Dr. Foreman's scholarly work consists of a reproduction of Whipple's "Itinerary"—a diurnal journal that was published in volume 3 of the *Pacific Railroad Reports*—with extensive annotations and a lengthy foreword. The only other account of the expedition available to Dr. Foreman was that of David S. Stanley, Whipple's quartermaster. Stanley's 271-page memoir was published in 1917; however, fewer than six pages are devoted to the Whipple survey.

Soon after Foreman's book was published, the Oklahoma Historical Society acquired the diary of Lieutenant David Sloane Stanley, Whipple's quartermaster; a few years later, the society added to its collection the papers of Lieutenant Whipple, including his personal journal. Sometime after that, the University of Arizona acquired one of Lieutenant John C. Tidball's diaries, covering the period from January 3 to February 22, 1854, along with Tidball's copy of volume 3 of the *Reports* in which he made marginal annotations. Meanwhile, a substantial body of journal literature on the Whipple expedition began to appear and has continued until the present.

All this material was available to Mary McDougall Gordon, whose annotated version of the journal of John P. Sherburne, another member of the expedition, was published in 1988, although Professor Gordon does not seem to have made use of Tidball's annotated copy of volume 3 of the *Reports*. Gordon's work *Through Indian Country to California*, the second book-length publication on the Whipple expedition, which is still in print, is a fine scholarly work; the annotations, introduction, afterword, and biographical appendix are packed with a bounty of useful information that I drew upon liberally for background. But Foreman's and Gordon's books, both annotated journals, necessarily suffer from the confining limitations of that genre; verbatim journals contain a lot of mundane, sometimes uninteresting information that the average reader would just as soon skip. Alternatively, the narrative form that I chose allows the interweaving of selected excerpts from the firsthand accounts of the diarists, along with comments reflecting the author's viewpoint, as well as material from secondary sources.

When I had nearly finished my biography of John Tidball,[1] I discovered in the Beinecke Rare Book and Manuscript Library at Yale University an unexploited manuscript written by him about 1890, describing his adventures with the Whipple expedition. I hurriedly extracted three short segments for use in the biography. That manuscript, entitled "Itinerary," except for those brief excerpts, appears here in print for the first time, and it is the only new firsthand account of the 35th parallel survey to be discovered in nearly thirty years. It provided the impetus for this, the first book-length narrative of the Whipple expedition, and forms the spine of this volume.

Tidball proved to be the most versatile member of the expedition. In addition to commanding a detachment of thirty soldiers that formed a crucial part of the survey's military escort, he contributed a written account of the expedition in the forms of both a contemporary diary and a memoir, and also made over a dozen sketches that appear in the published *Reports* as woodcuts or lithographs. He was not only a competent artist, he was also a fine writer; he had an eye for character and color and a sense of dramatic situation. His account of the journey is replete with keen descriptions of the terrain and the adventures and foibles of members of the party, and detailed accounts of the colorful Mojaves, the largest group of Indians encountered on the trip—all related in vigorous, tactile prose. Alone of all the diarists, journal keepers, and memorialists, Tidball gives us cameos of the major participants and brings to the story a richly ironic sense of humor. This memoir of the Whipple expedition, written many years after the fact when Tidball was a retired Civil War general, reveals him to be an acutely perceptive observer and humorous storyteller—in sharp contrast to the impatient and caustic young first lieutenant we meet on the pages of his contemporaneous diary. Although his memoir appears to be a first draft, he wrote fluidly and spontaneously with few emendations, suggesting that his thoughts emerged fully formed from his pen. His writing is free of cant and is the writing of a literate man, one who read widely and was curious about the people and things around him.

In the end, what makes this book significantly different from previous accounts of the Whipple expedition is the inclusion of nearly all the material from this newly discovered manuscript, giving us John Tidball's fresh, pungent observations and his analysis and insights, as well as new information on his artwork. The primary purpose of this book, then, is not to supply another iteration of the Whipple expedition—grand adventure though that was. This book tells the story of John Tidball's part in that adventure—how his artistic and literary contributions enriched and enhanced our understanding of what the survey party saw and thought as they crossed the continent to the Pacific shores.

Although the perilous topography encountered by the expedition is an integral part of their enormous effort, my interest lies less in the geography of the route than in the diverse personalities of the men who traversed it and the fascinating character of the Native Americans they encountered. Melding the written observations and thoughts of the various diarists, distilled from their journals and diaries, allows the reader to compare and contrast their characters and personalities. In addition to Tidball, there is Whipple, thoughtful and conscientious, whose innermost thoughts confided to his unpublished journal reveal a romantic, utopian, mystical dreamer; Sherburne, cheery, full of callow enthusiasm; Stanley, of morbid state of mind, suffering from melancholy and hypochondria; and Möllhausen, irrepressible and buoyant.

From these diverse sources, we are presented with an absorbing mosaic of human emotions as we follow this stalwart band of scientists and soldiers, urging their mules across the forbidding deserts and mountains of the mid–nineteenth-century Southwest. The first part of the journey was comparatively easy, but after passing Zuñi, about the time Tidball and his military escort joined the party, they broke all communications with the civilized world, and conditions quickly worsened. They were pointing toward a known destination, but the route was unknown, and in their quest—all day long astride their mules, and at night sleeping on the hard ground—these men struggled against the harsh climate and terrain. Fatigue, hunger, thirst, disease, the stinging mountain snow, and the broiling desert heat were all part of the daily routine. Every day they searched for water to sustain them, and for vegetation to nourish their precious mules; the men would turn aside to give their animals a nibble at any chance bunch grass among the rocks, and when water was scarce they would share it with them from their canteens. Every day they apprehensively scanned the horizon, knowing that each expedition that preceded them had encountered violence and injury at the hands of hostile Indians. Every day they looked for a way through the mountains—the seemingly endless serrated peaks that always blocked their way. And every day they searched for the elusive rivers whose very existence they had begun to doubt. In the end they succeeded. There were days of distress, doubt, and despair, but with measureless courage and stamina, one of the last great transcontinental expeditions attained its goal.

Acknowledgments

Before the manuscript went to the publisher, Ardith Sehulster, my wife, first reader and trusted critic, reviewed it and as always significantly improved it.

Patti Hartmann, acquiring editor for the University of Arizona Press, deftly maneuvered the manuscript through the early and sometimes uncertain stages; I greatly appreciate her patience and persistence. Along the way I was guided by the expert advice of Al Schroder, assistant managing editor of the University of Arizona Press, who was both helpful and supportive. Melanie Mallon, my meticulous and analytical copyeditor, deployed expertise and restraint in exactly the right proportions.

I am greatly indebted to my two friends from academia, history professor David Miller of Cameron University and history professor emeritus Andrew Wallace of Northern Arizona University, who read and critiqued my manuscript and patiently offered much useful advice. Andy has specialized in southwestern history for years and possesses an almost actuarial knowledge of events and terrain. In addition to thoroughly understanding the history and topography of the region, Dave has studied and written extensively about Balduin Möllhausen and was a great help as I tried to unravel the mystery of which artist drew what. Their collective depth of knowledge of nineteenth-century southwestern history greatly exceeds mine, and they both care deeply about the integrity of historical writing. It was clear to me that they wanted this book to be professional, accurate, and complete. If that turns out to be the case, as I believe it will, they deserve some of the credit; however good this book is judged to be, it is better because of their involvement.

The Arizona Historical Society is a great resource. Bruce Dinges, director of publications, with whom I have worked for many years, was helpful in identifying sources of information, and in many other ways. The AHS Photo Services Division made photocopies for use in this book of all of the illustrations in the *Pacific Railroad Reports* attributed to John Tidball; the AHS Archives is a congenial and efficient research group.

In the preface to this book, I acknowledge the importance of the published works devoted exclusively or primarily to the Whipple expedition. I employed a great many other publications in the writing of this book, but I want to give special recognition to two works by William H. Goetzmann: *Exploration and Empire* and *Army Exploration in the American West, 1803–1863*. Anyone dipping a toe into the vast pool of nineteenth-century western military history will find these magisterial and seminal works indispensable as a starting point; they provided me an essential framework and a context for the early chapters of my book.

Finally I acknowledge the invaluable assistance of those stalwart explorers and journal keepers, whose accounts I quoted so abundantly and paraphrased so liberally—and whose words were with me all the time I composed this book. For the record, I used modern spelling, abbreviation, and punctuation when required for clarity.

Soldier-Artist of
the Great Reconnaissance

Chapter 1

Glory Grabber or Reliable Wheelhorse?

The best-known expedition to explore the American West was led by two U.S. Army officers, Captain Meriwether Lewis and Lieutenant William Clark. Their renowned passage across the wide North American continent at the dawn of the nineteenth century was systematic, pursuant to an elaborate set of instructions fashioned by that master of scientific method Thomas Jefferson. They returned with maps of previously uncharted rivers and mountains, specimens of plants and animals unknown to easterners, anthropological data, daily logs of temperatures and weather, astronomical observations, and tabulations of longitude and latitude. The abundant information the expedition produced brought to a close three centuries of searching for the Northwest Passage and refocused attention on the continent itself. As Michael L. Tate observed, "From out of the towering accomplishments of this corps of discovery emerged a century-long tradition" of military and scientific exploration.

But for decades after this seminal journey, the western heart of the continent remained largely unknown, a mysterious land mass whose interior was only tentatively probed, and whose limits were only gradually defined by occasional travelers: fur traders, mountain men, and European sportsmen. To the extent that methodical inquiry was instigated, U.S. Army officers conducting infrequent expeditions over the next half century produced the few maps and relatively scant data describing this great expanse: Lieutenant Zebulon Pike in 1806, Major Stephen H. Long in 1819, Captain Benjamin Louis Eulalie Bonneville in 1832, and in a self-declared triumphant finale to the first half of the nineteenth century, Captain John C. Frémont, "The Pathfinder," in the 1840s.[1]

While the United States went to war with Mexico, western exploration continued, but when the war ended and the United States had gained a vast stretch of territory—taking about 50 percent of Mexico's land—incentives to explore this unfamiliar territory multiplied. The acquisition of a Pacific empire forced Americans to think about a Pacific railroad—a prerequisite to populating, developing, and defending their new western domain. Colonel John J. Abert of the U.S. Corps of Topographical Engineers sounded the alarm. "The consequences of such a road are immense. They probably involve the integrity of the Union. Unless some easy, cheap, and rapid means of communicating with these distant provinces be accomplished, there is danger, great danger, that they will not constitute parts of our Union." The discovery of gold in California added new voices to the national clamor for a transcontinental railroad. In 1849 and again in 1851, Abert urged a plan to construct first a wagon road, then a railroad, along the 32d parallel route, which would help police the Mexican border and at the same time link up with California. In the words of William H. Goetzmann, "It would run east from the Rio Grande below Santa Fe, across Texas and come to a great fork at Nacogdoches, where one branch of the road would continue on to Vicksburg, Savannah, Charleston, Wilmington, Norfolk and Washington. The other fork would slant north to Little Rock, St. Louis, Pittsburgh and New York. Thus, in Abert's view, it was to be a truly national road, a great compromise in which everyone, North and South, would get something."[2]

John C. Tidball was to become a part of this Great Reconnaissance. Along with many other graduates of the United States Military Academy at West Point, he would join the vast exploratory effort seeking a path for the transcontinental railroad. This assignment was typical of John Tidball's career—happenstance seemed to place him at the fore of momentous national events. Just as he was called to defend Harper's Ferry at the time of John Brown's attack, just as he was to position his battery of flying artillery on the White House grounds to protect President Lincoln at his inauguration, just as he found himself effectively in charge of the entire territory of Alaska a few years after it was purchased from Russia, he would find himself at the center of this great national endeavor, searching for a railroad route to the Pacific shores, not only as the commander of a military escort but as an artist and commentator. In addition to his unique artistic contributions to the final report, Tidball left us his contemporary reactions, recorded in his diary as the expedition progressed westward and then, written in a more reflective mood many years later, in his memoirs describing his experiences from the perspective of a retired general. These two writings together would comprise an entirely fresh and critical look at the personalities and accomplishments of the men who made up the 35th parallel survey party.

While the nation debated railroad routes, western exploration continued, and Abert acted to implement his plan. In response to urgent pleas of Congressional delegates from Arkansas and Texas, in the spring of 1849, Abert dispatched Lieutenant James Hervy Simpson of the topographical engineers, an 1832 West Point graduate, to join an expedition westward out of Fort Smith, Arkansas, bound for Santa Fe, led by Captain Randolph Barnes Marcy of the Fifth Infantry. The search for an iron trail was on. Marcy, a West Point classmate of Simpson's, was accompanied by two companies of the Fifth Infantry and one company of the First Dragoons. Marcy left on April 4, 1849, without Simpson, but the lieutenant caught up with him twenty-six miles outside Fort Smith. They crossed present-day Oklahoma and the Panhandle of Texas and rode into Santa Fe on June 28. "The route we traveled," wrote Marcy, "is 819½ miles; and for so long a distance, I have never passed over a country where wagons could move along with as much ease and facility, without the expenditure of any labor in making a road, as upon this route." Simpson was more conservative but deemed the route "practicable" for a railroad because of its freedom from snow; the level nature of the topography; the abundance of timber, coal, and building stone; and the fact that it ran parallel to but was never forced to cross the two great rivers of the region. It was the route Lieutenant Amiel Weeks Whipple would endeavor to follow four years later on the first leg of his expedition to the Pacific Coast.[3]

> After the arrival at Santa Fe of Captain Marcy and his force in 1849, Lieutenant Simpson was detached from it and assigned to another expedition commanded by Colonel J. M. Washington, who was ordered out from Santa Fe to operate against the still marauding Navajo Indians. This expedition of about 175 men departed from Santa Fe on August 16, 1849. They crossed the Rio Grande at Santo Domingo and pursued a northwest course to the Cañon de Chelly, thence almost south to Zuni, and from [there] east to Albuquerque on the course to be traveled four years later by Whipple.

Simpson, supplementing his own observations with information given him by the mountain man Richard Campbell, concluded that a good route existed from the Rio Grande due west past Zuñi and across the Colorado to California, although his exploration had not gone west of Zuñi.[4]

Simpson's suggestions for a road west of Zuñi were followed up in an expedition in 1851 under the command of Captain Lorenzo Sitgreaves of the topographical engineers. As Andrew Wallace wrote, "The government expected the officer, a member of the elite Corps of Topographical Engineers, to determine if a practical wagon road existed midway between the roundabout northern caravan route (popularly called the Old Spanish Trail, suitable only for pack animals) and the long southern road that lay within the Republic of Mexico south of the Gila River." Sitgreaves was to ascertain whether the Zuñi River afforded an approach to California and was also to estimate the navigability of the Big Colorado. The party included Lieutenant John G. Parke, also a topographical engineer; an experienced artist-cartographer, Richard Kern; a physician and amateur naturalist, Samuel W. Woodhouse; and Antoine Leroux, a well-known mountain man, as guide. "Starting on September 24 with poor mules, insufficient food, and a small escort, Sitgreaves' tattered party finally reached the Yuma Crossing of the Big Colorado ten weeks later, having traveled afoot the last thirteen days and buried two men on the trail."[5]

Sitgreaves was an 1832 graduate of West Point. Parke, much his junior, also graduated from West Point, where he and John Tidball had been friends; he graduated second in his class of 1849, a year after Tidball. Parke was to distinguish himself during the Civil War as commander of the IX Corps during the Petersburg and Appomattox campaigns, when Tidball would be his chief of artillery. In command of Sitgreaves's military escort was Brevet Major Henry Lane Kendrick, Company B, Second Artillery, an 1835 graduate of West Point, with thirty artillerymen mounted on mules. Kendrick, whom Tidball would refer to as "Old Dad" Kendrick, would be Tidball's company commander when he was transferred to Company B at Fort Defiance two years later.

The Sitgreaves party encountered violence and hardship. They were attacked by Hualapai—Leroux was wounded by a Hualapai arrow—and later by Yumas. Kendrick managed to get his men into a battle line, and after killing four of the attackers, including their leader, drove them off. One private was mortally wounded in that skirmish. By early November they began slaughtering the weakest mules for food, and by late November many of the soldiers had worn out their boot soles and were reduced to repairing their boots with rawhide from slaughtered mules. Professor Andrew Wallace wrote, "Their hunger was now extreme, and scurvy had set in among the weakest men." Despite these travails, the expedition accomplished little: Sitgreaves's report had "failed to describe the land he passed through in sufficient detail for a roadway to be evaluated." But lithographs made from Richard Kern's sketches were the first pictures printed of scenes west of Canyon de Chelly and of the Lower Colorado Valley, and Kern's map for a decade was the most accurate portrayal of the far Southwest. Sitgreaves's disappointingly brief report was not published until the summer of 1853 and was a pitiful return for so much hardship. It contained an itinerary, but the presentation was inexact and lacked detail, and it appeared too late to be of use to Whipple, who was to take to the field in the spring of 1853. Whipple did obtain a copy of Kern's map, and he would hire Leroux as his own guide, but unfortunately he was deprived of detailed information that Sitgreaves could have imparted.[6]

The stage was now set for the centerpiece of the Great Reconnaissance—the Pacific railroad surveys. The nation was acutely conscious, as President Franklin Pierce would declare in his message to Congress in 1853, that "the thirteen States have grown to be thirty-one, with relations reaching to Europe on the one side, and on the other to the distant realms of Asia." In William H. Goetzmann's words, "to southern political leaders the annexation of Texas and the Mexican cession had raised the possibility of a new era for the South"—a chance to expand as far as the Pacific. "Every commercially minded Southerner believed that the Southwest offered the only ice-free, mountain-free route for a railroad." As a consequence, the South always led in the race to start construction, and its "statesmen were the most aggressive in advancing their cause in Congress." Jefferson Davis was in a unique position to appreciate the value of the army surveys in the Southwest. He had served on the Senate Committee for Military Affairs for three years, and now, in 1853, as the nation was poised to select a transcontinental railroad route, he was secretary of war and could capitalize on the bias of the topographical engineers favoring a southern route. But Goetzmann believes that because of Davis's rigid mind, he was unable to appreciate the political realities of the time.[7]

The sharp division of congressional opinion rendered any agreement virtually impossible because, as Goetzmann wrote, "apart from the complicated issue of financing the railroad, the most divisive factor was the location of the line," with every city and town in the Mississippi valley a potential terminus. Since more than one road was considered financially unthinkable, "competition over railroad routes and termini was fervent and bitter. Not only was North pitted against South, but within each section, up and down the Mississippi Valley, local rivalries flourished." The survey finally mandated by Congress "promised to substitute the impartial judgment of science for the passions of the politicos and the promoters." Just as Jefferson had found it useful to rely on the scientific findings of Lewis and Clark to implement his western plans, federal policy-makers sought recourse in a scientific solution. Congress enacted a bill on March 3, 1853, handing to Secretary of War Jefferson Davis and the U.S. Army an impossible task: to submit within ten months a full report to Congress on *all* the practicable railroad routes across the trans–Mississippi West to the Pacific Ocean, grounded on a solid scientific and engineering examination of the terrain.[8]

Davis had his southern route picked out and had good reason to believe that a comparison of routes would favor his prejudices. Some congressmen may have been biased or naive enough to think the route most advantageous to their district or state would prevail. But it is just as likely that the underlying impetus to the grand Pacific railroad survey scheme was to stifle political debate, silence Congress, and by altogether taking the issue from the indecisive hands of the politicians, move this disruptive and insoluble hot potato off the national agenda—at least for the time being. Did this scattergun approach to resolving sectional and political animosity offer any reasonable opportunity for success—if success is defined as producing a single, indisputably superior transcontinental railroad route? It did not. In that narrow sense the surveys were doomed to failure. There was another definition of success, however, a larger goal that was at first little discussed. That was the underlying objective to advance knowledge by gathering scientific data on the vast expanse of land to be traversed, and artistically portraying the majestic wonders of the largely unknown American West. Thus, a verdict on the success or failure of the surveys would have to be judged on more than the resolution of a political problem—on more than the lone criterion of proving the superiority of a route for a railroad across the continent.

Secretary Davis drew up a plan establishing as many survey parties as there were feasible routes, and then he sent them all out simultaneously. But because of the magnitude of the assignment, the army could conduct only a series of general topographical reconnaissances aimed at determining the relative merits of the competing routes, rather than detailed right-of-way surveys. Financed by an initial appropriation of $150,000, four parties were ordered into the field to pursue the four routes that had dominated the congressional debate: a northern route through Washington Territory from St. Paul to Seattle; a central route beginning at Kansas City, extending to California through the central West; a route beginning at Fort Smith, Arkansas, following the 35th parallel to Los Angeles; and a southern route along the 32d parallel. For most of the work, Davis planned to use officers of the topographical engineers, "but instead of placing the surveys under Colonel Abert's authority, he established a separate Bureau of Explorations and Surveys, accountable to him and with his old friend Major [William H.] Emory as its commander."[9]

First to take the field was the northern party under Isaac I. Stevens, governor of the newly created Washington Territory. Stevens led the main contingent that marched west from St. Paul; on the western end of the route, Capt. George B. McClellan explored the Cascade Mountains. Stevens was the only civilian to lead a Pacific railroad survey, but his military credentials were impeccable. He graduated first in his class from the U.S. Military Academy in 1839. During the Mexican War, as an engineer on General Winfield Scott's staff, he was brevetted major for judgment and cool daring in several campaigns and had been wounded in the capture of Mexico City.[10]

The exploration for a central route between the 38th and 39th parallels was commanded by Lieutenant John W. Gunnison, who had graduated second in his West Point class of 1837 and had accompanied Captain Howard Stansbury on the expedition to the Great Salt Lake in 1850. While wintering in Salt Lake, he wrote a treatise on the Mormons, which was published in 1852. He was appointed to lead the central route expedition in May 1853; his chief assistant was Lieutenant E. G. Beckwith of the Third Artillery, an 1842 West Point graduate.[11]

The southernmost route was divided into two distinct surveys. Lieutenant John G. Parke, who was ordered to explore the 32d parallel route between the Pima villages and the Rio Grande, started from San Diego. Captain John Pope was to survey the eastern part of the 32d parallel route between the Rio Grande and Preston on the Red River. Parke, it will be recalled, was a topographical engineer who traveled as an assistant on the Sitgreaves expedition in 1851. Pope, who graduated from West Point in 1842, would, like Parke, become a Civil War general.[12]

At the head of the 35th parallel survey was Amiel Weeks Whipple, the army officer best qualified, both technically and temperamentally, to lead a major scientific expedition across the western half of the continent. Born in Massachusetts, he received an appointment to West Point in 1837. He graduated fifth in his class of 1841 and was assigned to the topographical engineers. In 1843 he married Eleanor Sherburne, who was connected with most of the old Portsmouth, New Hampshire, families. From 1844 to 1849 he was in charge of the instrumental work of the Northeastern Boundary Survey with Canada. In 1849 Whipple again found himself engaged in boundary survey work, but this time several thousand miles to the south, as a member of what historian Grant Foreman characterized as "the ill-starred Weller Boundary Commission." Whipple's involvement in the Mexican Boundary Survey is of interest here because while doing the commission's work, he attained maturity as a reliable and seasoned scientist and explorer; it is of subsidiary interest because of some rare, and probably unwarranted, criticism of Whipple left on the record by one of his fellow officers.[13]

"The survey of the boundary between the United States and Mexico was the first large-scale project undertaken by the Topographical Corps in the trans-Mississippi West." Its job was to implement the 1848 Treaty of Guadalupe Hidalgo between Mexico and the United States by establishing the international boundary between the two countries. The American Boundary Commission was a mixture of civilians and officers of the topographical engineers operating under orders of the secretary of state. President James K. Polk appointed John B. Weller, a former Democratic congressman from Ohio, to head the commission, and Andrew B. Gray to the post of surveyor. Brevet Major William Hemsley Emory was the senior military officer, assisted by topographical engineers Lieutenant Amiel Weeks Whipple and Lieutenant Edmund L. F. Hardcastle. The personnel of the commission consisted of thirty-nine men, plus an army escort of about 105 soldiers. By July 7, 1849, three field parties had begun survey operations. Gray was to survey the Port of San Diego; Whipple's job was to establish the exact point of confluence of the Gila and Colorado rivers; and Hardcastle, to explore the barren country between these two points and connect them. Disputes arose almost immediately.[14]

Amiel Weeks Whipple. This conscientious, competent officer, whom Tidball
described as "a lovable person," was the most qualified of all
the leaders of the Pacific railroad surveys.

Whipple's task was considered more difficult and extensive than those
of the other two. He and his men would travel the farthest distance from
the base camp in San Diego, crossing the desert through an area for the
most part unmapped and inhabited only by unpredictable Indian tribes.
Company A, First Dragoons, commanded by a twenty-eight-year-old
Tennessean, Cave Johnson Couts, was the military escort. Couts was a
West Pointer, graduating in 1843 with Ulysses Simpson Grant. En route
to the rivers, while encamped at Vallecito, the thermometer stood at 104
degrees, and, as Thomas L. Scharf observed, "tempers as well as temperatures rose." According to Couts's journal, Whipple curtly informed him

that only the official commission would receive public acknowledgment for operations conducted at the Colorado and Rio Gila, and that, should Indians or immigrants ask to whom credit for the job belonged, Couts was to designate Whipple and the commission, because what the public heard "was published to the world and from the world to the newspapers." In his journal, Couts made Whipple out to be a glory grabber, although this opinion is contrary to Whipple's reputation as a modest and dignified officer; he seems to have been, with this single exception, universally admired. Explorer and artist Balduin Möllhausen's description of him as a man with "special professional qualifications united [with] the advantage of particularly pleasing manners," who "inspired confidence in all who approached him," was typical. But from this point on, Couts continued to refer to Whipple in derogatory terms. Concluding his description of his dispute with Whipple, Couts remarked: "Washington City dandies with white kid gloves, etc., don't like roughing it any more than having to get up early in the morning, saying nothing of losing a night's sleep."[15]

In Whipple's personal journals, this incident is not mentioned, but we do find there early examples of his propensity to engage in flights of fanciful poetic descriptions of his surroundings. "The scenery here, by moonlight, was beautiful. The hills in the background, with angles sharp and sides perpendicular, were singular in the extreme. By the dim light it was hard to believe that they were not the ruins of ancient works of art— one had been a temple to the gods, another a regularly bastioned fort." When the party finally reached the Colorado, Whipple made a crossing but in the process drowned a mule, provoking this entry in Couts's journal. "Take him away from his books, and he is not worth a tinker's damn for anything under God's heaven. I now doubt his capacity for determining the position of the mouth of the Gila." Soon after, they encountered the Yumas. Whipple, the amateur ethnologist, was fascinated by the Indians, but Couts mistrusted them and wrote in his journal that in the event of hostilities between the Indians and immigrants, "God only knows what Whipple would do!" But to Couts's chagrin, Whipple had little fear of the Indians and continued to study them, describing their customs and patterns of social organization in his journal.[16]

What of this dragoon who so mercilessly disparaged Whipple? After Couts resigned from the army in 1851 and settled near San Diego, he earned a reputation as a violent man who did not hesitate to take the law into his own hands. One historian suggested "Couts' actions were sometimes the result of haste, anger, and the belief that he was always right," while another wrote that "Couts had an unfortunate propensity to commit acts of violence" caused by excessive drinking. Couts and Whipple clashed, probably due to their strikingly different personalities. Couts, the dragoon, evidently regarded the reserved engineer as prissy, if not effete. His opinion of Whipple, who went on to a most distinguished career, is not corroborated elsewhere; considering Couts's volatile personality, his pejorative remarks deserve to be peremptorily dismissed.[17]

Whipple successfully completed his assignment at the Colorado and left his camp there on December 1. On December 18, 1849, Weller was dismissed; the Whigs had been against the appointment from the beginning, and the new administration of President Zachary Taylor wanted him out. After Weller's dismissal, the American Boundary Commission was in effect disbanded; Whipple's work at the mouth of the Rio Gila proved to be one of the few significant accomplishments of the Weller-led commission. In the words of one writer, "Upon Whipple's departure from San Diego, he left behind an enviable record of achievement. He had demonstrated a high level of ability both as a surveyor and as an amateur diplomat. His reports on the Yuma Indian tribes and their language would be of value to ethnographers and scientists in later years."[18]

On May 4, 1850, President Zachary Taylor appointed a new boundary commissioner, John Russell Bartlett, a bibliophile and amateur ethnologist, but soon his commission also was enveloped in controversy. Lieutenant Colonel James Duncan Graham of the topographical engineers was appointed chief astronomer and head of the scientific corps, with Whipple as his assistant; Graham and A. B. Gray, the surveyor, disagreed with Bartlett on an agreement reached between Bartlett and the Mexicans. Graham and Gray also disagreed over who had the highest rank in the scientific corps. The squabbling continued, and late in 1851, Gray was dismissed and Major William H. Emory was appointed chief astronomer and surveyor, in effect succeeding both Gray and Graham. It was a commission, in the words of Mary McDougall Gordon, "in which wastefulness, political intrigue, and petty jealousies assumed almost comic proportions." Meanwhile, Whipple, described by Edward S. Wallace as "the reliable wheel horse," continued to make astronomical observations and surveyed the nearly two hundred miles of southern boundary of New Mexico, connecting the Rio Grande with the Gila.[19]

The squabbling that typified the Bartlett survey did not end when the survey ended. In late 1853, as Emory began preparing segments of a manuscript of the survey, he learned that Bartlett was planning a private publication of his version of the survey. Emory, who confided to a friend that he considered Bartlett a "putrid carcass," at first decided to shun the former commissioner but became infuriated in 1854 when he received a copy of Bartlett's published *Personal Narrative,* which criticized Emory's reconnaissance along the Gila River. Because he could vindicate himself only by public denials, which he was concerned would make him appear petty, he attempted to enlist the aid of his former subordinate Lieutenant Whipple. He asked Whipple to inform the press of the manner "in which Whipple's name has been used to throw discredit on my professional labors by this unprincipled plagiarist." The ever-judicious Whipple diplomatically counseled Emory that he believed a public reply would be a "useless tactic" on Emory's part; after his temper cooled, Emory realized the wisdom of Whipple's advice and let the matter drop.

In the words of historian Edward S. Wallace, "The one man who seemed to mind his own business was the quiet, industrious and capable Lieutenant Whipple, who remained on with Major Emory after all the others had left." Whipple's survey duties along the Mexican border continued until 1853, when he returned to the East. There his reputation for reliability, technical competence, and even-temperedness was rewarded by an appointment to head his own expedition—the 35th Parallel Pacific Railroad Survey. He learned of his new assignment in April 1853 and at once addressed the job of organizing and outfitting the expedition.[20]

Chapter 2

The Ultimate Destination Is India

By 1853, America was an internationalist and expansionist nation. As Allan Nevins wrote, "The republic which had seized the vast Southwest by a few swift and inexpensive victories, and had then found it filled with dazzling treasures, was intoxicated by its success. It felt the exhilaration of commercial prosperity, rapid growth in population, and boundless opportunities in the exploitation of natural wealth." America looked beyond internal development alone; it looked abroad to assert what the *New York Herald* called its title to "national glory, national greatness." Lewis Cass typified the exuberance of the still young nation when he reminded the Senate that men still lived who were alive when only "a narrow strip upon the sea-coast, thirteen remote and dependant colonies, and less than three millions of people, constituted what is now this vast Republic, stretching across the continent and extending almost from the Northern Tropic to the Arctic Circle."[1]

The national enthusiasm exhibited itself in an assertion of American rights, real or fancied, toward the isthmian area of Central America in the hope of constructing a canal; an abortive filibustering expedition aimed at the conquest of Cuba; and—hard to believe today—the "liberation" of Canada. It was manifest destiny running rampant. The railroad fever that was sweeping the country was but another manifestation of this boisterous era. The greatest economic fact of the fifties was the throwing up of a network of rails from the eastern seaboard into the upper Mississippi Valley; in early 1852 the United States had some 10,800 miles of railroad, and the head of the census bureau predicted that by the end of the fifties, the nation would possess at least 30,000 miles of finished track. He was right, for then it had 30,626.[2]

The drive for a Pacific railroad was fueled not only by the need to secure newly conquered territories, but also by the surge of westward settlement. When Whipple came to Washington in the spring of 1853, there was a hot debate in the Senate on the bill to organize the territory of Nebraska. Based on the Missouri Compromise, it assumed the exclusion of slavery, encountered fierce southern resistance, and then became embroiled in the rivalry between the Platte Valley railroad route through what is now Nebraska, and the Kansas Valley route through what is now Kansas. These debates would have intrigued Whipple, but he had a more immediate task—to ready an expedition to chart the course of a railroad to the distant Pacific—and the conscientious engineer did not allow his attention or energies to be diverted by transitory political arguments.[3]

At the time of his assignment to the 35th parallel survey, Lieutenant Amiel Whipple was thirty-six years old, "five feet ten inches tall with a slender but athletic build. His hair was brown and worn down almost over his collar in the style of the officers who served in the West." He was said to possess an active mind and was a keen observer of everything he saw. Like the well-trained West Pointer he was, he immediately started a journal in which to record the many events he knew would occur while fulfilling this important assignment; it would fill twenty-eight notebooks by the time the party reached California. Meticulous, opinionated, and, at times, expansive, he wrote poetic passages extolling the beauty of the sky and inserted philosophical commentaries fretting about the future of the Indians and other moral questions, but he was careful to see that none of this personal material found its way into the official, published reports.[4]

The first journal entry was a copy of a letter dated April 27, 1853, addressed to Colonel J. J. Abert, chief of the Corps of Topographical Engineers. "In compliance with instructions this day rec from Bvt. Maj. W. H. Emory I have the honor to report to you for duty. I shall endeavor to reach Washington on Saturday next to report in person." Emory's old friend Jefferson Davis, it will be recalled, had appointed Emory commander of a separate Office of Explorations and Surveys to supervise the Pacific railroad surveys. By this time Emory was well along in what was to be a long and distinguished career. He had graduated from West Point in 1831 at the age of twenty and served with distinction in the Mexican War, winning two brevets. By the time the Pacific railroad surveys were being organized, he had played an important part in all the topographical engineers' southwestern projects, including, as we have seen, the Weller and Bartlett Mexican Boundary survey. He was the ideal example of the soldier-scientist and a close friend of many of the leading scientists of the day. Whipple worked under him on both surveys and knew him well.[5]

Whipple arrived in Washington in late April and began organizing his expedition, including the formidable task of selecting personnel. While so engaged, his marching orders from the War Department arrived. Secretary Davis's travel instructions to Whipple, which comprised less than two pages but covered half a continent, directed him to proceed westward from the Mississippi River toward Rio del Norte. "The reconnaissance will continue," Davis ordered, "along the headwaters of the Canadian [River], cross the Rio Pecos, turn the mountains east of the Rio del Norte, and enter the valley of that river at some available point near Albuquerque."

> From thence westward [he continued], extensive explorations must determine the most practicable pass for a railway through the Sierra Madre, and the mountains west of the Zuñi and Moqui countries, to the Colorado. . . . From Walker's Pass it would be advisable to pursue the most direct and practicable line to the Pacific Ocean, which will probably lead to San Pedro, the port of Los Angeles, or San Diego. . . . Over such portions of the route as evidently afford no material obstacle to the construction of a railway, a rapid reconnaissance will suffice. This work, however, must be checked by numerous geographical points determined by astronomical observations. Through mountain passes greater accuracy will be necessary, in order to determine (roughly) the grades and curves to be adopted, and the probable expense of their construction.

Perhaps harkening back to Jefferson's exacting instructions to Lewis and Clark, the secretary instructed Whipple also to give attention to collateral branches of science—"the nature of the rocks and soils; the means of obtaining water upon arid plains—whether by tanks or artesian wells; the products of the country—animal, mineral and vegetable; its population and resources; its supply of timber and other materials for the construction of a railway; the location, character, habits, tradition, and language of the Indian tribes." Forty thousand dollars was made available to defray the expenses of the survey.[6]

To meet this demanding criteria, Whipple assembled an impressive contingent of natural scientists. Historian William H. Goetzmann wrote, "The role of theoretical science was to provide a backlog of basic knowledge concerning the resources of the new country and its potential for supporting a railroad with its accompanying population. Here, as never before, was a chance to compile a great scientific inventory on all levels and at the same time to make that data relevant to the national problem at hand. The opportunity for science to serve as the positive instrument of public policy had never been greater."[7]

Whipple's scholarly background, interest in astronomy, and professional experience with civilian technicians and engineers, as well as his connections with scientists at the Smithsonian Institution, informed his selection of scientific corps members. Because of his interest in Indian culture, "he appointed himself as the ethnologist for the railroad expedition. He consulted with Smithsonian experts and acquired the first volume of a history of Indian tribes by Henry Schoolcraft, regarded as the foremost authority on ethnology, a science then only in its infancy." He also obtained funds from George Manypenny, of the Office of Indian Affairs, to buy presents for Indians. "Whipple was conscious, he wrote to Manypenny, of the importance of 'lifting the veil which yet covers to a great extent the past & present history of this singular people,' who were melting away before 'the westward march of the Anglo Saxon race.' "[8]

Applications for membership in the company far exceeded requirements, and Whipple turned away many well-recommended aspirants. By the middle of May, he, in consultation with Smithsonian officials, completed the selection of the scientific corps. In one instance, however, Whipple may have been influenced by family loyalty, when he appointed his brother-in-law, John Sherburne, as a junior member of the scientific corps. Sherburne had good family connections, and several years earlier had no trouble getting into the U.S. Military Academy. On February 7, 1849, his congressman recommended him for admission, and less than a month later Sherburne acknowledged receipt of Secretary of War William Marcy's appointment. He did, however, have trouble staying at West Point; he was dismissed on January 31, 1853, because of "deficiency" in chemistry. In 1853 he was unemployed in Portsmouth, and Whipple was most likely under pressure from the Sherburne family to appoint his failed brother-in-law to a position with the survey. Of the other fourteen scientists and technicians comprising the scientific corps, only two were army officers—Whipple himself, who held the titles of chief engineer, surveyor, and astronomer, as well as ethnologist, and his second-in-command, the relatively inexperienced Lieutenant Joseph Christmas Ives, an 1852 West Point graduate who was assigned to the survey by the Office of Pacific Railroad Explorations and Surveys.[9]

The senior members of the civilian scientific corps were Dr. John M. Bigelow, Albert H. Campbell, Dr. C.B.R. Kennerly, H. Balduin Möllhausen, and Jules Marcou; the Smithsonian Institution chose all but Albert Campbell. Dr. Bigelow of Ohio, the expedition's surgeon and botanist, "had served with Whipple on the Mexican Boundary Commission, where he collected botanical specimens for the Smithsonian 'with zeal and enthusiasm.'" His absent-minded devotion to collecting would occasion several humorous anecdotes. "Albert Campbell, a Virginian and graduate of Brown University, was appointed the principal assistant engineer and surveyor. A civil engineer, Campbell may have been recommended by his mentor, Jefferson Davis. The physician and zoologist Dr. Caleb Kennerly, another Virginian, had collaborated with the Smithsonian for years and was a protégé of its assistant secretary, Spencer F. Baird."[10]

Another member of the party, Heinrich Balduin Möllhausen, was born on the Rhine near Bonn in 1825. Discouraged from attending a university, he served a year in the Prussian military service, and in the fall of 1849, sailed to America. After accompanying Duke Paul Wilhelm von Wurttemburg on several expeditions in the Midwest and on the Oregon Trail, he returned to Germany, where the aging scientist-geographer Alexander von Humboldt befriended him. Before long Möllhausen's sketches became known and appreciated by King Friedrich Wilhelm IV, and he was on his way back to America with a letter of recommendation from Humboldt. With the help of the Prussian ambassador Baron Leo Gerolt, he was appointed topographer and naturalist for Whipple's expedition. Möllhausen, not an academically trained naturalist, was nevertheless brought to the survey by the Smithsonian to help collect zoological specimens. In contrast to the novice Möllhausen was the experienced scientist Jules Marcou, a French geologist and mining engineer, Ecole Polytechnique graduate, and mineralogy professor at Sorbonne, who was probably the most distinguished member of the group and who would prove to be John Tidball's benefactor. Marcou emigrated to the United States in 1847, where he became a protégé of Professor Louis Agassiz at Harvard.[11]

Balduin Möllhausen. The German artist, whom Tidball described as "a brawny, hairy Teuton, full to overflowing with amiability and kindness to everyone," liked to pose for photos dressed as a frontiersman.

The remaining six men who made up the scientific corps were the junior assistants in the various "departments," as Whipple called them. He appointed Hugh Campbell of Texas, George G. Garner of Maryland, and Thomas Parke of Pennsylvania as assistant astronomers, and William White of Pennsylvania as a meteorological assistant. The assistant surveyors were N. Henry Hutton and Walter Jones, both from Washington, and most likely recommended by Albert Campbell. . . . Hugh Campbell, Garner and White had served as Whipple's valued assistants on the Mexican Boundary Commission. The others were making their first western journey.[12]

In the words of William H. Goetzmann, speaking of the 106 scientists assigned to the four Pacific railroad surveys, "Not since Napoleon had taken his company of savants into Egypt had the world seen such an assemblage of scientists and technicians marshaled under one banner." Unfortunately, as Lieutenant Whipple discovered, his elite scientific corps would not immediately be as well equipped as he would have liked; they were competing for instruments with a number of other scientific expeditions. He complained that "Commodore Perry had just gone on his mission to Japan; Captain Ringgold was completing his preparations to explore the North Pacific ocean; Dr. Kane was in readiness to recommence his search for the lost ship of Sir John Franklin; and Governor Stevens, in charge of a party to examine the northern route for a Pacific railroad, had secured the few instruments of the kind referred to which the others had left." Consequently, every portable transit, magnetometer, and barometer that could have been purchased or borrowed had been already appropriated, and Whipple had to wait until barometers were manufactured.[13]

The Office of Pacific Railroad Explorations and Surveys soon recruited nonscientific members of the party: Lieutenant David Sloan Stanley as quartermaster and Lieutenant John Marshall Jones as military escort commander. Stanley was fresh out of West Point, having graduated with Lieutenant Ives in 1852. At the time of his appointment, his regiment of dragoons was stationed at St. Louis; he left immediately for Cincinnati to purchase army rations. Stanley's proclivity for grousing surfaced early; in his memoirs he expressed regret for joining the expedition after only one day out. "Anyone who has served as quartermaster can appreciate the miseries of my first day's start . . . How I wish I had never started." Then he added the peculiar remark, "Lieutenant Whipple was a pious man and why he should start on a Sunday I could not imagine." Whipple was a pious man, although not as obsessed with religion as Stanley, and he did not let his observance of the Sabbath interrupt the relentless westward march of his expedition. Stanley's religiosity—he at times seemed overwhelmed with guilt and self-loathing—also became apparent soon after departure. He "did some swearing," he remembered, and lamented "his wickedness and hard words at the day's closing." He then prayed for "God's help that I may spend the next day more like a Christian."

Jones, a Virginian, was much senior to both Ives and Stanley, having graduated with Whipple in 1841; prior to his appointment, he had taught in the tactical department at West Point for seven years. He was stationed with the Seventh Infantry Regiment at Fort Gibson, in Indian Territory. With thirty soldiers mounted on mules, he would join the company near the time of departure.[14]

Easily the most important single member of the nonscientific contingent was the celebrated French-Canadian guide Antoine Leroux. His thorough knowledge of the country Whipple was about to explore, and the Indians who occupied it, would contribute greatly to whatever success the expedition achieved. He had lived in Taos for twenty-four years when army officers had engaged him during the Mexican War. A few years later he scouted for the army during several Indian campaigns, and in 1851, as we have seen, had served as a guide from Zuñi to the Colorado River and California for Captain Lorenzo Sitgreaves. The next year he helped John R. Bartlett, who was engaged in surveying the Mexican boundary, get through to New Mexico from San Diego. He then traveled with the Gunnison party for a few weeks in the fall of 1853 but left it at the present western boundary of Colorado to keep his engagement with Whipple a month before Indians killed Gunnison and several members of his party near Sevier Lake.[15]

As indispensable as Leroux was to the expedition, when Whipple and his men were wandering westward in search of Bill Williams Fork, and ultimately the Colorado, Whipple's loss of confidence in Leroux was so severe it amounted to distrust. Whatever the underlying causes or merits of Whipple's suspicion—perhaps a momentary failure on the part of the mountain man—Leroux was a peerless guide to the Southwest, who knew the Indians and the terrain like no other. And of the survey members, no one would describe Leroux—especially his genius in sniffing out water in the parched desert—except John Tidball, who employed his descriptive powers and humor to bring to life Leroux and his inimitable talents.

The entire expedition numbered 110 men, including the armed escort and some thirty herders, teamsters, drivers, packers, cooks, and orderlies. The wagon train consisted of thirteen wagons and two *carretellas* that had distance-measuring devices attached to the wheels. The *mulada,* or mule herd, numbered two hundred forty mules. According to Conrad, "The men were armed with muzzle loading 'Mississippi rifles,' Sharps carbines, and Colt six shooting pistols." The so-called .54 caliber Mississippi rifle was a Model 1841 Harper's Ferry manufacture and used a primer cap. The Sharps carbine was approximately the same caliber but was a breechloader. The expedition was well armed, although the only repeating weapons were the Colt pistols.[16]

In his May 13, 1853, instructions, Secretary Davis ordered Whipple to "immediately detail an officer, with a small party, to proceed directly to Albuquerque, in New Mexico, in order to make in that place a cardinal astronomical point in the survey, and to hasten preparations for the necessary explorations in the mountainous regions of New Mexico before the approach of winter." Less than three weeks later, Whipple dispatched Lieutenant Ives, Dr. Kennerly, and Hugh Campbell to San Antonio, Texas. From there Ives was to proceed under military escort to Albuquerque via Magoffinsville, near El Paso, where he was to collect much-needed scientific instruments borrowed from the United States and Mexico Boundary Commission. "Whipple ordered them to conduct scientific observations and collect specimens of plant life as well as Indian artifacts and vocabularies." Ives was also to survey the Albuquerque area and choose a suitable railroad crossing of the Rio Grande.[17]

Although Secretary Davis "had instructed Whipple to assemble at some spot on the Mississippi River, by May 30 the commander reached the conclusion that Fort Smith, Arkansas was the logical place for departure. Located near the 35th parallel, it was both a military post and a fair-sized town able to furnish the additional laborers and supplies needed for the expedition." Upon arrival on July 2, Whipple "put his staff to work surveying the Poteau River for a suitable crossing, testing the instruments, training rodmen and chain bearers for the surveying party, conducting scientific observations, and exploring a nearby mountain. He hired teamsters, herders, cooks and servants," and bought 240 mules and a huge flock of sheep for the commissary.[18]

Railroad fever had taken hold of the people of Arkansas, and the enactment by the Arkansas legislature of a measure encouraging the construction of the Arkansas Central Railroad aroused much enthusiasm. In this, Fort Smith was like many other towns within reach of a railroad connection. As Goetzmann wrote, "Every city, town and crossroads hamlet in the entire Mississippi Valley was a potential eastern terminus—an emporium of transcontinental trade, or a port on the vast inland sea of Western commerce whose ultimate destination, as Senator Thomas Hart Benton never tired of saying, was 'India.'" Möllhausen, in his typically breezy style, goes on to describe the railroad fever that had pervaded Fort Smith, and how the inhabitants thought that locomotives from this point would

> hereafter rush fearlessly through the territories of hostile Indians, establish a connection between the two oceans, and bring the gold mines of California within easy reach. For a long time this matter of the construction of a railroad had been a favorite subject of conversation, as well as of more serious debate, in all the western settlements; no one of the numerous little towns had neglected to furnish, in their newspapers, the most exhaustive proofs that the line must absolutely run through their district if the advantages of good coal, excellent timber, and an admirable supply of water were not to be neglected.[19]

It would be easy to dismiss Möllhausen, or at least not take him too seriously, because of his florid writing style, his propensity to dramatically pose in outrageously exaggerated mountain man costumes, and his flashy career as a fiction writer. But he was in fact an experienced frontiersman, who had earned his spurs by undergoing a series of extraordinary experiences. His first visit to the plains was in 1851 in the company of Duke Paul von Wurttemburg, a widely traveled scientist. Duke Paul preferred that his traveling companion be a mountain man but against his better judgement accepted the twenty-six-year-old Möllhausen for the job. Their return journey from Fort Laramie to St. Louis was punctuated by what Professor David Miller described as a "series of adventures and accidents"; their encounters with Plains Indians "were at times unpleasant and annoying, at other times dangerous." In a driving rain in late October, "Möllhausen veered off course in mid-stream and the wagon plunged into quicksand. The wagon stuck fast. The duke, refusing to leave his valuable collections, spent the remainder of the night in his wagon" in the middle of the south fork of the Platte while Möllhausen camped on the opposite bank, wrapping himself in a leather teepee. As the Germans continued their journey, an Indian stole Möllhausen's bowie knife and took it back to his camp. The duke insisted that his young assistant demand the return of his knife. Möllhausen recalled that his scalp seemed to him somewhat more valuable than the knife, but nevertheless, he rode into the Indian camp, demanded his knife, and was utterly surprised when it was returned. "However, while he was victoriously riding out of the camp, the Indian shot the Prussian's cap from his head. Yet Möllhausen was philosophical: 'A miss is a miss, whether by an inch or a mile,' I thought to myself as I pulled up my horse . . . picked up my cap, swung back into the saddle, and greeting the Indian for a final time, rode away." Now, signing up with Whipple, Möllhausen was ready for more excitement.[20]

With the authorization by Congress of the Pacific railroad survey west from Fort Smith, there was great rejoicing in the town, and during the party's nearly two weeks there, the townspeople lavishly entertained the men with balls and parties. But Whipple was anxious to begin the journey, although he had received no word of the arrival of William White with the supplies, wagons, and tents. On July 11, he was informed that White had difficulties with river transportation and had only reached Louisville. Resolved to move forward without further delay, he borrowed wagons and tents at the fort and left Lieutenant Stanley and the military escort at Fort Smith until White's arrival. He crossed the Poteau River on July 15, 1853.[21]

As Whipple assembled his expedition, yet another West Pointer, who would join the party seven months later, was preoccupied with an unrelated event. On May 27, 1853, twenty-eight-year-old First Lieutenant John C. Tidball married Mary Hunt Davis of Newport, Rhode Island. Tidball's unit, Company M, U.S. Second Artillery, was stationed at Fort Moultrie, South Carolina; the June 1853 regimental records there contain an unmilitary-like entry noting Tidball's departure for his wedding: "Left Co. M April 29. Not heard from since."

John C. Tidball was born in western Virginia, but his parents took him to Ohio when he was an infant. His parents were strict Presbyterians, and he recounts vividly in his unpublished memoirs a flogging he received at the age of six or seven from a church member for picking berries on Sunday. Historian James L. Morrison Jr. believes that his strict upbringing "created the taciturnity, the sternness, and the austerity which sometimes unnerved his subordinates in later years and which successfully camouflaged a lively sense of humor from all but his most intimate associates. However, the same experience also produced the flinty integrity and the unswerving devotion to duty which were equally Tidball's hallmarks as a soldier."[22]

He graduated eleventh in the class of 1848, and selected the Artillery Corps as his branch of service. He wrote in his memoirs that on his way home to Ohio on postgraduation leave, he went by way of Washington because he wanted to "interview the President upon a matter that was giving my class no little concern." This apparently naive statement is surprising enough, but more surprising is the fact that he did just what he declared as his intention. His concern was the announced policy of the War Department to fill vacancies for commissioned officers by the appointment of civilians ahead of West Pointers. "As it turned out," Tidball said of his graduating class, "I was the only one bold enough or fool enough, to move in the matter." He arranged to accompany a friend on an evening social call at the White House, where he stepped up and informed President Polk of the "great injustice" of this policy. According to Tidball, the chief executive responded imperiously: "Young gentleman, the Executive commits no acts of injustice; his official acts are guided by the best lights of his conscience, and his motives are pure." When the young subaltern pressed his argument, the president abruptly terminated the interview. This astonishing picture of a brash, newly commissioned second lieutenant, standing toe-to-toe with the president—"dignified to chilliness," which was the way Tidball described him—for the purpose of impertinently challenging the executive's policies, is so far out of the present realm of experience as to be unimaginable. He could be admired for boldness or damned for brashness, but it is an early example of the audacity that typified Tidball's entire career; never irresolute when duty called him to press forward, no matter how formidable the odds.

Following his unsuccessful petition to the president, he departed Washington for Fort Brown, Texas, and later was transferred to Fort Adams, Rhode Island. Then, after serving at two Georgia posts—Oglethorpe Barracks in Savannah and the Augusta Arsenal—he was sent to Florida when the Seminole War again flared up in 1849. Then, he was stationed at Castle Pinckney and Fort Moultrie, South Carolina, for nearly three years before ordered to New Mexico.[23]

Tidball had met Mary Hunt Davis while stationed at Fort Adams near

Newport in 1849. They had corresponded steadily, and he spent two months visiting her while on leave from Fort Moultrie in 1851. Friendship gradually glided into love, and love into an engagement. There was, however, a thick cloud of uncertainty hanging over them. As a second lieutenant of artillery, he earned only sixty-five dollars per month—barely sufficient for his own support, with poor prospects for promotion. "She had nothing, and although I would have cheerfully shared with her my small pittance, I was unwilling to take her from a home where she enjoyed comfort and plenty to follow me through the various inconveniences that a subaltern's wife must be subjected to." The thought of immediate marriage was set aside, and they parted "sorrowfully though hopefully." John returned alone to Fort Moultrie.[24]

Then he was promoted to first lieutenant on March 31, 1853, and ordered to join his company at Fort Defiance, New Mexico. This order, as Tidball put it in regard to his and Mary's relationship, "gave our expectations a new aspect." He had to go almost immediately, and there was not time to make arrangements for taking her upon so long a journey, even if he "had possessed the means of procuring the necessary outfit for crossing the plains." In other words, he did not have enough money to buy a wagon, team, and the other paraphernalia for the trip. John arranged to meet Mary in New Orleans, where they discussed their plans; she was not only willing but eager to accompany him to the wilds of New Mexico. But this would be impossible to do unless he could get his orders to depart immediately changed. He applied to the War Department to have his departure delayed until fall.

To their profound disappointment, the War Department refused his application. "This was the point upon which everything turned," Tidball later wrote, "and it had turned against our prospects." She was to proceed on to Newport, he to New Mexico, and then, should he not be able to come east permanently, he would apply for a leave of absence for a few months when they would be married. Each of the young lovers, however, was plagued with the same tearing concerns: the separation would be long with few opportunities of communication; they thought that without a marriage binding them together, they might never see each other again. As the moment approached for bidding farewell, Mary's grief overcame her, and her distress proved to John "how deeply her heart was involved," and he proposed that they be married in a few days; then she would proceed on to Newport and he to New Mexico. They were married in Philadelphia on Friday, May 27, 1853. "In our happiness we endeavored to forget that we had again to part on the following Monday, she to go Eastward and I to go Westward, trusting in a kind providence to bring us again together."[25]

So it was that First Lieutenant John Tidball's newly betrothed returned to Newport to reside with her uncle to await as "patiently as possible" his return from New Mexico. "My promotion to a first lieutenancy in 1853," he wrote, "carried me to 'Old Dad' Kendrick's Company B, 2d Arty., then stationed in New Mexico. Situated at Cañon Cito Barrito [Cañoncita Bonita] . . . it was then considered the most frontier post of the army and the one most difficult of access. It was in the country of the Navajos, whose stronghold was in the region of Cañon de Chelly." Brevet Major Kendrick, who subsequently became a professor at the military academy, was described by Tidball as "one of the most lovable characters—for character he was—that I ever met with. My journey across the plains to reach this remote region, although tedious, afforded me valuable experience and some pleasure."[26]

Fort Leavenworth was the starting point of trains for New Mexico and what is now the eastern part of Arizona. Tidball's party was a large one, consisting of some three hundred recruits for various posts in New Mexico, a hundred or so remount horses for dragoons, a supply and baggage train, and numerous ambulances, the private property of officers for the accommodation of themselves and families. There were quite a number of families, and a large number of officers, many of whom were returning from leave of absence for another tour of exile in that remote region. Among the officers Tidball mentioned were "General Garland (Col. 8th Inf.), going out to relieve Col. (afterward General) Sumner as commander of the Department of New Mexico" and "Col. Mansfield—afterwards General Mansfield, a Corps Commander killed at Antietam." In the party there was also a group of civil officers going out to organize a territorial government of New Mexico, headed by Governor David Meriwether. He was from Kentucky, Tidball noted, and had served out Henry Clay's unexpired term in the U.S. Senate.

In addition there were several territorial judges, secretaries, and Indian agents, along with a fair sprinkling of ladies in the party—wives and daughters of the officers. "Altogether the party was a very agreeable one, and so far as the tedious dreariness of the plains would permit, the journey was pleasant. The length of the days' travel depended, to a great degree, upon distance between water. Upon an average it was about sixteen miles, including one day of rest during the week." It required about fifty days to reach Fort Union, the first post in New Mexico, and about twenty more, including a few days' stop at Santa Fe and Albuquerque, to reach Fort Defiance—in all, seventy days. At Fort Union, Santa Fe, and Albuquerque, various parts of the military outfit either halted or branched off to other posts. The civil outfit stopped at the capital—Santa Fe. "Up to this time N. Mexico had been under military government. . . . These were the days of the Empire for N. Mexico, and the army swayed things with a rollicking hand." Tidball finally arrived at Ft. Defiance where the post records noted: "Joined Company 8/28—acting post adjutant."[27]

Meanwhile Whipple and his abbreviated party had been driving westward for more than a month, but it had not been a propitious start. On the first day, July 15, one of the carretellas broke down, and they proceeded on foot.

Their troubles worsened when a storm came up, with thunder and lightning and a flood of rain. As the "last glimmering of twilight faded away," Whipple recorded in the *Reports*, they reached an Indian farmhouse where camp was to have been pitched and found that the wagon master had taken it two and a half miles farther. "Resuming our march," Whipple continued, "the darkness, except when relieved by vivid forks of lightning, was so intense beneath the dense foliage of trees that twined their arched branches overhead, that we were obliged at every turn to wait for the next flash to guide us. Through mud and pools of water we actually waded up to our thighs." On reaching camp, Whipple found that no tents had been pitched, and some of the party had taken shelter from "the pitiless storm" in a nearby house. Möllhausen described the first day's march as "somewhat dolorous." They were not yet organized, and the night found them ill prepared. Some of them took refuge from the storm under the wagons and others under shrubs. Whipple, making a disciplinary example early on, fired the wagon master for disobedience to orders.[28]

Chapter 3

Across the Ocean Prairie

"We enter upon the country ceded to the Choctaw nation," Whipple wrote as he continued west from Fort Smith, "where no white man can in his own right acquire a land-title or residence without permission of the Indians and their agents." It was July 16, and for the next three weeks the expedition would be traveling through Indian Territory, following the Canadian River, and adhering closely to the tracks left by the Marcy-Simpson expedition of four years earlier. But Whipple was not merely exploring. This was a scientific excursion to determine the engineering feasibility of a railroad; every day survey lines were run, meteorological and astronomical observations were dutifully recorded, and biological and geological specimens were collected. Those weeks when the party rolled through present-day Oklahoma are chiefly interesting for intercourse with the Indians, who were mostly "civilized" and peaceful, but as the western reaches of the Indian Territory were approached, became unfriendly and threatening.[1]

On July 19 the party reached Scullyville, a village consisting of about thirty houses and the seat of the Choctaw agency, where it camped for a week awaiting the military escort and the stores to be brought by Mr. White. Möllhausen found Scullyville a lively place, especially since a council of Choctaw chiefs was being held at the same time the party set up camp there. "Men and women all appeared in their best clothes," he observed, "which, though cut in European fashion, exhibited glaring contrasts of colours and many fantastic and most untasteful decorations. The camp was the great point of attraction, and as I had set up a kind of studio in my tent, many of the Indians came crowding that way, evidently speculating on the chance of having their portraits taken in their splendid full dress." In an entry in the official report, Whipple described a less attractive side to some of the Choctaws he encountered, who said they had been to Little Rock to draw their annuities and were on their return to their homes in Mississippi. If this were true, Whipple thought, it would appear that some imposition had been practiced on the government. "They had certainly obtained money somewhere, which was fast finding its way to the whiskey shops. They were a merry set, decked out with ornaments such as the half-civilized admire; the most popular being a tall beaver hat, with wide silver band. Several were in an advanced state of intoxication." The effect of alcohol was not to make them quarrelsome, but to put them in good humor. The next morning "one pleasant looking fellow" complained that while he had been asleep in the street, his pockets had been picked, and his money stolen. But he added that it served him right: "Indian a fool to get drunk."

But Whipple reported positively on Thompson McKinney, a Choctaw interpreter, who lived in a fine home, and whose family's pleasing manners attracted Whipple. McKinney's eldest son attended the Choctaw high school and studied algebra, geography, and history. "Neither bloodthirstiness, nor cruelty of any kind," reported Whipple, "is characteristic of this tribe. There is no new country upon the frontier where theft and robbery are less frequent—where human life is more sacred. Persons ride alone and unarmed without fear of molestation, from one end of the Choctaw nation to the other."[2]

On July 26, Lieutenant Jones having arrived with his escort, camp was struck early in the morning. The next day the wagon train moved only five miles. The forests were difficult to penetrate, and the operations of the survey were many miles in the rear. Two other members of the party also made early entries in their diaries—David S. Stanley and John P. Sherburne each noted his sickness, the nature of the ailment not being specified in either case. The next day near a stream in a valley they found many Indian farmhouses, surrounded by patches of corn and gardens. The residents could not speak English and could impart little information. Whipple reported, "They were kind and civil, however, willing to share with us their scanty stores of food." The next day Mr. Campbell was sick "from fatigue and exposure" and, unable to ride his mule, was compelled to take a seat in the ambulance.[3]

On July 30 Whipple recorded that the survey thus far showed no great difficulty in selecting ground for a railway. Building materials such as timber and stone were found in abundance, and nearly on the spot where required. In order to speed up the work, he resolved to allow the survey to follow the general route of the wagons as a base of operations, and whenever the ground became unfavorable, "make explorations to the right or left, till the route by which the obstacles may be avoided can be reconnoitered and sketched."

On August 1 it was Marcou's turn to be sick. Whipple wrote that his health had for some time been delicate; he was quite ill and thinking of turning back. But the lusty Möllhausen was relishing every minute and related how in the late evening he sat on the bank of the San Bois Creek pulling out fish after fish, while the loud flapping of wings told of wild turkeys seeking roosting places for the night on limbs in the highest trees, and the call of the sentinel, as he walked his beat around the camp not far away, gave him a sense of security in the solitude.[4]

Whipple found a fine campsite on August 3, on a grassy prairie near a small creek, and decided to spend the day there while the astronomical and meteorological assistants carried out their computations and others explored twelve miles north to the Canadian River. Lieutenant Stanley found nothing pleasant in his environment. His diary reveals a curiously dyspeptic disposition for a young officer on the brink of a distinguished military career. It is peppered with dolorous complaints about his health and disposition, and characterized by an obsessively guilt-ridden religious despondency. During that week he wrote in his diary, "Bad humor and too high a sense of my own wickedness to even feel fit to open my bible. . . . OH! That God may forgive me the wickedness I have and am constantly guilty of on this expedition, owing to the constant crosses and consequent fits of bad temper I fall into. . . . Prayed to God to preserve me from the wickedness one is so much liable to commit from the state of humor produced by such trying journeys . . . the self reproach of having spent the Lord's day in perfect thoughtlessness."[5]

On August 9 they entered a Shawnee village and refreshed themselves with melons at a comfortable farmhouse. Whipple's ethnocentric observations, which were typical of the times, found the Indian men to be robust and intelligent, and the women, dressed in neat calico frocks with silver earrings and brooches of Shawnee manufacture, to be very attractive.

Some of the young girls were almost white, with regular and pretty features, by far the best looking of their race that we had ever seen. But an indication of the savage appears in the fact that the women perform the duties of the field as well as of the household. They break the soil, plant, gather the crops, and grind the corn. Most families, however, are provided with Negro or Mexican slaves. In such cases these relieve the mistress of the more laborious duties. The Shawnee men hunt deer and shoot turkeys, but are too lazy and too proud to work.[6]

Meriwether Lewis expressed identical sentiments a half century earlier when he wrote that Indian men "treat their women but with little rispect [sic], and compel them to perform every species of drudgery . . . the man does little else except attend his horses, hunt and fish." And Lieutenant John Mullan, with the Stevens expedition the previous year, thought that the Flatheads were a fine-looking, noble race of Indians, and the men athletic and exceedingly intelligent, but wrote, "The women are kept in the same state of wretched drudgery as the women of all other tribes of Indians; they pack and unpack the horses, pitch and strike the lodges, cook, carry wood, water, and, in fact, do everything but hunt." Presumably, Lewis, Mullan, and Whipple all intended to be fair and objective in their description of the Indians, but all were caught in the persistent trap of having to judge them by the standards of their own limited view of the world—in terms of white Christian culture, which elevated and idealized its females in a way American Indian culture did not. Although the societal standing of Native American women was different from the place of Indian men, they were not necessarily without stature. The workday of the Indian woman was long and hard, but she was not merely a drudge; the mother, in fact, dominated affairs of the home, and she exerted paramount authority over the children until they reached adolescence.[7]

Slavery flourished among the so-called "five civilized tribes" in the Indian Territory. Earlier, the party had camped near the house of Stephen Perry, a member of a numerous and prominent family of the Chickasaw Nation. "Upon his farm," Whipple recorded, "are several Negro slaves who seem to have the principal management of the estate, buying and selling, and as close at a bargain as if the profits were their own. They appear healthy and happy, the children especially so. No work is required of them till they arrive at the age of ten or twelve, and even then their duties are light." Then on August 11, at Shawneetown, an Indian surprised them by speaking Spanish to a young boy. Upon inquiry they found that the boy, who called himself Pablo, was a Mexican captive and

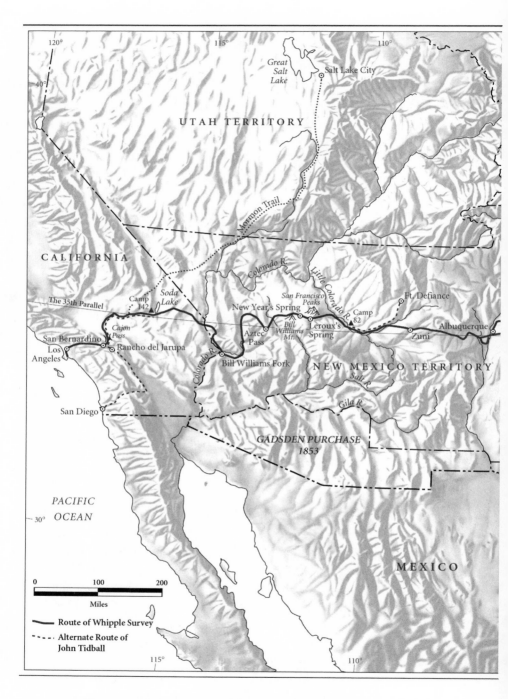

The route of the 35th Parallel Pacific Railroad Survey

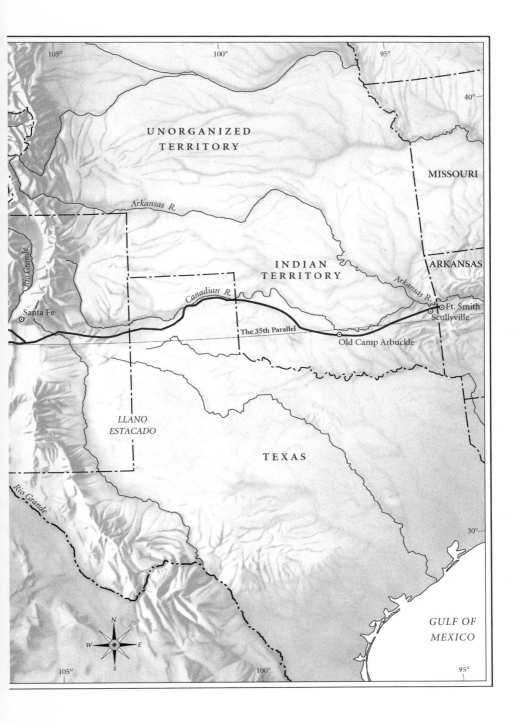

105° 100° 95°

40°

UNORGANIZED
TERRITORY

MISSOURI

Arkansas R.

INDIAN
TERRITORY

ARKANSAS

Rio Grande

Canadian R.

Arkansas R.

Santa Fe

Ft. Smith
Scullyville

The 35th Parallel

Old Camp Arbuckle

LLANO
ESTACADO

TEXAS

Rio Grande

30°

N
W   E
S

GULF OF
MEXICO

105° 100° 95°

slave, ten or twelve years old, who spoke Spanish. He said when he was very young Comanches stole him, and it had been three and a half years since he was purchased from them by an Indian trader and sold to his Shawnee master. "He seems quite happy in his present condition," Whipple said, but "would prefer to return to his parents. Another 'Spanish boy,' as they are called here, lives with Johnson, a Shawnee. Several are owned by Jesse Chisholm, the famous Cherokee guide. One of these captive boys is valued at two or three hundred dollars. Nearly all of the more wealthy Indians of this country—Shawnees, Creeks, Chickasaws, Choctaws, Cherokees and Delawares—possess either African or Mexican slaves." Whipple entered in his diary a comment that did not make it into the official report: "It is a singular state of things where almost universally the master appears to be in mental capacity inferior to his slave."[8]

In the vicinity of the trading post of Little River, they encountered several Quapaw Indians, and also two Creeks, one of whom Whipple thought had "face and features almost Grecian." They did not move camp for several days while they attempted to engage a guide. Stanley's disposition must have temporarily improved; while waiting he celebrated with Marcou the anniversary of the birth of Napoleon Bonaparte. Both Black Beaver, a Delaware chief, and Jesse Chisholm, "celebrated as a bold guide and good Indian interpreter," were approached about guiding the party, but both refused. Then a famed Shawnee hunter named Johnson agreed to accompany them, and on August 17 they reached the site of old Camp Arbuckle, which was occupied by about a hundred Delaware Indians, with Black Beaver, their chief.[9]

The next day Whipple recorded, "We have now traversed the whole extent of country occupied by the semi-civilized Indians of the Choctaw nation, and are upon the verge of the great western prairies, over which wild savages held almost undisputed sway." At this point their guide, Johnson, refused to continue the trip "for fear of savages," and they hoped to hire John Bushman, a Delaware guide of some celebrity, but he declined. They were all, Whipple wrote in his diary, "afraid of Indians on their return." Möllhausen described their dilemma: "John Bushman, with his little son and a beautiful squaw, paid us a visit in our camp; but it was only to declare how impossible it was for him at present to leave his land. Johnson, the Shawnee, too was now going back to his tribe; so that all that remained for us was to find our way for ourselves as we best might, from wood to wood and from water to water, through the desolate grassy wilderness already on fire in many places." Meanwhile, Whipple, as always, conscientiously compiled vocabularies of the language of local tribes—this time of the Comanche and Delaware—and interviewed Jesse Chisholm at length about Indian customs.[10]

"Jesse Chisholm," recorded Whipple, "is a Cherokee man of excellent sense and has traveled far among Mexicans, Americans and various tribes of Indians. He speaks—beside his native tongue—English, Spanish, Comanche, Creek, Kioway, Keechi and I believe Delaware, Shawnee, Chickasaw and Choctaw." Chisholm was born in Tennessee in 1805, the son of a Scottish trader and Cherokee mother; his family immigrated to a Cherokee community near Fort Smith in about 1816. Because of his language skills and knowledge of the region, he found work as a guide and interpreter for numerous military expeditions. Along with Black Beaver he worked for the 1834 expedition of General Henry Leavenworth and Colonel Henry Dodge. Whipple described his lengthy interview of Chisholm on Indian history, customs, and religion in his diary, but not in the official report. He concluded, mystically, "One is struck with this resemblance of many of these ceremonies & customs to the ancient Jewish rites. How unfortunate that there is no hand able to lift the dark veil and penetrate the cloud which envelops the origin of this race in unfathomable obscurity."[11]

August 20 was notable for the loss of fifty mules. Parties were immediately dispatched from camp to search in all directions. Stanley said he "rode hard all afternoon . . . up and down the Canadian a long way." The next night the beef cattle purchased from Chisholm escaped from the herders, and another day was required to secure them. Whipple was disgusted. "White men make indifferent herders. For taking care of mules, one Mexican is worth a half dozen of them." Three mules remained lost, but at least the party had an interpreter. One of the slaves Chisholm purchased from the Comanches was Vincente, who spoke the Comanche language perfectly.

Whipple said, "[H]e is a bright, active lad, and Chisholm is very fond of him; but on account of our need of an interpreter, he has kindly given him permission to join our party." On August 22, two Indians were discovered setting fire to the prairie; the fire soon threatened the camp, and the party was obliged to burn a wide space around the camp for protection. Whipple described its appearance as sublime. "Huge waves of flame, with a roaring sound like that of the ocean, were rolling over the rank grass, and rushing onward with fearful rapidity." Sherburne reported flames as high as ten feet—"a magnificent sight."[12]

They continued to pursue the trail of Captain Marcy, "which follows the almost inappreciable ridge that divides the waters of Red river from those of the Canadian." Whipple recorded that the results of the survey thus far were highly satisfactory—the grades being light, and timber and water abundant. Whipple was quite taken by the Mexican boy Vincente who, with his sister, was taken from Parras by the Comanches when he was a child; many of the inhabitants, including probably his parents, were murdered. For many years he was a slave among the Comanches, taking care of their horses and performing other services. Wandering about with them from place to place, he learned their language and the signs they employed in conversing with other tribes. Eventually, he was seen by Chisholm when on a trading expedition and purchased for goods valued two hundred dollars. His sister was married to a Comanche and was still living with the tribe against her will. "It is easy to see," Whipple thought, "that his character has been formed among the savages, for he displays in a marked degree the apparent indifference and obstinacy peculiar to the Indian race." Vincente proved his aptitude as an interpreter when a Huéco (Waco) Indian came into camp. He understood a few Comanche words, and with the aid of "expressive signs," Vincente conversed with him easily. Inevitably, before the Indian departed, Whipple obtained a Huéco vocabulary from him.[13]

Stanley also remarked on the appearance of the Huéco Indians. "Great excitement this afternoon caused by the appearance in our camp of the real wild Indian. Two Wacohs came in with no covering but a fold of deerskin about the loins. They are armed with bows of the bois d'arc and carry a large sheaf of arrows, tipped with stone, in quivers made of raw deer skin." Sherburne and Möllhausen described them differently—with buckskin leggings and a blue cloth wrapper around the waist, and that is the way Möllhausen drew them. Whipple later criticized Möllhausen's rendition: "They have high cheek bones, and a wild look, (which the artist has failed to represent)."

However wild their guests may have been, civilization prevailed in camp. Stanley reported that they "had an oyster supper given by Mr. Whipple as payment of a bet made . . . upon our last presidential election." In a letter Stanley further explained that the supper of canned oysters was made to settle a bet with one of the members of the party who had served with the Mexican Boundary Commission in 1852. Whipple had bet on the Whig candidate, Winfield Scott, who was defeated by Democrat Franklin Pierce. With these minor diversions, the party rolled onward through promising terrain. "Through country like that we have been traversing, there can be no difficulty in selecting a route for a railway. There is plenty of material for its construction. The soil of the valley is rich, and eminently adapted to agriculture, while the prairies afford abundant pasture for flocks and herds. Mills could be erected upon the streams, which seem to be unfailing." In his personal journal Whipple was less prosaic: "We have passed today the prettiest country in the world for a railroad." The rich land was also abundant with game. Sherburne observed one stream "full of large green turtle, fish called *gar*, buffalo & cat fish. On the banks were partridges & wild ducks. Two bears and several deer were seen today. . . . One of our mess shot an immense turkey, which served as two meals for eleven men."[14]

The next few days were uneventful until the party crossed into the Texas Panhandle, when Sherburne reported "one of the most exciting scenes occurred on the route today that we've yet had." A dozen shots were heard, and when Lieutenant Jones went to investigate, he thought he saw two horsemen in the distance. He took six mounted soldiers in pursuit at full gallop, but no Comanches were found. Whipple placed in the official report an entertaining account of what really happened, describing how Dr. Bigelow wandered far from the train in search of new species of plants and near the river encountered a rattlesnake of such remarkable size that he determined to secure it for a specimen. He obtained a club but, as the doctor approached, the coiled reptile leaped erect, nearly to the full height of a man, "his neck proudly curved, his head flattened with anger, and his protruding fangs swollen with deadly venom." It was evident to the doctor that, in western parlance, "he had waked the wrong passenger." There was a struggle and at length both became weary, "and a successful blow placed his snakeship *hors du combat.*"

Then the doctor fired eight shots in rapid succession, and supposing him to be in a desperate fight with Indians, a party galloped off to his rescue. Meanwhile, Stanley, who also thought "the Doctor was attacked by Indians," went galloping near the river and found that a member of the party had been firing at a buffalo and had wounded one that had come to bay in the river. "I immediately went in pursuit and, when within fifty yards, fired and rolled him over by a single shot." It was the first killed on the trip, and consequently, in Whipple's words, "a glorious achievement," although the glory achieved by gunning down a wounded animal at close range would seem to be dubious. Stanley admitted it was "an old bull and quite poor." They cut out the animal's tongue and left the carcass.[15]

Miles away at Fort Defiance, John Tidball was settling in to the routine of frontier garrison duty. In the "old army" this meant physical hardship, low pay, danger, and perhaps worst of all, ennui. Many officers felt that they were "buried in oblivion," and this was surely true to as great an extent at Tidball's remote post in New Mexico as it was at any other garrison in the country. One of the few diversions from the routine was sitting on the occasional court martial, and on September 6, Tidball was notified by the commanding officer of the Ninth Military District in Albuquerque that a general court martial was being assembled at Fort Defiance on the 20th "of which you have been appointed the Judge Advocate." Without knowing what lay ahead, he undoubtedly regarded this as a welcome change from what he expected to be a long, arduous, and boring confinement at his remote posting.[16]

On September 9, Whipple came upon a large Kiowa encampment, completely surprising its inhabitants. On one side of the stream was a "crowd of wild Indians," apparently in great excitement, and on the other, the survey party, each ignorant of the other. The Indians were evidently prepared for battle, decked out in their gayest attire, mounted on spirited horses, holding bows in their hands and arrows between their fingers. As Whipple advanced, Vincente placed a white handkerchief at the end of a ramrod and waved it as a signal. Upon sight of the banner the Indians set up a shout and rode rapidly to meet them. They called themselves Kái-ò-wàs and professed friendship. "They looked splendidly," Whipple thought, "as they rode from point to point; their horses prancing, and their gay silver trappings glittering in the sun. The old fellow who appeared to be the chief, or probably medicine man, was on foot and almost naked. He begged to ride in the carretela; and, by aid of Vincente, informed us that as friends we ought to encamp at the village and hold council with them."

They drove to the village and found a heterogeneous mass of old men, women, and children, as well as two Mexican traders. To their surprise, they also saw a blue-eyed three-year-old boy and found that his mother was a Mexican captive. She had been captured by the Comanches seven years ago and now wished to leave her hard masters and accompany the Americans, but she was watched and hardly dared to speak to them. Whipple wrote in his journal that "her Indian husband would not sell her and to take her by force would raise all the Comanches and Kiowas against us. Lt. Jones agrees with me, that it is not our mission to relieve these captives of whom there are several in every tribe of Indians and every party upon our route. I must content myself by making a representation of facts to our government."

A council was then had with the Indians, of whom Whipple had a low opinion. "A wilder-looking set can scarcely be imagined. Cunning, duplicity, and treachery, seemed stamped upon every lineament of their features." The Indians disdained the small presents offered to them, and at one point "the old chief seemed almost convulsed with anger. The placid expression of his countenance was changed to one of black malignity." After trying once more to secure release of the captives, in Sherburne's words, "It was resolved not to interfere with them but leave them to their fate." The Kiowas were fierce and formidable fighters, and one writer believed that only "the strength of Whipple's column caused the Indians to decide against attacking it." They departed from the Indian camp and crossed the Canadian, a quarter of a mile wide, two or three feet deep, and full of quicksand. "The difficulties encountered in this operation," Whipple reported, "nearly banished the Indians from our thoughts."[17]

Somewhere along the route at this time, Möllhausen made a sketch later turned into an etching, *Columns of Sandstone, South Bank of the Canadian River*, critiqued by a present-day writer: "This etching reflected once again his appreciation of the physical geography of the region, a perceptual slant inspired by Humboldt and promoted by Marcou. This faithful but lifeless illustration was included in . . . the *Report*."[18]

They continued up the valley of the Canadian at an average daily rate of fifteen to twenty miles. September 16 began with an unusual atmospheric phenomenon. In the cool predawn morning, as corps members scurried with preparations for an early start, the men suddenly observed a vast, glowing crown of bright light, as shafts of white divided the eastern sky. Whipple recorded, "an extraordinary refraction . . . of sufficient brightness to cast a shadow." His journal entry describes bright orange sunbeams "singularly contrasted with the indigo blue that seemed to hang like a curtain behind them." Inspired by this atmospheric wonder, Whipple sketched the magnificent predawn sunrise; a woodcut taken from his drawing appears in volume 3, part 4 of the *Reports*. Soon after, a violent wind sprang up and blew all day as they slowly ascended the Llano bluffs. Their route passed two large pools of water before arriving at Rincon de la Crux. "Here we encamped," Whipple wrote, "beside a spring and a natural vineyard of wild grapes. The fruit is as large as a hazelnut, with thin skin and deep purple juice. It could be greatly improved by cultivation. Mr. Marcou thinks it would make an excellent wine similar to Port."[19]

The next day all were roused at 4:30 A.M. to cross the Llano Estacado. This high, barren plain stretched from western Texas to southeastern New Mexico. The Llano Estacado, or "Staked Plain," was given its name by early Spanish explorers who found the plain so vast and trackless that the only way to mark roads and trails was with stakes. Whipple described the scene as the party set out. "Not a cloud was visible; and the moon being full, created a pretty effect of light and shade upon the distant peaks. Ascending about two hundred and fifty feet, in about a mile from camp we reached the top to the Llano. Here, for the first time, we saw what one might call an ocean prairie; so smooth, level, and boundless does it appear. It is covered with a carpet of closely cropped buffalo grass and no other green thing is to be seen." Even Stanley was impressed, apparently drawn from his usual funk by the spectacle. "As far as the eye reaches a level, beautiful plain stretches out without an object to arrest the eye, except the antelope which roam over this beautiful, but destitute region, with nothing to disturb their peaceful existence." On September 19, "as summer blended into autumn on the prairie" they passed from Texas into New Mexico Territory.[20]

The following day Whipple reflected on the plight of Indians and recorded his private and poetic thoughts in his journal.

"Lo the poor Indian," a pathetic phrase which everybody sighs, speaks so plainly of a race passing away. Linked with the red man as if in the bond of Brotherhood is the buffalo with the same wild and proud nature. They roam the same plains and drink of the same fountains. Equally they recede from the trend of civilization and soon the exciting scenes of a buffalo chase will be but as legends of yore. The region we are traversing was formerly their favorite haunt but no trace of them exists except here and there bones bleaching in the sun.[21]

On September 25, to avoid leaving their foot-sore and weary cattle behind, they stopped for a day, and the adventurous and single-minded

Dr. Bigelow immediately set out on a botanical excursion. About four miles southwest, he struck the bend of a river, probably the Gallinas, and, following it down, found cacti and other interesting plants. "Time was beguiled away, and night came upon him unawares," wrote Whipple, and alarmed for the doctor's safety, he kindled signal fires on the hill and discharged guns to direct him in the darkness toward camp. Finally a party went out to search and "met him on his return weary almost to fainting," with the weight of his herbarium. As David Conrad suggested, "Most military commanders would have been intolerant of this eccentric behavior by a subordinate but Whipple was lenient" with the idiosyncrasies of the scientists, "whose zeal for scientific pursuits sometimes outweighed consideration of their own safety," or led them to disregard Whipple's orders. Whipple himself was a scientist, both an astronomer and meteorologist, which doubtless accounts for his leniency toward the scientific "gentlemen" of the corps. The next day, after a fifteen-mile drive, they reached the crest of a hill overlooking the Pecos at Anton Chico, a town of about five hundred inhabitants.[22]

The principal part of the town stood on the west bank of the river, on the first rise of ground above the irrigated fields. The houses were built of adobes and were singularly festooned in front by strings of red peppers—the much prized chili colorado—intended less for ornament than use. Their entrance, Whipple said, "was greeted by wolfish-looking dogs—which, by the by, are celebrated for sagacity in guarding sheep—and a large number of children; the latter dressed in loose cotton robes, generally torn from the feet to the very neck, and gracefully flowing behind. Having no other covering, they looked cool, if not comfortable."[23]

"In the evening," Sherburne wrote, "they made a fandango for us. Of course we all attended & no one was sorry for doing so." The lovely local females even cheered up the usually morose Stanley. "We had a fandango given us at night and here, for the first time, I had the opportunity of seeing the Spanish dance in the true Spanish style and witnessing that remarkable grace and beauty of carriage remarked by so many of our travelers. Some of the young senoritas were very pretty and the dancing was beautiful. They use the violin and guitar and accompany the music of these instruments with the voice." The next night the *alcalde*—the headman of the town—gave another fandango, and the irrepressible Möllhausen described how the explorers all set to work to rummage up the most elegant ball costumes that circumstances permitted. "Needles and thread were seen in brisk motion in all quarters, and chasms and openings in our well-worn garments, originating either in accident or in severe service on our long journey, disappeared as if by magic." An artificial black was obtained for their shoes, and "the most gorgeous shirt collars and fronts were manufactured out of stiff drawing paper." They set off in the evening to the festive scene, being summoned by the church bells, and soon the dancing began. "The bright-eyed Senoritas were indefatigable," according to Möllhausen; "the degenerate descendants of the Spaniards looked with evident complacency at their own nimble limbs, and the wildest excitement gleamed from the bearded visages of the Americans."[24]

On September 29, the party split up, the main contingent to proceed with the survey directly to Albuquerque, while Bigelow, Marcou, Möllhausen, and Sherburne accompanied Whipple to search for another possible route for a railroad. On October 5, Whipple led his group into Albuquerque and saw the white wagons and tents of the advance party—nearly as conspicuous as the adobe village itself. Albuquerque's population was about 2,500, less than that of Santa Fe, but its situation was more central with regard to the inhabited portions of New Mexico, and General Garland selected it for the headquarters of the military department.

It was in Albuquerque where Whipple heard unsettling stories of the territory ahead—unknown country of difficult terrain, controlled by the Navajos. And it was in Albuquerque where he first began to doubt his mission's success. These doubts and his anxiety over the safety of his party would ultimately lead to First Lieutenant John C. Tidball joining the 35th parallel survey, resulting in the addition of a new and different voice to those of the other diarists and commentators; it would be a voice critical, yet humorous, and one that would offer a singular viewpoint when describing the events that overtook the expedition.[25]

Chapter 4

Twenty-Five Wild, Daring-Looking Fellows
Join the Expedition

In his official report, Whipple only generally alluded to the predicted difficulty of the routes westward from Albuquerque. In his personal journal, however, he recorded in agonizing detail the abundant and discouraging information that came to him as a result of his inquiries. "Since my arrival at this place I have received much information regarding the country between Zuñi to Rio Colorado, all of which tends to convince us that the difficulties attending the railroad exploration and surveys expected to be performed by my party are far greater than were anticipated when we left Washington." Three previous expeditions in the near north and south of the 35th parallel had been difficult and nearly disastrous crossings.[1]

One of these trips was made early in 1853 by Francois X. Aubry, a French-Canadian trader in sheep who, in an article in the Albuquerque *Amigo del País*, was reported to have found a wagon route to California. David Conrad described how "Whipple went out to a ranch near Isleta, where Aubry was preparing for another sheep drive to California, and talked to him. . . . It was true that he and seventeen men had traveled from Tejon Pass in the Sierra Nevadas across present-day Arizona to Zuñi earlier that year, but they had experienced great hardship." They had been constantly harassed by Paiute, Mojave, Cuchane (Yuma), Tonto Apache, and other Indians, and were forced to go into the mountains to escape and to find water. "Aubry and most of his party had been wounded, and they eventually were reduced to eating their pack mules to survive." He assured Whipple that the account of his finding a wagon route to California had been greatly exaggerated.[2]

"The second expedition Whipple learned about was that of Joseph Rutherford Walker, a famous scout and mountain man, who had led a party west from Zuñi to Southern California in 1852," according to Conrad. "His route was through the area north of the Bill Williams and San Francisco Mountains and south of the Grand Canyon." Whipple searched out an old mountain man who had been with Walker. "Saw today Mr. Thomas, a mountaineer and guide who went to California with Walker. He advises not to attempt to take wagons across. Says it will be impossible for me to do so. . . . Thomas describes the country traversed as terrible—volcanic mountains piled on mountains denying passage almost to pack mules." Whipple was already familiar with the third expedition, having read the account of Captain Lorenzo Sitgreaves. In his journal he summarized that officer's ordeal: "Capt. Sitgreaves . . . passed over a country worse than language could express. Even with pack mules they with difficulty reached their destination. Their advice to followers is to avoid their route."[3]

"No wagon road has yet been discovered," was Whipple's inescapable conclusion. "When 3 such enterprising parties have failed I myself begin to look doubtingly upon the success of the trip." Not only had Whipple's anxiety been heightened by his failure to obtain a guide, but he doubted that his military escort was sufficient to protect the party through the Indian Territory ahead. "The three distinguished guides of this country therefore," the unsettled lieutenant wrote, "each following the route of his selection have signally failed in their object. This conclusively proves the great difficulties which we must be prepared to contend with or doubtless fail likewise. One of these difficulties is the hostility of Indians. Each of these parties referred to fought their way and the latter, that of Mr. Aubry, has left various tribes apparently greatly irritated against Americans." Whipple had by now concluded that the escort accompanying the party from Fort Smith, commanded by Lieutenant Jones, would be insufficient because reconnoitering parties would be continually far in advance, and a permanent division of the survey party could be required. "I feel constrained to apply for an additional escort—25 mounted men, to protect operations through this department to the boundary of California."[4]

Lieutenant Ives, with the party dispatched from Washington before the main party left, was supposed to reach Albuquerque before Whipple to make advance preparations for the expedition but did not arrive until a day after Whipple. He did succeed in obtaining at El Paso the instruments loaned by the Department of the Interior, good news that Whipple said would greatly increase the facilities for making scientific observations. On October 22, bad news arrived: Antoine Leroux of Taos wrote Whipple that he was too sick to accompany the expedition as a guide. In his place the lieutenant employed José Manuel Savedra, a Mexican who claimed he had once accompanied the Moqui Indians to the Colorado River in an expedition against the Mojave Indians. On October 27 General Garland visited Whipple; in response to Whipple's plea for an additional military escort, he informed the lieutenant that he could not have the dragoons he asked for, but instead could have "infantry on mules." Then just before the expedition left Albuquerque, Leroux agreed to accompany the expedition; Whipple, however, felt obliged also to retain Savedra as a guide. Whipple was now ready to move. Stanley captured the mood of the party in his November 10 diary entry: "After a busy day packing, hustling and discomfort we started at a late hour in the afternoon on our march over the unknown, but dreaded country we are to explore this winter."[5]

Three days later they came upon the Pueblo de la Laguna, one of the old Indian pueblos, founded in the 1690s after the Pueblo revolt and said to contain one thousand persons. "The inhabitants," Whipple reported, "are reputed honest, sober, and to a certain degree industrious. Encamping near by, we visited by invitation the family of the Rev. Mr. Gorman, a missionary of the Baptist persuasion, who has established himself among this singular people." The minister's school for children was well attended, and adults also listened respectfully to his instructions. In the center of the pueblo was a plaza, or sort of court, surrounded by houses facing inward. The dwellings of the Pueblo were so closely built as to give admittance by two crooked alleys only. "Here the Indians collect upon certain festivals which no Mexican is allowed to witness. Americans, however, are freely admitted; because, they say, facetiously perhaps, we are of the same race and people with themselves."[6]

Whipple also observed a cemetery in the interior of the main building where the space was so limited that, in digging a new grave, the Indians would frequently turn up a previously interred body, in which case it was taken out and thrown into a little enclosure where, Whipple reported, "there is now an immense pile of bones, skeletons, and carcasses."

Möllhausen recalled his visit to the town, where "in the burial place of the Indians my friend Kennerly contrived to pocket, unobserved, a very well-preserved skull, which he triumphantly exhibited to me when we got beyond the reach of the sharp Indian eyes . . . but if the Indians had had any idea of the robbery we had committed, we should probably not have been allowed to escape so easily. We did succeed, however, in carrying it off unobserved to the camp, and there made all possible haste to hide it in one of the waggons." Whipple more dispassionately, but somewhat disingenuously, reported, "Our naturalist, for the cause of science, succeeded in abstracting a skull."[7]

November 14 found the party at Covero, a town of about sixty families. Being a frontier Mexican settlement, Whipple said, its people had suffered greatly from incursions of the Navajos and occasionally had been driven from their village to take refuge among the neighboring cliffs. Whipple described how that night the fandango given by the alcalde was interrupted by a great disturbance outside. People rushed out to see what was the matter, and everybody, "as is usual among Mexicans whenever there is the slightest cause," seemed to be in a high state of excitement. Menacing words were bandied, knives flourished, and pistols drawn. The whole town was in an uproar, and no one seemed to know what it was about. Finally it was ascertained that one of Whipple's herders, named Torrivio, had been recognized as a peon, and a man wished to seize and imprison him till he could be restored to his original state of servitude. "The Mexican had tasted freedom," Whipple added, "and was manfully defending it. The claim was only fifteen or twenty dollars; so the money was advanced, and order immediately restored. Had it not been paid, this little debt might have kept the poor fellow bound to his master for life. In New Mexico the system of peonage has been abolished in law, but not in practice. Written statutes are a sealed book to the laboring classes, and nearly a dead letter to the alcaldes." Torrivio would not long enjoy his freedom. Before the end of the journey he would meet death at the hands of the Paiutes.

The next day they passed within six or eight miles of Mount Taylor, named for the president by Lieutenant Simpson when he was in the country in 1849. They made camp in a valley abundant with grama grass near what Sherburne described as "a fine stream of water" and Whipple described as a "pleasant spot." Stanley contrarily found the country "barren and desolate," and wrote that the scenery was "extremely gloomy from the prevalence of black volcanic rock in our vicinity."[8]

Whipple was still uneasy about traversing the largely unknown country and was anxious for the arrival of the men promised by General Garland. "To hasten the escort," he dispatched Lieutenant Jones, accompanied by Leroux, A. H. Campbell, and a small party, to Fort Defiance, about fifty miles to the northwest, noting, "An additional escort being ordered from that post, we hope it may be prepared to join us at Zuñi, or at least upon the Colorado Chiquito." On November 18 the main party crossed the continental divide, an event that stimulated Stanley's memory and imagination, causing him to recall that on one side the water ran to the Atlantic; a few feet distant a neighboring drop of water set out on its long tour to the Pacific. "My mind could not but indulge in a few strange musings, as I thought that I stood upon the summit of this mighty chain of mountains, that used in my boyhood days to be the enchanted region of everything dreadful and wild. The grizzly bear, the sheep that threw itself down from cliff to cliff safely, by falling on its horns. All the little tales of the story books which I perused as a child and which fancy had dwelt upon were recalled to my thought."

The same day, in a wide valley, they found *El Morro,* called by Simpson "Inscription Rock." The following morning Whipple took some time to examine the inscriptions and described his findings. "We passed by the more modern records of Spanish origin, from 1620 to 1736. . . . Many of them are beautifully carved, and though doubtless faithful in their statement of date, seem but slightly affected by atmospheric action upon the rock. The Indian hieroglyphics, which we examined more carefully, are, however, much time-worn and defaced—some are scarcely traceable."[9]

The morning of November 20 broke upon them bright, clear, and cold—19 degrees according to Sherburne's thermometer. By the end of the day they were within sight of the "dark pueblo of Zuñi." Whipple did not want to move until Lieutenant Jones and his party returned from Fort Defiance; he was still hoping that they would bring the additional escort back with them. The governor of Zuñi paid them a visit, and Whipple told him that his government desired them to furnish a guide. "He listened attentively to the explanations of the object of the expedition, of the general course we proposed to follow, and the requisites necessary to make the expedition satisfactory." With dignified reserve the governor said he would consult with the caciques, or chiefs. It is doubtful whether the Indians understood that the primary purpose of the survey was to find a route to enable the Americans to drive hundreds of miles of steel rail through the heart of their traditional tribal homeland and hunting grounds, first disrupting and then forever destroying their traditional way of life. After a few days, Whipple with a small party visited the pueblo, but upon reaching the town of Zuñi, "a most revolting spectacle" met their view. "Smallpox had been making terrible ravages among the people, and we were soon surrounded by great numbers—men, women, and children—exhibiting this loathsome disease in various stages of its progress."[10]

On November 24, Möllhausen reported the return of Mr. Campbell and the other members of the expedition from Fort Defiance, "not, however, bringing with them the promised military escort, but only the information that it was detained by the preparations for the march, and would not be able to leave for some days; and that it would then take the direction of the little Colorado, find out the track of the Expedition, and follow it in rapid marches." A few days later, the Zuñi war chief arrived to inform Whipple that a council had been held the previous night by the caciques and governor. "They approved of the objects of our expedition," Whipple reported, "and determined to afford all the aid in their power," including guides to show a better route than that which Savedra proposed. The trail west was across desert country that was one of their favorite hunting grounds. But the land beyond the Little Colorado was *terra incognita* to them, and they would have to turn back there.[11]

With some misgivings, the expedition left Zuñi on November 29 and moved west toward the Little Colorado River. At sunset the following day, a smoke signal was sighted in the distance, and soon after, two Navajo Indians rode into camp; they said they had come on a hunting trip from Canyon de Chelly, their tribal stronghold to the north. "Whipple asked if they had seen a party of soldiers, explaining that he was expecting a detachment from Fort Defiance to join his expedition," perhaps to let the Navajos know that his party would soon be stronger than it then appeared. When the Indians learned that the expedition had recently been in Zuñi, they were afraid of catching smallpox and hastily departed. Their fear of contracting the dreaded disease was well founded, for there were several cases among the party. On the evening of November 30, Whipple and Dr. Bigelow were summoned to the tent of a soldier who "was out of his mind" with fever from the disease.[12]

On December 1, the party crossed the 109th meridian—the present boundary between New Mexico and Arizona—and the following day reached Lithodendron Creek and a forest of petrified trees. "One trunk,"

Fort Defiance, 1860. Perhaps the most remote army post in the country, it was nicknamed "Hell's Gate" by the soldiers posted there.

Whipple noted, "measured ten feet in diameter, and more than one hundred feet in length." On Sunday, December 4, Whipple wrote in his journal that they "rested from their labor," and then nervously added, "The additional escort from Ft. Defiance has not yet arrived." Whipple would have been relieved to know that the previous day First Lieutenant John C. Tidball and the long-awaited escort had started from Fort Defiance.[13]

The genesis of Fort Defiance lay in the bitter enmity between the New Mexicans, the Navajos, and the Pueblo Indians; hatred centuries old had been fostered by the actions of each nation. One of General Stephen Watts Kearny's first acts when he entered Santa Fe in 1846 was to proclaim all New Mexicans citizens of the United States and promise them protection against depredations by their ancient enemies, the Indians. The United States' attempt to secure peace with the Navajo by means of treaties was futile, however, and the tribe continued to raid communities as though no treaties existed. Major George A. McCall reported from Santa Fe on July 15, 1850, that "the principal pursuits of life . . . have, up to the time of the cession of the territory to the United States, been blighted by the presence of formidable tribes of Indians, who *still* infest the country," and that the future prosperity of the state would in a great measure depend on the pacification of the eight tribes of wild Indians who inhabited the mountains and plains of New Mexico and the contiguous country, of which the Navajos and Apaches were "the most formidable as enemies and the most troublesome as neighbors."

Finally, in 1851, the War Department decided to regroup its forces to equalize contests with the Indians, and five new posts were created: Fort Union, Fort Conrad, Fort Fillmore, Fort Massachusetts, and Fort Defiance. Fort Defiance was established on September 18, 1851, located sixty miles north of Zuñi and fifteen miles south of Canyon de Chelly. It was a fort in name only, having no stockade, trenches, blockhouses, or other defensive works; all military operations from the fort were to be offensive. Located in one of the "loneliest corners of the United States," with extreme weather conditions in both summer and winter, the fort was nicknamed "Hell's Gate" by soldiers posted there.[14]

"My sojourn at Fort Defiance was short," Tidball recalled. "On the 3d of December I started for the Pacific coast with Whipple's exploring party in search of a route for an overland railroad," although he was not yet "with" Whipple's party, but hastening to catch up with it. The route that he assisted to explore, he wrote many years later, "is now occupied by the Atlantic and Pacific [Railroad], but at the time, a large portion of it from Albuquerque had never before been explored and was quite unknown to the white man." We do not know if Tidball was given a choice to command the additional escort to bolster Whipple's military capability, but if he was given an opportunity to volunteer, we may be sure he jumped at the chance to escape from his solitary desert garrison. We know from his writings that he was curious about the world around him, and the prospect of journeying to the Pacific shore would have excited him. More importantly, perhaps, he knew that he would return to his post via the isthmus of Panama and the East Coast of the United States, there to be reunited with Mary, his bride of only a few months. He would have been aware of the danger and hardships ahead, but he surely preferred this assignment to sitting out the lonely winter at Fort Defiance, regarded as one of the most undesirable of all army posts.[15]

The party Tidball assembled at Fort Defiance consisted of twenty-five enlisted men and one packer—Jim Horan, an ex-dragoon soldier. His principal sergeant was Curwen B. McLellan. The men were taken from the three companies of the Third Infantry and the company of the Second Artillery at Fort Defiance. "It was not difficult to obtain volunteers for this expedition," he remembered. "Those selected were those whose times of enlistment would soon expire, and they were thus afforded the opportunity of being discharged in California—a great favor." Tidball gives us a preview, a unique view, of what it was like to pack across the Southwest in the mid-nineteenth century. Each man had two mules, one for riding and the other for carrying his provisions and blankets. They started with a three-month supply of provisions, but as it required about four months to reach the first settlement, San Bernardino on the Pacific Slope, they were to run extremely short during the last period of the journey. There was no game to be had, although frequently they saw signs of it, and during the last days mule meat sufficed to get them through. They carried along no camp equipage whatsoever, trusting to the lee side of rocks or the spreading branches of trees for shelter. "With the exception of snow there was but little necessity of shelter. The wind was the chief inclemency to guard against, and from this we were better without than with tents. Without tents we could snuggle closer to our fires." At times the weather was extremely cold, but they suffered little on this account. "We were well provided with blankets, and for my part, as the weather became colder I put on an additional undershirt, until in the end I had five or six on. As we neared the Pacific Slope and the weather became warmer I removed them, as I had put them on, one at a time." The most difficult problem to overcome was footgear. Although they started well provided, the sharp volcanic rocks soon played havoc with their boots. Saddle skirts and rawhide from the mules were resorted to, and great ingenuity was displayed in manufacturing extemporary soles. "For meat ration I drove along sheep and goats, starting with about two hundred. These soon became familiar with traveling in company with mules, and followed along like dogs. Only occasionally the goats would lead the flock upon some overhanging precipice from which it would be difficult to extricate it. They required no herding but kept close to the mules for protection against wolves who nightly serenaded us with their long drawn howls."[16]

Tidball estimated that he was about ninety miles from Whipple when he started to track him. He took the trail to Zuñi, passing Ojo del Oso (Bear Springs), where at the time of his writing, he said, stood Fort Wingate. On the third day he came in sight of Zuñi but passed it several miles to the west, and encamped for the night without finding water.

Tidball wanted to avoid Zuñi, being aware of the smallpox then raging among its inhabitants. Unfortunately, the mules, having been without water all the previous day, were uneasy, and during the night several of them escaped and made their way straight for a creek near the village. "Early in the morning I started a party in pursuit, charging the men not to enter Zuñi on any account. It was about sixteen miles back to the village, and the party, instead of starting immediately back with the re-captured mules, remained that night among the small pox inhabitants and returned the next day, bringing with them sundry robes, blankets, etc., most excellent forms for small pox. Happily none of my men took the disease."

Tidball found that the trail from Fort Defiance to Zuñi, although on the crest of the Sierra Madre, followed chiefly a succession of valleys, varying in width from a few hundred yards to a dozen or so miles, and enclosed on their sides by lofty mesas with precipitous walls. The erosion left sandstone strata molded into fantastic shapes. "Some resemble Egyptian architecture, others old feudal castles, others again huge statues, columns and in fact anything of which the imagination can conceive. The action of the weather and water has carried away the softer portions of the rocks leaving the harder portions in their natural layers, piled one on top of another, often with the utmost nicety and regularity, so much so as to be readily mistaken for works of art, and monuments of a giant race now lost to the earth and to history." Nearly all of the small detached mesas that formed islands in the valleys, Tidball observed, were, or had been, occupied by the pueblos of the aborigines. "Such for instance is the present pueblo of Zuñi. These pueblos were built by a peace-loving race that clustered their dwellings upon these almost inaccessible points with a view of defense against their warlike neighbors—the Navajos and Apaches."

Upon striking Whipple's trail, Tidball found he was several days' march behind him, following a trail over a rolling prairie and gravelly country, along the Lithodendron Creek to the Little Colorado. "The Lithodendron was so named by Whipple on account of the immense quantity of petrified wood found in its valley. A whole forest of huge trees seems to have been turned into stone, and the whole region is macadamized with broken pieces. The woody texture is faithfully preserved in silex, producing jasper variegated with rich and bright colors."[17]

While Tidball closed in on the expedition, Whipple's march was abruptly stalled. "Last night there occurred that dreaded calamity of the

John C. Tidball. This photo was taken about the time Tidball was promoted to first lieutenant, and shortly before he embarked from Fort Defiance to meet up with Whipple.

prairies, a stampede of the mules," Whipple reported on December 10. The herd was quietly grazing when suddenly a pony took fright and created a panic among the animals; they all fled. Their heavy trampling awoke the party, and seizing arms, the men rushed out, thinking that Indians were the cause of the disturbance. The night was so dark that nothing could be seen at a distance, and they followed the sound. Some mules were overtaken and brought back, but at daybreak it was found that many were missing. No trace of Indian footsteps was found, and it appeared that the animals had taken the back track at full run toward Zuñi. "The swiftest were gone," Whipple continued. "Only the tired and lazy remained. But a party, without waiting for breakfast, was quickly mounted and in pursuit, hoping to overtake them before they might fall into the hands of Indians." Party after party followed the trail of the wandering mules and horses. For thirty-two miles they continued the pursuit, and finally overtaking the frightened horses that led the herd, turned them back. "One of the mules had broken a leg in leaping an arroyo," Whipple reported. "Another had wearied herself out. The rest were driven back to camp."[18]

On December 12th, while the party spent its second day in camp allowing the mules to recover from their fatigue, the arrival of reinforcements was tersely recorded in Stanley's diary: "Lt. Tidball and party arrived to-day, bringing us late newspapers from the States." As an example of how a single reported event can be transformed by differing observers, Whipple, whose official version in the *Reports* matches Stanley's for brevity, was inspired to write these effusive remarks in his unpublished journal:

Lt. Titbald [*sic*] has today arrived with our additional escort of 25 men from Ft. Defiance. Our party now numbers about 110, perhaps one hundred and fifteen men all told. There are 13 wagons, 2 carretelas and about 240 mules. Lt. Titbald brought a mail very acceptable, each one of us receiving good tidings from home. It is not within the pale of civilization that the value of a mail and the blessing of a letter is fully appreciated. Far away from friends, upon the dreary desert where the sky shuts down upon lands unknown, in the midst of perils, now seeking to avoid the danger of perishing with thirst upon the arid plains ahead, now looking for grass to save the famishing mules, now rushing onward to avoid starvation as provisions rapidly diminish, while in the midst of all these difficulties savage foes are lurking around to wipe us out of existence, there comes a message from loved ones at home and the . . . memory brightens our hopes and dissipates our fears. Invigorated and refreshed, difficulties are surmounted, dangers are spurned. Hope like a pillar of fire leads us onward.[19]

The irrepressible Möllhausen sketched yet another, more colorful, description of the arrival of Tidball, whose name gave either him or his translator trouble, just as it did Whipple.

On the second day after the stampede there was again a stir and excitement in our camp, but this time it had an agreeable cause, namely, the arrival of Lieutenant Fitzball with the men under his command—five-and-twenty wild daring-looking fellows, whose physiognomies, and entire bearing, were strongly indicative of their having been long in remote, uncivilized territories. They were provided with pack mules, and also with so many for the saddle that half the men could be mounted; and the journey from Fort Defiance had been made very quickly, especially as this party carried with them neither waggons nor tents, and though they had to dispense with many comforts, they were also thus relieved of a great burden. Most cordially did we salute the new comers, and within half an hour of their arrival, they were making merry round our blazing fires, and roaring jovial songs, which afforded satisfactory indication of their spirits not having been at all affected by the hardships of a life in the wilderness.[20]

John Tidball's parents, who, it will be recalled, were strict Presbyterians, would not have approved of this rollicking event, which surely included the consumption of spirituous liquors. But while Tidball inherited his father's probity and work ethic, he left behind at the Ohio farm his parent's abstemious habits. He seemed to balance quite well the sometimes-severe hardships of frontier military life with a few earthly pleasures; he liked his whiskey and an occasional cigar.

In his memoirs Tidball sketched arresting and often humorous word portraits of his traveling companions, something no other diarist had done; consequently, we are for the first time presented with glimpses into the personalities of party members, as well as additional insights into Tidball's personality. First he described the officers, only briefly mentioning the gentle Whipple, whom he remembered as a "lovable" person, a word John Tidball is not known to have employed to characterize any other army officer. Whipple had considerable experience in surveys and explorations, Tidball went on to say, "and from his zeal, perseverance and aptitude was well adapted for the work which he now had charge of."

Ives had been in service only a few years, but Tidball charitably described him as bright, active, and zealous and well qualified for an assistant. But, contrarily, as revealed in deprecating marginal notes in his copy of the *Reports,* Tidball at the time also found Ives an unenergetic and obdurate officer, and would have trouble with him before the expedition ended. In his memoir, written many years after the Civil War, it was clear that by then he thought little of Ives, who as a turncoat northerner was not likely to arouse his enthusiasm, and described him as "a great courtier and admirer of those whom he considered his superiors. His duties in Washington, after he returned from this exploration, threw him in contest with many of the southern ladies whose arrogance of manners and opinions impressed him to the extent that when the rebellion broke out he went south, and although himself a New England man, joined the war against the Union." Ives, Tidball concluded with evident satisfaction, made no mark at all as an officer in the Confederate Army. After the war he returned to New York City, destitute and degraded. "Such was the fate of all, without an exception, of those officers from the North who went south and joined in the rebellion."

Tidball liked Lieutenant Jones, of the Seventh Infantry (Rum Jones as he was called), who commanded the other escort of about twenty-five infantrymen. "Jones was a good boon companion: a fairly good officer, but being from Virginia he left the Union and joined the Confederate Army." Lieutenant Stanley, Second Dragoons, was Whipple's quartermaster, and the most junior officer. We have seen from Stanley's own diary how morose and unenergetic he was. Tidball concurred: "At that time he appeared to be an indolent, unenterprising young man who gave but little promise of the energy and capacity for command which has since marked his career. He is now a Brigadier in the regular Army; a grade well earned by his courage and skill during the rebellion." There may have been something in the experience gained by this recent West Point graduate in crossing the continent under dangerous and challenging conditions that molded and reformed his character, and contributed to his later success.

With Tidball's arrival, the army had committed five lieutenants to the

35th parallel survey party. In less than eight years, when the Confederate artillery pounded Fort Sumter and the nation exploded into Civil War, all five would still be in uniform. Before the end of that great conflict, four would become generals, and two would die.[21]

It is said that a shadow of the Civil War—in the form of a sectional dispute—was cast over the regular army on the frontier, and that this quarrel even had an impact on the Pacific railroad survey. Foreshadow would be a better term, but at the time of the railroad surveys it was a faint and fleeting shadow of slight consequence. Professor Durwood Ball, however, alleges that "the sharp edge of slavery politics" sliced its way through the interwar regular army and, employing the same slashing metaphor, claims that the "the North-South schism sliced into the heart of the regular army," in a manner that somehow "undermined its natural-ization, professionalism and cohesion." This is fine rhetoric, but Pro-fessor Ball offers only anecdotal evidence in the form of random remarks and conversation among a few officers over more than a decade, and does not describe a single instance during the long antebellum era of any officer neglecting or refusing to carry out his duties in accordance with his oath of office because of "slavery politics," nor does he allege even the slightest destabilization of the army, much less any overall impairment in its ability to discharge effectively its national mission.[22]

Of course there was conversation—and debate, sometimes heated. Mid-nineteenth-century America was a highly charged political commu-nity, and rural stump speeches by politicians were enthusiastically at-tended. But the American hierarchy of political credos was complex and confusing, and slavery was not the only contentious issue. In the political fabric of the country there were North and South politics, Whig and Democratic politics, and abolitionist and free soil politics, to name a few. The officer corps of the army constituted just one of many informal debating societies where politics were avidly argued, but there is no evidence that the army was rendered dysfunctional by internal dissen-sion. Indeed, all of the evidence suggests that well-trained and disci-plined officers, when the mess hall debate ended, stolidly carried out their assigned duties as ordered.

John Tidball himself remembered how at West Point, politics became a hot topic during the election year of 1844 and were avidly debated, especially by southern cadets. Tidball observed the sectional differ-ences himself. New Englanders and Southerners, the two extremes, were equally unfamiliar to him. At this period, he recalled, some very bizarre notions prevailed as to customs and habits among those but a little way off geographically. "From various sources I had acquired the idea that a Yankee was a pert jack-knife-trading sort of an individual, ever on the alert to invent something, or to outwit his neighbor in a bargain; while the Southerner was a saturnine person, armed with whip and bowie-knife, equally ready to thrash a 'nigger' or to disembowel an abolitionist. Among my associates I recognized no such picture. Differences there were, it is true, and very marked, but chiefly in the manner of doing the same thing in a different way." He found that his New England friends had an idea that the West was some vast, wild region, of wonderful promise to speculators and enterprising school teachers, while those in the South knew it only as a place of refuge for runaway Negroes, confusing Ohio in their minds with Oberlin, then famous for its college of co-education of blacks and whites. Tidball revealed his own bias when he described peculiarities of pronunciation, referring to sectional expressions as "mere distortions of proper expressions, and not genuine coinage like the crisp expressive phrases of the West," an opinion his fellow cadets from New England and the South would have jeered. But in the end, Tidball concluded, "in point of general manners and bearing I could perceive but little difference among us all. With occasional exceptions we averaged up about the same," and that was the attitude he carried into the army, as did most regular army officers.[23]

As the 1850s advanced, and talk of secession grew, the debate inevitably became more intense, and the 1860 election of Lincoln pushed most southerners closer to choosing loyalty to their states over the Union. The fact that one third of the officer corps defected is unremarkable—when the choice finally had to be made, they went to serve their states, where their strongest loyalties resided. Shelby Foote once perceptively noted that before the Civil War, people would say, "They are the United States." After the war it became "It is the United States." Foote said, the Civil war made us an "is," but in the days and weeks preceding the war, loyalties to the individual southern states were intense and predominate. But all this tumult, which unquestionably acted as a momentary distraction to the army, occurred in the few months immediately preceding the war, and right up until that time the army, aside from a lot of talk, did not seem much affected; after this disruptive incident, both the northern and southern segments, again with credit to their previous training and discipline, quickly organized into viable, if not immediately fully efficient, separate fighting forces.[24]

There is no evidence at all that the 35th parallel railroad survey was infected with any sectional malaise. John Tidball served in the antebellum army for twelve years before the Civil War, and like most professional soldiers, got on well with his fellow officers from all sections of the country, often referring to southerners in the most affectionate terms. Of the officers on the survey, he thought Lieutenant Jones of Virginia was "a good boon companion" and a "fairly good officer." The two officers he didn't think much of were Stanley from his own state of Ohio and Ives of New York, and that was at a time when he had no reason to suspect that Ives would later defect to the South. Even when the war started, Tidball, who disliked politicians generally, thought little of sectionalism. In a letter home he wrote, "I love the Union and in proportion as I love it, I hate those of the North or South who are causing it to be irremediably broken." He spread blame for the war impartially and intersectionally, and when called to the field, he put politics out of his head and performed his duties gallantly and efficiently, as did nearly all soldiers of that era.

Chapter 5

A Continuous Succession of
Mountain Ranges Lay in Our Path

Throughout his career, Tidball observed what was going on about him and remembered what he saw. After he joined the Whipple party, he scrutinized his traveling companions, and when he wrote his memoirs many years later, he called on his considerable powers of observation and description—as well as his arch humor—to evoke the personalities and characters of the civilian members of the party. The entertaining manner in which he describes his traveling companions tells us not only about them, but also much about himself. He left us with these artful, sometimes sardonic, vignettes.

J. M. Bigelow, M.D., surgeon and botanist, had been a wagoner boy in the War of 1812 and was the oldest of the party, being then about fifty-five, "but hale and hearty; one of the strut and twist sort," capable of great endurance, said Tidball. Whatever he was as a surgeon, he was certainly an enthusiastic botanist. "He was especially cranked upon the subject of cacti." During the days' march he wandered from side to side exploring every nook for new species. He would come into camp, Tidball recalled, with his haversack filled with the "prickly abominations." Much to the disgust of party members, he would spread them out on their blankets to explain their beauty. "His amiability was, in such cases, always equal to the emergency and saved his venerable head. He moved around in such a way that we were fearful that some skulking Indian might take a fancy to his dingy clothes and give him a stealthy *coup*. He did me the favor of naming a new variety of his villainous favorite plant after me— *Apuntia Tidballia*."

Tidball did not get the name quite right, but the doctor did indeed honor him in the manner described. In "Report on Botany of the Expedition," Bigelow wrote that at the southern base of Bill Williams Mountain, he found an *Opuntia* never before seen on their route, and from its peculiar appearance, predicted, "it will doubtless prove to be a new species." It was an upright flat-jointed species, thickly beset with yellow spines, of a much lighter green color than most other species, or indeed, any other that they had seen. "Lieutenant Tidball, of our escort, kindly sketched it for me and [I] provisionally named it after him, to distinguish from other allied species. . . . As we proceed westward into the neighborhood of Pichaco and Val de China, the *O. Tidballii* becomes much more frequent." But it does not appear that the name honoring Tidball survived; there is evidently no cactus now so named.[1]

Tidball described Jules Marcou, geologist and mining engineer, as a native of France, highly educated and intelligent, and master of his profession: quick of observation and alive to the importance of his work. "He was very tall, about six feet four, slender, flaxen haired, blue-eyed and ruddy complexion, but of consumptive tendency. In fact he was then a very sick man, but is notwithstanding, yet living. It is probable that this journey, with its wholesome fresh air exercise, gave him a new lease on life."

C.B.R. Kennerly, M.D., physician and naturalist, was a long-legged Virginian, capable of wading deep into pools and creeks in search of specimens. He was industrious and loaded many mules with his skins of birds and beasts, fishes and reptiles in alcohol, and specimens of Indian work. Tidball observed that he was quiet and unobtrusive, "given to sitting upon banks of streams in deep meditation—no doubt upon what they might contain in way of specimens. His great ambition was to secure a Gila 'Monster,' but as we did not strike that river he no doubt went down to his grave a disappointed man."

Tidball thought that A. H. Campbell, principal assistant railroad engineer, was a man who appeared to understand his business; amiable, without ostentations, pretensions, and altogether an agreeable companion, despite his tendency toward hypochondria. He made much amusement for other members of the party describing his numerous imagined ills. Every morning he woke up with some new disorder. "We soon learned that it was all in his imagination, and would often wager with each other as to what would be his next." He was from Norfolk, Virginia, but Tidball never knew what became of him and thought perhaps the rebellion swept him away. The only thing Tidball had against Campbell "was his stealing for himself the name of a pass on the Continental Divide, on the road from Albuquerque to Fort Defiance." This pass was, and had been for years, well known as the Ojo del Oso Pass, and "it was rank sacrilege for Campbell to attempt to rub out the Spanish name and substitute his own, however beautiful he might think it." This pass is near the present Fort Wingate, and the railroad, the route for which they were exploring, eventually passed through it. Campbell was one of the three artists on the expedition, and produced a few sketches that appeared in the final *Reports.*[2]

H. B. Möllhausen, the topographer and artist, Tidball said claimed to be a natural son of Baron Humboldt, and consequently to have inherited great talent, but Tidball thought his talents slight. "He knew nothing of topography and was but little of an artist, except that he could most admirably delineate plants, and small animals and birds. He was nothing on landscape. He was a brawny, hairy Teuton, full to overflowing with amiability and kindness to everyone. Although a very thoughtful man he had the gift of his supposed progenitor in relating adventures, a fact which suggested—but unjustly—a slight change of name. We called him by way of pleasantry Baron Munchhausen."[3]

Hugh Campbell, assistant astronomer, was a native born Irishman with a "whining brogue, a good recorder and computer of observations. A jolly companion, light hearted and making the best of every difficulty." Tidball did not know what became of him, and said the last time he saw him was in the winter after the war had commenced, on 15th Street in Washington in front of where the Riggs House now stands. "He had in his hands quite a bagful of gold coin, his hard earned savings, which he appeared not to know what to do with. I advised him to invest in seven thirty U.S. Bonds; he shook his head with an incredulous laugh, evidently not having full faith at that time in the stability of the government."

William White was assistant meteorological observer and surveyor, a young man fresh from college, modest, unpretentious, and efficient up to the time, about the first of January, when he was seized with rheumatism in the legs, which made traveling and camp-life exceedingly painful to him. "Captivated by the loveliness of the country, he remained in southern California to try ranching, but failed at this. Now dead." George Gibson Garner, assistant astronomer and surveyor, was a large, stout, hearty young man, full of song and jolly good fellowship. Soon after the expedition, Tidball said, he was appointed second lieutenant in the Second Artillery but resigned within two or three years thereafter. N. H. Hutton, assistant engineer, was a refined young man and a valuable assistant. After the survey he became connected with the engineer office at Baltimore.

John P. Sherburne, who we have seen was Whipple's brother-in-law, was assistant meteorologist, observer, and surveyor, and Tidball thought, a young man fully up to the requirements of attending to the few meteorological instruments used in the exploration. "He was a very pleasant companion. Soon after returning to the States he was made a second lieutenant of infantry, and about the beginning of the war was advanced to the Adjutant General's Department. His last service was on the Pacific Coast, which proving too festive for him, he fell into disfavor and upon the reduction of the army in 1870 he was *benzined* out, the only instance of a staff officer being at that time reduced out of service."[4]

Thomas H. Parke, assistant astronomer and computer, was a brother of the officer who would become General Parke during the Civil War. He was a young man who quietly attended to his own business, pleasant and affable to all. Tidball remembered, "He reached Southern California when the whole country was green with spring grass and carpeted with flowers. This was such a contrast to the sterile and rugged region through which we had been so long journeying, that he and White—before mentioned—were captivated by the prospect and decided to remain and try their fortune at cattle and sheep raising. They were, however, unsuccessful—perhaps because discouraged too soon, and gave it up. He died long since."

Antoine Leroux, guide, was perhaps the most essential and important civilian member of the survey. Tidball thought perhaps he was a native of New Mexico; he was, however, of French-Canadian origin, a "genuine voyageur type," and a thorough mountaineer. Tidball greatly admired his "canine-like instinct" for locality and for finding his way to places even though unknown to him, and described this unique ability as no other member of the party did. As noted earlier, however, Whipple, in his frustration at not finding the major rivers of the region where he thought they should be, would come close to accusing Leroux of deliberate deception. "The nature of mountain ranges and what lay beyond them," Tidball said, "appeared to be as well known to him as though he could see through their rocky diaphragms." His highest gift as a guide, however, was his aptitude for finding water. So much had he roamed, in his trapping and hunting excursions, through the arid mountains of New Mexico, where the finding or not finding of water means either life or death to the traveler, that his powers in this respect seemed to the uninitiated as pure instinct, and hence his services were invaluable to not only the survey party but to other parties whom he had guided through these unwatered regions. "He was rather under the standard size," as Tidball described him, "but every ounce of him was genuine man. His muscles were unencumbered by fat, his wiry form in a manner indicative of the endurance required of one pursuing his mode of life. Swarthy of complexion, with straight black hair and clear black eyes, he showed in his whole make up a man equal to the occasion. His native language was the Spanish of New Mexico, but his broken English was quite intelligible. He, however, talked but little, and never boastingly of himself. He was no swashbuckler cowboy, but a genuine mountaineer of a pair with Kit Carson."

"Water," Tidball remembered, "was the great desideration." Their course was generally perpendicular to the mountain ranges and but seldom along the few streams they encountered. Flowing springs were rare almost to total absence, and their chief water supply was to be found only in holes or pockets in the sides of mountains. John Tidball's description of the guide's "canine-like instinct" for locating places and water is a good example of his evocative talents.

Finding these holes was Leroux' great art. From an eminence he would gaze long and steadily at the dreary prospect before him, a prospect that generally gave but little hope of water for ourselves and our thirsty animals. Presently he would say in his quiet way: "Dare is de wat." "Where?" someone would ask. "Dare at de foot of dat butte." "But which butte?" would be asked, there being a multitude of buttes. He would indicate by giving his hand a horizontal swing of a quarter of a circle taking in a scope of country often greater in extent than the state of Delaware, mostly of jagged mountains which if they had been flattened would have covered more than the area of Pennsylvania. This was his method of pointing. He never aimed directly at the mark with his finger as others do, but gave a sweep with his hand. A few more questions, however, would fix the attention to the exact spot, which generally proved to be a gigantic cliff of basaltic rock appearing at such great distance as a mere speck against the mountain side. Many tedious hours would be consumed in toiling over and winding around spurs of mountains to reach the indicated spot. But we never failed to find the water.

According to Tidball, a clump of small cottonwood trees was a never-failing sign of water in this region. At that season of the year, they were leafless and difficult to see at a distance. "But Leroux' practiced eye always proved more keen than our field glasses."[5]

José Manuel Savedra was assistant guide, "a full-blooded New Mexican." He had wandered extensively through the western part of New Mexico, and Tidball said that he even professed to have been at the Moqui villages, but he did not possess the broad views of mountain guide craft so eminently displayed by Leroux. "Nevertheless he made himself highly useful in *buskering* around in a local sort of way," finding where chasms could be crossed, precipices turned, the best places for camps, and the like. Tidball remembered him as rather above the usual size of the New Mexican, slightly stout, and if dressed up would have been a fair specimen of the hidalgo type of Spaniard. "His great trouble of life was dread of Indians, and any sign of them, however old it might be, would cause him to cry out, *'las Indians!'* and cling close to the column of march." His knowledge of the country was obtained while on expeditions to capture Indian children to make peon slaves of, in former times one of the business pursuits of the New Mexicans.[6]

The remainder of the Whipple party, Tidball wrote, consisted of the twenty-five men under Lieutenant Jones, a few Americans as teamsters, and many New Mexicans as mule packers. He also recalled that Whipple had a dozen or so army wagons, and a spring wagon of the kind used in very rough parts of the Pacific Slope for stage purposes, and known as *jerkies* from the motion of which the name is suggestive. "He had brought these from Fort Smith, Arkansas, and they had served a good purpose while on the plains and until we struck the Sierra Madras, which proved too rough for them and they were abandoned here and there along the way." Whipple was ambitious to take them through to the Pacific and thus demonstrate beyond doubt a practicable route for wheeled vehicles, and "by dint of main strength in lifting, carrying and crossing," one jerky was taken through.

Tidball had joined Whipple on the Little Colorado, "a good sized creek which we crossed without difficulty." He wasted no time in engaging in reconnaissance. On December 13, Stanley wrote, "Lt. Tidball and myself, having found that the grass was becoming scarce in our present position, crossed the river to search for a new camp." Throughout the entire trip Tidball would display the energy, determination and zeal for action that later would characterize his Civil War performance as commander of a battery of flying artillery.

Soon after he joined the party, Tidball remembered, they "commenced the rugged ascent of that branch of the Sierras of which San Francisco is the highest and most pronounced peak. It is an extinct volcano about three hundred and fifty miles west of Albuquerque." This mountain seemed to Tidball to rise from a great swell of the surface of the earth that had an elevation above sea level of about 8,500 feet. Above this, the cone or peak rose an additional 4,500 feet, giving a total elevation of 13,000 feet. To the southwest of these mountains, the plateau from which they rose descended as a wide spreading plain toward the Little Colorado and seemed to offer a fair prospect for the expedition, but before attempting it an exploration was made. "To the great surprise of the party," they unexpectedly found themselves on the edge of a deep chasm in the plain of magnesium limestone, over one hundred feet in depth, the sides precipitous, and about three hundred feet across at top.[7]

On December 13, Whipple started on a reconnaissance with a small party consisting of several members of the scientific party, Lieutenant Jones and thirteen soldiers. He reported encountering on December 14 the chasm described by Tidball: "The cañon which interrupted our march today has been named Cañon Diablo." On December 15 they recrossed the Colorado Chiquito and turned again westward toward the peaks; two days later they turned the southwest point of San Francisco Mountain and, after traveling about seven miles, reached a permanent spring that poured from a hillside and was lost in the grassy plain below. "In honor of the guide," Whipple wrote, "it was called Leroux's spring." In his memoirs, Tidball also recalled, " 'Leroux' Spring flows from the base of one of these hills. The accompanying picture is from a sketch, which I took at the time. The ground was covered with snow, hiding the luxuriant growth of grass."[8]

"The accompanying picture" is a copy of a lithograph, made by Sarony and Company, New York, entitled *San Francisco Mountain*, which appears facing page 80 in part 1, volume 3 of the *Reports*. Some litho-

San Francisco Mountain. When Tidball drew this peak, he said
"the ground was covered with snow, hiding the luxuriant grass."
Möllhausen also sketched the mountain, and this lithograph
could have come from either drawing.

graphs of the same scene are attributed to Möllhausen, but this one is
unattributed, and on his copy he wrote in the lower lefthand corner,
where the name of the artist or delineator normally appears, "Lieut. J. C.
Tidball, U.S. Army." It is a majestic depiction of a mountain powerfully
thrusting upward from a pine forest, with a campsite far below, nestled
tidily among the lower trees.

There has always been and always will be uncertainty as to who is
responsible for the artwork in the *Reports.* Robert Taft said the lithograph
San Francisco Mountain, for which Tidball unequivocally takes credit, "is
not credited in all volumes to Möllhausen but since practically the same
view appears in [Möllhausen's] *Diary* (both in the German and the English editions) it is virtually certain that Möllhausen drew the original
sketch upon which the lithograph was based." Tidball's memoirs and his
description of how and when he made his drawing were not available to
Taft when he wrote his book, and he had no way of knowing that Tidball
also sketched the mountain. The Möllhausen illustration Taft refers to,
although it may be "practically the same view," differs from the view

depicted in the Sarony lithograph in important respects, and Möll-hausen's drawing is, at best, indirect and circumstantial evidence that it was the basis for one of the lithographs. Without having Tidball's sketch to examine, we can never be sure if he was responsible for a published lithograph. Tidball was easily a good enough artist to have produced such a drawing, but the mystery of which drawing or drawings formed the basis for one or more of the published lithographs, at least for now, must remain unsolved.[9]

Tidball, noting that Leroux's name would lastingly "be preserved in a copious spring flowing from the base of the snow-capped San Francisco Mountain," added some derisive comments on the practice of naming geographic features after people.

> It is thought to be a great honor to a person to confer his name upon a mountain; and so it is if mere bulk is considered; but throughout the regions in which we were traveling, mountains were abundant and springs infrequent. Such mountains! Apparently the Saturday nights' leavings after the good work of Creation had been completed. The name borne by any one of them would be muttered in curses by those toiling to pass their earth encumbering masses. Not so with the spring. It would be hailed with delight by the weary traveler, and between each refreshing swallow would go up a blessing upon its name. A spring has a fascination peculiarly its own; all animated nature capable of move-ment is attracted by it. The fowls of the air and beasts of the field are attracted to it. Insects and reptiles seek its freshness. The path of the explorer leads to it; by its side the pioneer builds his cabin and near it later on the country schoolhouse is located. Everyone turns aside to view a spring, and in the almost springless regions of the western mountains and plains the thirsty traveler remembers with keenest longing the springs of his eastern home with the welcome shade of their ever spreading trees. A spring is always an oasis in those desert regions and when discovered by the pioneer is noted by a name or is allowed to retain that of the aborigines to whom it was of like impor-tance, and it is the most cherished landmark of this desolate country. Highly honored is he who has his name thus perpetuated.

Tidball also recalled that on the flanks of San Francisco Peak were two lesser mountains, to which the party gave the honored names of Kendrick and Sitgreaves. "Their names were given to these mountains through mistaken compliment to them, certainly not through premeditated malice." And on the south, San Francisco Mountain was flanked by Bill Williams Mountain, "so called after a worthy of that name, a mountain trapper who belonged to that *sui generis* class of frontier wanderers who in pursuit of adventures or peltry left no nook of the wilderness untrodden."[10]

On December 18, not far from Leroux Spring, Whipple reflected on the peace and plentitude of the surrounding country. "Two years ago, when Leroux was here with Captain Sitgreaves, the hills were covered with savages, who occasioned them considerable annoyance by hostile demonstrations. But thus far, since leaving the Navajo country, we have not seen the fresh track of a wild Indian. The snow is untrodden, except by beasts and birds, which afford plenty of game. Antelope, deer, hares, and turkeys are abundant." John Tidball did not quite agree. In his personal copy of volume 3 of the *Reports* he made marginal notes, often contradicting the narrative of Whipple's "Itinerary"; in this case, in place of "are abundant," he wrote the words, "are scarce." Stanley was also unimpressed. Referring to the Colorado Chiquito, he wrote, "This River is perhaps one of the most uninteresting streams in North America." Whipple's group rejoined the main party on December 20.[11]

Christmas eve dawned cold, 3.5 degrees below zero. Several of the party went out to hunt turkeys for a feast but were unsuccessful. Tidball wrote in his copy of the *Reports*: "I was the only one who got anything. I shot three large blackish squirrels." But nothing would dampen the mood for celebration. John Sherburne loved parties, and perhaps for that reason, his descriptions of fandangos and other celebrations experienced by the explorers are always the most exuberant. He lovingly described how just after dark, Lieutenant Jones came with the compliments of his mess for them to celebrate "Buenos noches" by partaking of eggnog. Repairing to his tent, they found "an abundant supply of bottles & glasses in the center of which was a bucket of 'eggnog.'" The remainder of the party had already assembled. After taking a round or so and having a few songs, they sent for the Mexican songsters. They came numbering three or four. After having been instilled with the "proper spirit" they performed a theatrical play in which "The Devil" played no small part. After this was finished, the two opposition singers gave another song, extemporaneously, first one singing a verse and then the other. They sang an hour or so, without ceasing, and continued until obliged to stop from exhaustion.

"In the course of the song," Sherburne remembered, "they brought in every one of the parties a number of times making some very laughable and amusing rhymes. The celebration broke up about 12 with every one of the party more or less merry. Even the steady old Dr. was unable to relieve his feet of his boots and was obliged to call in his Mexy boy to pull them off."

Even the grumpy Stanley had a good time: "A huge egg–nog was manufactured and hilarity and boisterous mirth made the solitary mountains resound." Characteristically, the serious and somewhat romantic Whipple searched for a more profound meaning in the evening's entertainment. "The plaintive tones of the singers, and the strange simplicity of the people, lead one's fancy back to the middle ages. In this state of society, so free from ambition for wealth or power, where the realities of life are in a great measure subject to the ideal, there is a tinge of romance that would well repay the researches of a literary explorer. Their impromptu ballads alone would make an interesting collection."[12]

On December 27, Whipple confided to his journal, "The sick list of camp seems unfortunately to be on the increase. . . . Dr. Kennerly for some days has been suffering an attack of variola [smallpox]. Mr. Parke has been unable to move under the infection of inflammatory rheumatism. Mr. Möllhausen is recovering from chills and Mr. Sherburne and Mr. Campbell are threatened with variola or other disease. Several men have recovered from it." The smallpox epidemic went unreported in the official account. That same day Whipple noted in the *Reports* that traveling through the crusted snow became so fatiguing to the mules that it was necessary to add mules to some of the teams, which required leaving one wagon behind. The previous day Tidball had commented in his copy of the *Reports*: "Could go no further. Mules broke down." It was at this point that Leroux told Whipple they could neither proceed west nor southwest on account of successive mountains and canyons. Leroux proposed following the Sitgreaves route or going even farther to the north to keep on the dividing ridge until they reached the mountains that border the Colorado on the west, and then entering the valley.[13]

But Whipple was concerned about the engineering. "A uniform slope the whole distance would require a grade of forty feet to the mile. To keep upon the ridge, as he [Leroux] proposes, would diminish the distance at so great an expense of grade as to be objectionable. We therefore propose to follow Bill Williams' fork, which Capt. Sitgreaves has represented as rising near this place, and flowing west-southwest into Rio Colorado." But Sitgreaves, according to William Conrad, had made two serious errors in mapping Williams Fork. "First, he had mistaken the headwaters of the Verde River south of Bill Williams Mountain for the source of Williams Fork. The Verde flowed southward and emptied into the Salt River, which in turn entered the Gila. Second, he had miscomputed the latitude of the mouth of Williams Fork, placing it on his map almost a full degree (sixty miles) north of where it really was." Thus Whipple would encounter great difficulty in finding Williams Fork, "and once he had found it, he would be greatly alarmed when the stream dipped farther and farther south of the 35th Parallel."[14]

There was no good news in Whipple's December 28 journal entry: "By advice of Leroux we remained in camp to recruit the mules. Five of us, however, went to a volcanic peak 5 miles SW of Leroux Springs to reconnoiter. The country west looked dismal, hills covered with snow. On return to camp Lt. Jones was found ill, probably from an attack of small pox. Lt. Ives is worse. Mr. Campbell is quite sick. Dr. Kennerly and Mr. Parke are recovering. Mr. Sherburne is quite ill. Only one of the teamsters is now suffering with small pox, and strange it seems that thus far neither a Mexican nor soldier has been stricken."[15]

Stanley, although he enjoyed the scenery, unsurprisingly corroborated Whipple's pessimistic report on the terrain. He and Dr. Kennerly set out to climb San Francisco Mountain, but after ascending about two thousand feet, they found snow two feet deep, and traveling, in consequence, "exceedingly laborious." They continued, nevertheless, to push ahead, although they could not move more than twenty steps without stopping to take breath. After climbing more than two thirds of the way to the top, they stopped, made a fire, prepared their lunch, and made a sketch of the country at their feet. "Well did our trip repay in the magnificent prospect it unfolded to our view. With the excellent glass we had, I could see quite well an extent of country much greater than the state of Ohio . . . but if the view was magnificent it was equally disheartening to the explorer for a railroad route. The country is decidedly one of mountains and chain upon chain can be seen in every direction. Snow covered the ground for fully eighty miles to the west and the Doct. and I pronounced the fate of our wagons at a glance."[16]

While the party rested, speculation was rife as to the height of the San Francisco Peak above them. Sherburne wrote that it was measured on

December 29, but that the measurement was thought to be mistaken. The next day it was again measured, this time correctly. Tidball tells it this way.

> To settle the question some of the young surveyors of the party got out their instruments and made the necessary measurements. To our great astonishment, they made out the altitude to be about 15,000 feet above us or about 23,000 feet above sea level. This opened the discussion still hotter. The calculations were gone over again by the doubting ones until all were forced to believe that it must be so, and that it was therefore the highest mountain in the Western Hemisphere. In repacking the instruments it was discovered that a chain of 100 links, or 66 feet, had been taken for one of 100 feet, each link being supposed to be one foot. The laugh was then upon those who had made the measurement. A recomputation made the mountain stand above us a few feet less than 5,000.[17]

Not wishing to move the entire party until he was sure of the route, on December 30 Whipple set out with a small exploration party consisting of himself, Dr. Bigelow, Campbell, White, and Leroux, with Lieutenant Tidball and twenty-five men as escort, as well as cooks, servants, and pack mules. Sherburne wrote, "They do not intend returning to this Camp, but propose sending us directions where to proceed. They took ten days rations & expect to be ahead for that length of time finding a road & occasionally or semi-occasionally sending back dispatches." It was intensely cold. Stanley awoke that morning and wrote "the wind whistling not mournfully, but wrathfully through the pines of our camp during the whole night. . . . Propose to move tomorrow; I fear the attempt—*nous verrons*." The first day out, Whipple's exploratory party descended gently into a long prairie and bivouacked at the foot of a grassy hill. The next day they continued their march through the long prairie and that night camped on the side of a hill. From the top of the hill, Whipple wrote, "Looking west and southwest appeared an open country, with imperfectly defined valleys, among a dense growth of cedars; but it was difficult to say in what direction was the slope."[18]

But the distant terrain from the top of a hill could be deceptive, as Tidball tells us in his preview of the next leg of the journey. "The main thing in view was to find practicable passes through the mountains." From the San Francisco Mountain, where the difficulties of the route commenced, to the foot of the Coast Range on the Pacific, Tidball estimated to be a distance of about 650 miles, comprising a continuous succession of mountain ranges. The ranges had a general north and south direction, and while there were some elevated plateaus and some valleys of considerable extent, the principal part consisted of ranges of mountains one after another with trough-like valleys between. "These ranges lay directly across our path. They were rugged in the extreme, and so little weather worn in that dry climate as to appear fresh from their Titanic upheaval. They are simply huge masses of naked rocks of every size and form," standing upon a great swell of the earth having an average elevation of 7,500 feet above sea level. Above this swell, the mountains rose to a general height of 5,000 feet, and "the passes were mere depressions in the ranges." With the exception of the country about Leroux's Spring, Tidball added, the whole region was almost treeless. A species of cedar, hardly worthy the name of the tree, was found in most localities, giving the landscape the appearance of an old apple orchard. The wood of these cedars was extremely brittle; "a slight wrench brings off the stoutest limb and axes are not required in obtaining fuel."

As he often did, Tidball digressed, this time from mountains and valleys to trees, and then to a new subject—fauna, not flora—and then finally to the aboriginal inhabitants of the inhospitable land surrounding them. Many of the cedars were hollow from age, he noted, and afforded dry and comfortable homes for numerous colonies of pouched rats. "These animals bear but little resemblance to the repulsive vermin so familiar to us as infesting sewers and other loathsome places." When routed from their nests, they would hastily fill the pouches of their cheeks with the most precious of their stores and seek refuge in the hollow of another tree. The young, when themselves unable to run, would hold on to the teats of the mother and thus be carried to a place of safety. These rats, which also lived in holes in the ground among rocks, seemed to form the principal meat supply of the Indians in these regions, who were exceedingly expert in capturing them. "This they do with a crooked stick something like a Shepard's crook. The Indian stealthily slips the crooked end of the stick into the rat's hole, and then entices the animal out by imitating his squeak. As soon as the rat gets inside of the crook the Indian gives the stick a dexterous jerk and tosses him out. Before the rat recovers himself the Indian dispatches him by a quick blow of the same stick." The skins of the rats, after being dried, were lightly twisted and woven together and fashioned into rude capes that Tidball believed to be the only garment that the natives wore for warmth, except occasionally similar capes made of rabbit skins. Owing to the scarcity of deer and the means of taking them in so difficult a land, buckskin was not seen among the natives.

Aside from rats and occasionally lizards, Tidball thought that the food of the Indians was entirely vegetable, and of the coarsest kind, principally the berry of the cedar, and nuts from scrubby piñon. They also made considerable use of the *Agave mexicana,* commonly called the mescal, which grew abundantly but was of a "dwarfed and dried up variety." The heart of this, near the root, contained saccharine juice, which the Indians extracted by chewing, spitting out the fibrous refuse as swine do corn stalks chewed with the same object. The Indians also roasted the plant. "The coarse nature of this kind of food," Tidball observed, "makes the dried feces of the Indians resemble those of mules more than those of human beings. Although each Indian has more than ten thousand acres of land from which to draw his individual sustenance, he nevertheless is confined to short commons." Having so little to cook, they had no need of cooking utensils, except occasionally when from an extra catch of rats and lizards they wished to have an extra feast; they then scooped out with sharp stones the pulpous inside of an *Opuntia* cactus and made of the cactus a trough two or three feet long and about half that in breadth. In this trough they cooked their mess by means of heated stones placed inside. The pulp of the cactus contained a sweetish nutriment, as well as a supply of water, and was always used as a part of the stew.

Then Tidball departed from his factual description of how the Indians clothed and fed themselves and concluded with a brief and opinionated historical essay.

These Indians are tied to no particular locality by hut or teepee. Holes among rocks or a few bushes propped together are their abodes. They have no domestic animals, not even dogs. They themselves fulfill every condition of the lowest beasts. Yet these same Indians within less than a generation of the period referred to, having obtained horses, and supplied themselves with firearms, welcomed the white man with bloody hands to inhospitable graves in this, their inhospitable land. To hunt and subdue them demanded of Uncle Sam's soldiers untold toil, suffering and deprivation, and cost to the government the value of his full weight in gold for each buck sent to the happy hunting ground.

It was winter when the party traversed those parts described by Tidball, and the Indians, so derogatorily characterized by him, had left the higher and colder region of the mountains for the lower and warmer belt toward the Gila, as was their custom, and would not actually be seen until the party neared the Colorado.[19]

Chapter 6

The Artist as Hero of His Own Journey

As he set off with the reconnaissance party, Tidball described how they would thoroughly explore the country for several miles on each side of their line of march. Whipple, with a few of his assistants and a small escort, and Leroux as guide and advisor, would go ahead hunting to the right and left for suitable passes in the mountains. This sometimes required an absence of eight or ten days from the main party. "I generally accompanied Whipple on these tentative explorations," Tidball wrote, "and was thus made more familiar with the country. When a favorable route was discovered a courier was sent back and guided the main party forward." From high eminences they diligently scanned the ranges of mountains ahead and studied their trend, their breaks and their spurs, discussing the probability of finding a practicable route between or over or around them. "Many of these views were magnificent from their extent, looking over wide valleys to ranges of mountains far in the distance. The valleys when thus looked down upon appeared quite level, while in reality they are much broken by rounded ravines." Among the ravines the stunted cedars divided the landscape into farmlike regularity.[1]

The first day of 1854 was bright and clear. Whipple gave the name "New Year's Spring" to a pool ten or twelve feet in diameter with water twenty inches deep. "The amount of water was not perceptibly diminished by what the mules had drunk during the night," Whipple observed, and then concluded, "It therefore appeared to be a permanent spring," a conclusion Tidball challenged by writing in the margin of his copy of the *Reports*, "which it was not." This is an example of Tidball's running commentary and criticism of Whipple's official report. While Tidball may have wished to be accepted as a typical and well-fitting military member of the survey—and we can assume that in his cynically good humored way he was—in his writing, especially in his contemporaneous diary and marginalia in his copy of the *Reports*, he instinctively challenged the conventional wisdom of Whipple and some of the other survey principals.[2]

They proceeded southwest, and after traveling about twelve miles, spread their blankets beneath a cedar tree three miles west of Bill Williams Mountain. Within three weeks of joining the party, Tidball was to complete his second drawing; the first, it will be recalled, was *San Francisco Mountain*. On that New Year's Day, while they surveyed the rim country above Ash Fork, Arizona, Whipple, who finally got Tidball's name right, wrote in his journal "Lieut. Tidball has taken a sketch showing the Sierra de la Laja and Pichaco, some twenty-five miles distant, between which the trail crossed. A chain of blue hills appears in the distance, and extends towards the south-southeast; its crest evidently preserving nearly the same altitude; but the descent of the valley along its foot causes the southern portion, represented in the sketch, to appear a formidable range." This drawing, entitled *Aztec Range and Black Forest*, has survived and is in the Archives and Manuscripts Division of the Oklahoma Historical Society. A woodcut taken from the drawing appears on page 85, part 1, volume 3 of the *Reports*, with the slightly different title *Black Forest, Pichaco, and Mountains North of Aztec Pass*. Tidball offers a further explanatory note. "In looking southward from the San Francisco plateau the lay of the country—gradually sloping downward—brings the scrub cedars into such positions as to cut off from view the wide intervals between them: thus giving the landscape an appearance of a dense forest, the dark hue of which suggested the name *Black Forest*. It is in reality no forest at all." Whoever wrote the caption for this woodcut—it was probably Whipple—misstated the locality. Recent investigation and photographic comparisons reveal that in all likelihood the sketch matches more closely a view to the southwest showing Granite Mountain and Sullivan Buttes.[3]

Why were artists included in Pacific railroad survey parties? The answer is simple. Jefferson Davis's instructions required the investigation of flora, fauna, geology, and Indian life along the routes, and it was instantly perceived that drawings of these phenomena would liven up the reports. The old saying "One picture is worth a thousand words" was never truer

Black Forest, Pichaco, and Mountains North of Aztec Pass.
This drawing by Tidball was probably mislabeled by Whipple. In all
likelihood, the sketch shows a view to the southwest showing
Granite Mountain and Sullivan Buttes.

than in the case when Dr. Bigelow was attempting to describe the appearance of a new *Opuntia*. Competent draftsmen or illustrators would be needed then, and many of the artists who contributed to the *Reports* were no more than that. The drawings of fish, snakes, birds, mammals, plants, and aborigines fell within the ambit of Davis's charge to the scientific camp. But the most memorable contributions of the eleven artists who rode westward with the five surveys were not purely scientific—they were sweeping and often imaginative landscapes. Some of these drawings, made into lithographs, or woodcuts or wood engravings, could be said to advance slightly the geological knowledge of the country; but the intent of the artists in most cases was to produce an aesthetically pleasing image—an inspiring scenic portrait—a work of art.

There was in mid-nineteenth-century America a preoccupation with nature, and that preoccupation manifested itself in landscape painting—a continuation of the late-eighteenth-century notion of America as the "virgin land," a world unsullied by civilization. And as author Barbara Novak wrote, the landscape artist's prominent role in the exploration of the American continent was as diverse as that great adventure itself. "In style, it ran the gamut from the simple topographical description of the earlier western expeditions to the baroque glorification of the great surveys of the seventies. The artist was explorer, scientist, educator, frontiersman, and minister. He ran risks and suffered extreme hardships which certified his 'heroic' status. This heroism became a kind of tour de force in the vicinity of art."

Dr. Novak, who might have added the vocation of soldier to her list, believes that while in Europe, the tour de force generally received its scale from the artist's ambition, set resplendently within a major tradition, in America, it consisted in simply "getting there."

The artist became the hero of his own journey—which replaced the heroic themes of mythology—by vanquishing physical obstacles en route to a destination. For the ambition of the artistic enterprise was substituted the ambition of the artist's quest—itself a major nineteenth-century theme. In this displacement of the heroic from the work of art to the persona of the artist lay, perhaps, part of the attraction of unexplored territory for the American artist at mid-century.[4]

By the second decade of the nineteenth century, landscape artists had invaded the American West. In 1820 Samuel Seymour ended the Long expedition with over 150 pictures, although most of them have disappeared, including "what might have been a first comprehensive view of the plains and Rockies," according to Goetzmann and Goetzmann. Young Titian Peale's animal and bird drawings were "so admired as scientific art that he became one of the artists on Lt. Charles Wilkes's [expeditions] that between 1838 and 1842 sailed the South Seas . . . as well as the ice-bound shores of the Antarctic Continent for the first time." Titian Peale's was a heroic and adventurous life, but as he lived on into the 1870s, his "first visions of the far West seemed to haunt him more than anything else he had seen, and he painted them over and over again. In each rendition, science gave way more and more to art."

George Catlin, painting in the 1830s and 1840s, specialized in Indians. So did John Mix Stanley at first, but in 1846, Stanley, who was to become a Pacific railroad survey artist, accompanied Colonel Stephen Watts Kearny's army as it marched across the Southwest in 1846. "On this epic march, Stanley painted landscape scenes in stunningly beautiful fashion," although some were fanciful and romantic. Captain Seth Eastman, formerly a drawing teacher at West Point, painted Indians, but "did not paint vivid scenes of war, massacres or even buffalo hunts"; he concentrated on the everyday life of North American aborigines. Eastman was selected as the principal illustrator for Henry Rowe Schoolcraft's definitive study of the Indian, a position rejected by Catlin; later, John Tidball would succeed Eastman in that position.

In 1832 the German Prince Alexander Maximillian arrived in the United States, accompanied by the Swiss view painter Karl Bodmer. The next year Maximillian was at Fort Union, far up the Missouri, where Bodmer produced some of his best landscapes, two fine examples of which are *First Chain of the Rocky Mountains Above Fort McKenzie* and *View of the Junction of the Missouri and Yellowstone Rivers*. Alfred Jacob Miller, who went west in 1837, was another pioneering artist, who painted mountain men and Indians as well as landscapes. "Miller's paintings of these mountains and lakes were never meant to be geologically accurate renditions. They were created to evoke feelings of surpassing, almost unreal, beauty." By the mid-nineteenth century, the tradition of adventure and art in the vast American West was well established by those precursors to the artists of the Great Reconnaissance.[5]

The Goetzmanns believed that the genre of art produced by the military expeditions at mid-century "was a combination of romantic view painting and topographical renditions with pretensions to scientific accuracy. These Western views of the Manifest Destiny era were not art in the grand or painterly manner, but rather, sketches and watercolors." They were usually meant as scientific illustrations, appearing in the same context with detailed drawings of plants, animals, fossils, and Indians. The landscapes, designed to be made into lithographs, however, were typically examples of the symbiotic relationship between science and art typical of the period. The artists who accompanied scientific expeditions went "with the idea of accurate documentation, but so stunned were they by what they saw—ranging from rock formations to immense herds of buffalo—that they often produced romanticized interpretations of the unknown territory."[6]

The Pacific railroad survey artists—there were eleven in all, including Tidball—who contributed illustrations to the published reports of the surveys were to play a prominent role in the exploration and depiction of the American West. The work of these artists "varied in quality, but they shared the same dedication and suffered the same risks." They all "devoted their artistic as well as physical energies to enlighten and inspire the readers of the surveys."[7]

Among the better artists who accompanied the surveys were Richard Kern, John Mix Stanley, F. W. von Egloffstein, and Gustavus Sohon. Richard Kern was one of two artist brothers who headed west in 1848 with John Frémont. The expedition ended in disaster as Frémont and his mountain man guide, Old Bill Williams, led the party into the impassable mountains of northern New Mexico in the middle of winter. Ute Indians killed both Benjamin Kern and Old Bill Williams as they returned to reclaim baggage that the party had left behind. Richard Kern, who was a member of the Academy of Natural Sciences of Philadelphia, continued to sketch and paint and produced some splendid watercolors. On his return from the disastrous Frémont expedition, Kern painted the Taos Valley in watercolor, a painting that may be the first of this view. In 1849 both Richard and Edward Kern, another brother, accompanied Colonel John M. Washington's punitive expedition against the Navajos north and west of Santa Fe. On this trip Richard Kern painted the spectacular Canyon de Chelly, the first to do so. In 1851 he was with Captain Sitgreaves on his march across the Southwest and painted more memorable views. In 1853, while accompanying Gunnison on the central Pacific railroad survey, Kern, along with Gunnison, was murdered by Paiute Indians near Sevier Lake. After Kern and Gunnison were killed, Lieutenant E. G. Beckwith was left in charge and was soon joined by Baron F. W. von Egloffstein, a highly regarded western illustrator who painted immense and exacting panoramas illustrating the central railroad route. "His drawings, with place names below the picture, were perhaps the only drawings that would have been helpful to railroad builders or site engineers. Yet these drawings, too," wrote the Goetzmanns, "were highly romantic in content. One showed an Indian and his dog resting atop the mountains like some nature god sadly surveying all that he had once possessed." The instinct to find spiritual significance in nature was inherent in the broadly devout American consciousness.[8]

By the time he was twenty-one, John Mix Stanley had already studied with James Bowman, one of the foremost art teachers of the day. After seeing Catlin's Indian Gallery in Baltimore, Stanley was inspired to create his own gallery of American Indians," and in 1843 he was painting Cherokees in the Indian Territory. As we have seen, he accompanied

Kearny's Army of the West across the Southwest and later traveled up the West Coast to the Oregon Country, where he narrowly escaped the Whitman massacre. By 1853, when he was hired as artist-draftsman for the northern route Pacific railroad survey, Stanley's work had been displayed in the Smithsonian Institution, and he was being touted as Catlin's superior. Art historian Robert Taft believed Stanley was "by far the best equipped both by ability and experience, of any of the artists that accompanied the Pacific Railroad Surveys." Stanley proved to be a master at capturing perspective and distance, and at depicting geological phenomena. His drawings illustrate terrain, mountain passes, and important geographical or geological features such as the Marias River, the Falls of the Spokane, and Flathead Lake. One of his most striking drawings, *Herd of Bison, Near Lake Jesse*, captured the vast spaciousness of the plains filled with enormous herds spreading to the horizon. Using a spyglass, he could see the horizon fifteen miles in the distance but still not the entire herd. According to one art historian, it is the best existing illustration of a large prerailroad buffalo herd.[9]

One of the least known but most talented of the Pacific railroad artists was Gustavus Sohon. He was born in Germany in 1825 and immigrated to America in 1842 to avoid service in the Prussian army. In 1852, apparently deciding that some armies are better than others, he enlisted in the U.S. Army. A year later private Sohon found himself trekking across the plains of Montana with Isaac I. Stevens on the northern route Pacific railroad survey. He began to draw and eventually contributed ten or twelve drawings to the final report. The most unusual one was occasioned by Lieutenant John Mullan's crossing of the swollen Hellgate River during what turned out to be an afternoon of terror. Mullan pushed off in his raft, aiming for a piece of projecting land on the opposite shore of the dreaded river. But swept by the impetuous current, they moved in the channel with a headlong velocity. After being knocked overboard, they stripped to facilitate their swimming, but the raft was broken to pieces, and they found themselves on a desolate island, naked, with a broad stream still between them and their destination. Members from another raft finally rescued them. This was rich subject matter for an imaginative artist, and Gustav Sohon was just the man. His drawing, entitled *Crossing the Hellgate River May 5th 1854*, dramatic and full of action, is a masterpiece of composition. It depicts three men clambering across a log island while the current rages past them, and has been compared by one critic to

Gericault's *The Raft of the Medusa*. Another critic wrote that Sohon's drawings "surpass the work of Stanley, the expedition's official artist." Sohon went on to attend several Indian Treaty Councils with Governor Stevens, serving as interpreter as well as artist. He later joined John Mullan, who was spearheading the construction of a military road from Walla Walla to Fort Benton, and made a number of drawings while on that assignment. It has been said of Sohon, "[H]is talents put him in the same league with other, better known, western artists such as George Catlin and Paul Kane, though he is best compared to Karl Bodmer."[10]

How John Tidball came to offer his services as an expedition artist is unknown. Although his responsibilities were strictly military—to protect the civilian members of the scientific expedition—as we have seen, within five days of joining the party, Tidball had completed his first drawing. West Pointers were all taught to draw, and it was second nature for them to sketch topography. As all those artists who had roamed the sparsely inhabited reaches of the continent before him, he must also have been motivated and inspired by the scenic beauty—by the harsh grandeur of the American Southwest.

Besides Tidball, two other members of the Whipple expedition contributed artwork. One was Albert H. Campbell, engineer and surveyor, who like Tidball had a primary job not connected with drawing but whom Taft credits with "having considerable ability in sketching," and whom William H. and William N. Goetzmann describe as being "especially effective in rendering the Southwestern deserts and the ancient marine terraces." Three of the lithographic illustrations are usually credited to Campbell, one of which actually was drawn by Tidball. The third artist was, of course, the famous Balduin Möllhausen, the principal illustrator of the expedition, who produced by far the most drawings that ended up in Whipple's report as woodcuts or lithographs. "Campbell and Tidball evidently gave Möllhausen some serious artistic competition," notes critic Ben W. Huseman, "but how much influence they had on Möllhausen's work is more difficult to determine. Campbell had a good command of perspective and composition, and Tidball had a feel for landscape drawing, composition, perspective, and a fair ability to draw figures." Tidball, as we have seen, was fond of Möllhausen, whom he found "full to overflowing with amiability and kindness to everyone," but was unimpressed by his artistic ability. On this, his second trip to America, Möllhausen's sketches were still awkward; Huseman found that he had difficulty with proportions, "and was plagued by a lack of knowledge about the rules of perspective and by a poor sense of scale." Möllhausen continued to progress as an artist, however, and the watercolors he produced after his return to Prussia are superior to the ones he produced in the United States.[11]

Although Whipple did not criticize Möllhausen's landscapes, he had some doubts about his abilities to accurately portray Indians. The whimsical German artist drew Navajo warriors, described by Whipple as bright-eyed and enthusiastic, with eyes half closed and slumped over on their tired mounts. Whipple describes another of Möllhausen's portrayal of Indians this way: "*Plate 22* is intended to represent Navajos. The sketch is given as furnished by the artist; though, excepting the striped blanket of Navajo manufacture, the portraits differ little from those of the Pueblo Indians." And again, "*Plate 23* exhibits portraits of Tonto Indians. Their appearance, according to the sketch, certainly indicates stupidity sufficient to render their name appropriate. But our guide, who had been among them, and known their reputation for thieving, said that they were neither stupid nor foolish." Art historian Doris Ostrander Dawdy concluded, flatly: "Tidball's sketches are superior to Möllhausen's."[12]

Professor David Miller, who has written extensively about Möllhausen, said, "Möllhausen was not a professionally trained artist. His art never reached the level of competence of better-known western painters. Yet, although Möllhausen was not an artist of stature, his sketches and watercolors are useful historical documents." The same could be said of Tidball and Campbell. All three were competent, and none of them towered over the others in artistic ability. Great artists they were not, but they were skilled illustrators as well as great adventurers, and their renditions of the marvels of the undiscovered Southwest landscape thrilled thousands of Americans in the mid-nineteenth century when the *Reports* was published.[13]

Robert Taft, whose work remains one of the best sources on art created by Pacific railroad illustrators, reckons that ten of the lithographic illustrations are directly credited to Möllhausen, and two indirectly. Of the sixty-five woodcuts, Taft says, "thirty five appear to be credited" to the German. Taft admits the difficulty in accurately attributing many of the illustrations. "The question of passing final judgment in the case of pictorial records, too, is complicated by the fact that many times the *original* work of the artist is not available. The only record of the artist may be a reproduction in the form of a lithograph, a woodcut print, or an engraving." Discrepancies and variations in printing, dating, and entitling the lithographs adds further uncertainty; Taft concludes, "As a result of these variations one becomes cautious about making too definite statements concerning the illustrations." The discovery of Tidball's memoir, in which he takes credit for some drawings previously attributed to other artists, provides new insights that will be discussed in the context of specific illustrations.[14]

After Tidball finished his New Year's Day sketch, Whipple's exploratory party continued on and made camp on a dry branch of Bill Williams Fork. The next day they continued to descend; the snow had nearly disappeared, and they found in the vegetation an agreeable change from the higher country they had left. Whipple observed the *Agave mexicana,* as Tidball had, but expanded on his description. "It is the beautiful American aloe, or Century plant, called in this country Mezcal. The apaches roast it for food; Mexicans distil from it a spirituous liquor."[15]

On January 3, the first entry by a fourth diarist occurs. A fragment of the diary of John C. Tidball, covering the period from January 3, 1854, to February 22, 1854, was discovered fewer than thirty years ago. Concise, descriptive—and interesting for the frank observations by one who, as a member of the military escort, was essentially an outsider—it is punctuated with the mordant humor that typifies the writings of Tidball, especially as he ridiculed the nonmilitary component of the expedition. While he recorded matter-of-factly the mid-winter hardships encountered by the party as it trudged across the rugged ground of what is now northern Arizona, he did not dwell as incessantly as the melancholy Stanley on the party's discomfort. On that day Tidball saw from the west to the southeast extended ranges of mountains, apparently three running somewhat parallel to each other. "The intervening space between them and us was a gently rolling country covered to a great degree with cedars and cut with many ravines." Winding down through the ravines, he wrote, proved exceedingly difficult and hard on the mules because of the angular stones over which they picked their way.[16]

The next few days Whipple endeavored to communicate with the main surveying party by smoke signal, but intervening hills prevented their signals from being seen. From atop a hill he looked anxiously for smoke signals or campfires but saw neither. At the main camp Sherburne wrote that they kept signal fires burning nearly all day in hope of hearing from Whipple but heard nothing. At length Whipple saw Bill Williams Mountain before him. To the east-northeast were several volcanic hills, and at the foot of one of them was New Year's Spring. Here again, at sunset, they made the usual signal, but fruitlessly, as before. "Unable to account for this," Whipple said, "we had many misgivings with regard to the safety of our friends. The loss of mules by an Indian stampede is the great danger to be apprehended in a country like this. A plan for that purpose, well concerted by savages, is almost sure to succeed; and, however strong the sufferers may be, pursuit is hopeless."[17]

A cold sleet blowing in their faces awoke them before daybreak on January 6. They again tried to signal the main party and watched in vain for the smoke of campfires. Without stopping, they traveled over broken ground for fourteen miles to New Year's Spring, where to their delight, they found the main body encamped. That day Stanley wrote in his diary, "Kept in bed most of the day to keep warm." Sherburne said everyone was overjoyed to see them, but said of the explorers, "They were pretty well disgusted with the trip, as might easily be seen, tho' none would admit it." Möllhausen said that during the main party's stay at New Year's Spring, the smiths were constantly employed in examining the hoofs of the mules and shoeing them when necessary due to the damage done by traveling over the rough lava-covered ground. "After the return of the reconnoitering party, the same thing had to be done for their animals."[18]

The night of January 7, Whipple slept uneasily. "The whole nightlong through the tall pines that surrounded camp wind whistled," he remembered, "sometimes mournfully, sometimes with wild strains that seemed to threaten a calamity. It was a relief when morning broke to find that, with the thermometer at 30.6, our mules had not suffered badly." By January 10 the party had traversed Cedar Creek Valley and passed westwardly over a slight ridge into a wide ravine that led into the great basin of the Black Forest.

Four miles south brought them to large pools of water in a rocky glen called Partridge Creek and an excellent campground with rich grama grass and large cedar trees for fuel and shelter. Game was abundant. A black-tailed deer and many partridges were killed, and tracks of deer, antelope, bears, and turkeys were numerous. "Hares and rabbits are frequently started from their hiding places upon our trail. Singularly colored gophers, rats and mice are found in hollow trees and crevices of rocks."[19]

On January 11, Whipple again set out ahead with a reconnaissance party—with ten men for an escort. He thought he saw a break in the mountain range near the Pichaco and decided to explore in that direction. That night they found an excellent camp, and Whipple dispatched "a trusty Mexican to conduct the train hither," where it would await a signal from the advance party. The next day they turned toward the Southwest and after eleven miles, bivouacked among the cedars. Whipple was still looking for a way through the mountains. "Although no gap can be seen from any point of view we have had, yet it is possible that a nearer approach may show some break in the chain."[20]

Möllhausen said at first they thought Partridge Creek was the Bill Williams River but later realized their mistake.

> It was not easy, however, to identify a river of which we knew only the mouth, and presumed to have its source in the Bill Williams Mountains. All else that we knew concerning this river rested on the narratives and the testimony of a certain trapper, denominated Bill Williams, who, coming down the Great Colorado, had discovered the mouth of a river near some village of the Mohave Indians, and had followed it up to the neighborhood of some mountains, which were also called after him by the western hunters, until at last his name found its way to the newest maps.

On a hill they "made a smoke," as agreed upon with the main party, but saw no sign in reply. Whipple was starting to lose confidence in his guides and seemed to be depending on a higher power. "Thus far," he said, "we have been highly favored by providence, finding a route today with water, grama and fuel unobjectionable for a wagon road or a railway."[21]

On January 13, Whipple raised "a huge column of smoke," but again no answering signal was seen from the wagon camp; two soldiers were dispatched to conduct the train ahead. Back with the wagon train, Sherburne reported that at sundown a great smoke was discovered southwest of them. "We returned it & kept it up till dark. It is uncertain whether it was a campfire or not & even if it were a signal fire, what does it mean? Quien sabe?" Clearly, the smoke signal method of communication left something to be desired in the way of clarity and dependability. The wagon train decided to take a chance and the next morning struck their tents and started in the direction of the fire. Late that night the two soldiers came in; they had missed them on the trail on account of the intervening hills and canyons. The wagon train was instructed to watch for another smoke signal but the weather interfered. "'Tis not known whether any were made," wrote Sherburne, "as there has been a very high wind all day & heavy clouds, so as to obscure everything in the shape of smoke."[22]

Meanwhile Whipple, suffering from uncertainty and loss of confidence, was becoming distressed. He believed that there were two formidable ranges of mountains standing between their location and the Colorado River, which from all the information they could obtain formed a complete barrier. Moreover, not sharing Tidball's unbounded confidence in Leroux, he did not completely trust the mountain man. He confided his loss of confidence in the seasoned guide to his diary, noting that for two days they had traveled on the route without finding water, and neither Leroux nor Savedra had expressed confidence of finding water soon. They concluded to return to the Pichaco and follow the stream of Partridge Creek to its junction with Williams Fork. Whipple continued his sharp criticism of Leroux:

> Therefore, much to the discomfiture of Leroux, who has used every artifice to cause us to follow the route over which he led Capt. Sitgreaves, we decided to explore further. . . . When we first explored at the southern base of Williams Mt. and found it possible to reach the waters of the stream that flows south from it, Leroux first expressed a doubt whether the maps of Sitgreaves might not be in error and this stream really flows into the San Francisco. Contrary to his advice we reached Pichaco and found a fine passage south where he had said it was impossible to go even with pack mules. He then stoutly affirmed that Partridge creek which we had followed must flow into Rio Gila inasmuch as he then recollected that Bill Williams had told him that the fork named for him rose west of the Pichaco and flowed parallel to the big river.[23]

On January 15, without the aid of smoke, Whipple found the main party with the train and said, "They had been here two days, and the mules were literally rolling with satiety in the luxuriant grass of the valley." He reported securing a new species of pouched rats, which Tidball said he had caught, and an owl, which Tidball said, "I shot with my revolver." Sherburne reported that the exploration party had returned disgusted: "The accounts of the country are bad but there is no help for it. In fact nothing is known of the country as neither of the guides have been over it."[24]

The exploring party went out again on January 16 supplemented by

Lieutenant Jones and sixteen men. "The quick eye" of Mr. Campbell marked a promising passage through the overlapping mountains; Whipple thought the valley might break through the Sierra near the Black Mountain, and they decided to continue the reconnaissance farther south. They bivouacked on January 17, and ascended a high peak for a view of the terrain, but again found only discouragement. The slopes all appeared to tend in the direction of that valley, destroying their hopes of reaching the Colorado by any stream they had crossed. Whipple decided to return to Pueblo Creek and first explore that stream to its source.[25]

By this time Whipple had begun to doubt the existence of the Williams Fork. "Hope is the name given to the snowy peaks north of which we now desire to find a passage for the wagons," he wrote in his diary "thence to gain some branch of Williams Fork—should such a stream be found to exist." On January 18, they turned back and, finding a good camping place, sent back to Pichaco with orders to Lieutenant Ives to bring the train to the place, determining meanwhile to explore for a pass westward through the Aztec Range. Tidball later commented in his copy of the *Reports*, "I had anticipated these orders, on account of the water giving out, there being no fuel, and the weather being extremely cold. I gave orders to move across the valley to the next mountains where there was plenty of timber."[26]

Tidball described January 19 as "[t]he most disagreeable day I have ever experienced." It rained as they started, then hailed, he said, followed by sleet and snow so dense with the wind blowing directly in their faces that it was impossible at times to see a hundred yards in advance. Lost in the wilderness with undependable guides, Whipple had every reason to feel morose, but he managed to find beauty and some humor in the inclement weather.

> Morning light disclosed a scene fit for a painter's pencil. A sheet of snow four inches deep covered the earth and the sleepers of camp. The tardy risers were just beginning to seek a breath of fresh air, but as their heads were uncovered, masses of snow fell into the beds making the occupants anxious to restore the equilibrium. Popping back their heads like prairie dogs they had to await breakfast. But soon the melting snow trickling through the saturated blankets drove them forth into the pelting storm.[27]

After an uncomfortable breakfast, they packed up and marched. Following a fresh Indian trail, they ascended the summit hill, passing into the western branch. "The storm pelted us most piteously," Whipple wrote in his journal. "Snow and sleet were driven in our faces by the merciless wind cutting our faces badly. One of the soldiers exclaimed to a Frenchman, 'Now talk of your Buonaparte crossing the Alps.'" After sunset the wind came only in gusts "apparently wandering among the mountains, now rushing upon us with the roaring of an avalanche, now sighing in the distance among the pines. But not a cloud dims the brightness of the stars." At noon they had followed the western creek about four miles, finding a beautiful slope and fine valley and pools of water. "To distinguish this pass and the mountain of granite which bounds it upon the north, we call them Aztec Mountain & Aztec Pass. Who can say that an ancient people did not pass this way?" At last Whipple had found his passage through the seemingly impenetrable mountains.[28]

A woodcut depicting Aztec Pass appears in volume 3 of the *Reports*, on page 35 of part 2, "Report on the Topographical Features and Character of the Country." It was taken from a sketch by Tidball and is described by Whipple as being on the top of a low granitic spur, which seems to connect the northern with the southern portion of the Aztec Range. "The accompanying sketch," Whipple reported, "taken from the ancient ruins that crown a height upon the north, overlooking the pass, represents the summit of the dividing ridge and the prolongation of the Aztec range towards the south. In the distance, upon the left, is seen the top of Mount Hope and the Gemini mountain is shown upon the right. From the latter extends a sloping plain to the wide valley in which Williams River takes its rise."[29]

On January 21 two Mexicans were dispatched to meet the rear party. A few hours after their departure, Lieutenant Ives arrived. He had left Pichaco several days earlier, having seen Whipple's smoke signal on the previous evening. During the storm of that day, Whipple said, Ives had crossed the great valley to the entrance among the cedars, where the men Whipple first sent met him. Tidball, in a marginal note on his copy of the *Reports*, complained that he had to prod the recalcitrant Ives: "It was a terrific storm. Sometimes we could not see a rod in advance of account of the sleet in our faces. Ives wanted to stop every minute but I forced him on." The exploration party and the wagon train had now joined forces to start through the Aztec Pass together. The next day they traveled six miles and ascended 4,286 feet on what Stanley called "the worst road we have yet had since leaving Albuquerque." Sherburne described the scene

View of Aztec Pass from the Indian ruins, looking south.

View of Aztec Pass. Whipple named this pass sketched by Tidball, writing
"Who can say that an ancient people did not pass this way?"

at day's end. "When within a half mile of camp the road got very bad &
although the teams were doubled the mules could not draw the wagons.
They were entirely given out with the hard day's work. The soldiers,
teamsters & Mexys were turned out & taking one wagon at a time, then
finally pulled them all & pushed the mules into camp with all the cheers,
shrieks & uncouth noises imaginable."[30]

Oppressed by his gloomy surroundings, Möllhausen painted a more
somber picture.

We had before us the primeval wilderness, untouched, unchanged,
apparently as it came from the hands of the Creator. It was not, however, the grand primeval forest such as may be seen more to the East,
nor the dreary deserts characteristic of this mountain chain; but low
cedars, and scattered oaks and pines, growing as irregularly as if they
had been flung there at random among fantastically formed rocks, and
masses of rolled stones, that had much the appearance of masonry.
The utter deathlike stillness of this solitude, where every word spoken,

and every footfall were distinctly re-echoed, had something in it strangely oppressive. Even the animals appeared to shun the place.[31]

Stanley complained that to ascend the pass, all the wagons had to be unloaded and the contents packed on mules. "After marching a mile we came to the summit of the mountain, or summit of the pass, which we crossed our wagons over with the assistance of all the men." After the ordeal Sherburne was optimistic. "Prospects brightening & the wagons *may get through after all.*" The moody Whipple, looking beyond the immediate success, was not so sure. In the official report he wrote about relying on guides, compasses, and maps; in his diary he continued to look for help from a supernatural power. "Our first impressions are therefore confirmed that with a railway keeping the slope near the base of the Aztec ridge after rising from grama valley, would be able with slight cutting to pass the summit and descend the slope of the western valley. Beyond the country looks far from inviting. Mountain chains seem to encircle us. Many are the dark forebodings in camp. But the kind providence that has led us through several mountain ranges at a distance seemingly impenetrable will we trust guide us to the end."[32]

On January 24 they moved onward, following a well-beaten Indian trail. "South of the valley was a swelling ridge, and a remarkable mountain rising 2,000 feet above its sides, clothed with dark cedars, and, in the center, cut as it were into two equal peaks; hence called the Gemini." Whipple decided that it would again be necessary to proceed in advance with an exploring party; the next day, after rounding up forty mules that had stampeded, with a small contingent he resumed his westward course. Along with Bigelow, Campbell, White, and sixteen men, Tidball was a member of that party; within the next three days he would complete two of his finest sketches, both of which would adorn the final *Reports* as lithographs.[33]

Chapter 7

We Will Be on Mule Meat before We Are Through

On January 26 Whipple's advance party followed the direction of the canyon nearly south ten miles, to the southeast point of a small range of mountains that, from the numerous streams flowing from it, was called the Aquarius Range. There they spread their blankets under the cedars. From an elevated point of view, Whipple wrote, they could see back to where they had left the train. The general surface of the country, which consisted of great beds of lava and trap dikes, overlying or intersecting limestone and granite, appeared like a plain, but in various directions it was cut into small canyons, through which flowed rills of clear water. One branch, bearing a fine stream from the northwest, joined the main creek near this point of Aquarius Mountain. "The sides of these deep ravines are frequently perpendicular cliffs," Whipple the engineer opined, "forming narrow chasms which might easily be bridged. Occasionally the banks recede, affording a declivity by which a train may effect a passage." In his copy of the *Reports*, in another challenge to the survey leader's veracity, Tidball added caustically after Whipple's last sentence, "if it had wings." Reading the acerbic commentary in John Tidball's diary and his biting interpositions in his copy of volume 3 of the *Reports*, one is tempted to dismiss him as overzealous and intolerant, but his annotations in the *Reports* simply show that he was nettled at the publication's perceived inaccuracies.[1]

"From the hill the view toward the setting sun looks bright and cheering for the railway," Whipple wrote in his journal, adding anxiously, "but the piles of hills with cañons intervening threw dark shadows upon our hopes for the wagons." Then he reflected further on the solitude and the beauty of the scene and, as he often did when confiding to his diary, drifted into a mystical mode of thought.

> Those accustomed to tentless prairies can feel why the shepherds of old should have been the fathers of astronomy. The converging magnificence of heaven as witnessed in lonely watchings of night expands the soul and leads enquiry into fathomless regions of space. I would give much to know what the rude, untaught savage of this region thinks when gazing at such scenes. Houseless, homeless, sons of nature, roaming from mountain springs to valley streams, wild & free as the deer they chase, still they are formed in the image of man having human fears and hopes, and with a soul, doubtless aspiring to the infinite, the immortal.[2]

January 26 was a day bracketed by the birthdays of Möllhausen and Tidball. They were born within two days of each other twenty-eight years earlier; Tidball being the elder first saw the light of day on January 25, Möllhausen on the 27th. None of the journals indicates that time was taken off to celebrate either, or both, events.

Tidball described the encampment that afternoon as being "among the hills at the southern extremity of an immense trap dyke." This is the site of a major drawing by Tidball. Entitled *Bivouac, Jan. 26,* and lithographed by T. Sinclair of Philadelphia, it is found facing page 95 of part 1, volume 3 of the *Reports.* Whipple wrote, "The sides of these dark ravines are generally perpendicular cliffs, resting upon steep rocky slopes which neither man nor beast may climb." The camp was sited "upon one of the multitude of mountain rills which Aquarius has filled with water." The drawing depicts a tranquil scene with three men sitting around a campfire, with mules grazing in the distance under huge masses of rock. One of the gentlemen is holding a plant. This was, Tidball noted on his copy of the lithograph, "Dr. Bigelow studying his favorite cactus." Although this lithograph is credited in some printings to Möllhausen, and in some to Tidball, there is extraneous evidence to establish irrefutably that Tidball was the artist who rendered the scene.

On January 27, Tidball recorded, "Traveled today about 8 mi. in a general direction of N. W. over succession of high hills or mountains so steep and rocky that it was with the greatest difficulty that our mules could get along; between these hills were deep ravines running S. Westwardly. We could see nothing but deep cañons and broken mountains in every direction."[3]

Bivouac, Jan. 26. This lithograph was taken from John Tidball's drawing of a campsite described by Lieutenant Whipple as being situated "upon one of the multitude of mountain rills which Aquarius has filled with water."

The next day, Whipple wrote, they were "favored with another charming morning, mild and without a breeze," and they followed an Indian trail down White Cliff Valley. A short distance below, five Indians were seen. They would not come to the party nor allow themselves to be approached. After half an hour of vain efforts to induce them to friendly intercourse, the party continued down the creek. Tidball said they "were the first that we have seen," meaning of course the first Indians seen since he joined the expedition. Then they came upon a deserted Indian encampment from which a party of perhaps twenty had evidently fled in haste on their approach, leaving behind a fire and the remnants of their breakfast. Their fare had been dressed in novel style. A large *Echinocactus* furnished not only a portion of the food, but also the sole culinary apparatus. It was three feet long and two in diameter, cut upon one side and hollowed so as to make a trough. Into this were thrown the soft portions of the pulpy substance which surrounds the heart of the cactus; and to them had been added game, and plants gathered from the banks of the creek. Mingled with water, the whole had been cooked by stirring it up with heated stones. "They probably owed us no good will for disturbing their meal," Whipple remembered, "but nevertheless kept a

respectful distance." The party members saw Indians on all sides following them until early afternoon when they stopped to graze the mules and
fill their canteens for a trip to the apparently waterless hills to the north
where they hoped to find a passage for their wagons. With the Indians
still nearby, they took possession of a grassy spot among the cedars for a
night's rest.

At that grassy spot Tidball sketched another camp scene, which appears as the lithograph *Bivouac, Jan. 28,* opposite page 97 of part 1,
volume 3 of the *Reports,* and which depicts four nattily dressed members
of the party standing or seated on their bedrolls. In the background,
Tidball noted on his copy of the lithograph, "This picture shows the
farm like regularity or appearance of a valley as before mentioned."[4]

At daybreak on Sunday, January 29, Whipple wrote in his diary, that
no stars were visible, "but the rising sun with rosy blushes circled the
clouds showing cirro stratus stretching from east to west." While at
breakfast an Indian whoop was heard from a hill and "two Mexicans
armed with revolvers beneath their coats and a white napkin floating
upon a ramrod were sent to coax them into camp." After long parleying,
two Indians brought from behind a bush a firebrand and made a little
smoke as a signal of truce. "With slow and stately tread the Mexicans
approached & were received by one of these sons of the mountains with a
dignity that princes might covet. The other was a facetious beggar and
quickly appropriated the white towel and hat of one of the ambassadors."
Whipple perceived from the vehement gesticulations that they were not
likely to come to camp, so, he said, "Leroux and myself like Mahomet
went to the mountain." The Indians greeted them by placing their hands
upon their hearts and saying, "Hanna, Hanna," and invited them to be
seated by the fire, which they had replenished. By signs they then told the
white men how they had watched and followed them, fearing to approach
camp lest they should be killed.[5]

The Indians examined Leroux closely and then, pointing toward the
northwest, indicated that they had seen him before in that direction.
Whipple said Leroux blushed and stoutly denied the fact, at the same
time pulling his hat over one side of his head to conceal the wound they
had given him there two years ago. While guiding Sitgreaves's party in
1851, Leroux had received the discharge of a flight of arrows from a
concealed party of Indians. Three of the arrows struck him, inflicting
severe wounds in the head and wrist.[6]

To Leroux's relief, the subject was quickly changed, and Whipple

Bivouac, Jan. 28. The attire and stance of the men in this lithograph taken from a Tidball drawing suggest young boulevardiers rather than frontiersmen, corroborating Tidball's scornful description of the "young dandies" who accompanied the expedition.

inquired as to the route to the Mojave villages. The Indians pointed due west, across valleys and over low ridges, to a blue mountain chain at whose western base, they said, flowed the Colorado. The distance was an estimated seventy miles, with three small springs of water on the way. According to Conrad, "Whipple now seriously considered moving due west to the Colorado, rather than searching further for Williams Fork, . . . but he decided against it after studying the lofty ranges—the Hualpai and Black Mountains—which lay between him and the Colorado. He reasoned that the mountains ran along the eastern side of the river and would thus provide a steep grade descending to the river—too steep a grade for railroad building. . . . As he was hunting for a route that would provide a gradual descent, the Valley of Williams Fork, if he could find it," offered the best choice; he continued his search for the elusive stream. The decision made, he turned toward the east to rejoin the main party and found a route for wagons through a pass in the Cottonwood Mountains, which he named Cactus Pass. Once through the pass, he lighted a signal fire and sent scouts to bring on the main party.[7]

While awaiting the wagon train, Dr. Kennerly continued to enlarge his

We Will Be on Mule Meat / 99

collection with new specimens of birds, pouched rats, and lizards; he also found a skull, supposed to be that of a Yampais. Some of the party, not satisfied with a simple skull, having seen two Indians lurking about camp, captured them. Whipple described in his diary how the white men, wishing to create a little merriment, requested the Indians to sing and to dance. The Yampais thought that according to the customs in this wild country, a death song was required and a dance the prelude to death. They were surrounded by Americans and Mexicans but burst away and ran. One escaped, the other was caught and tied. Then by signs he was asked to tell the distance to the Mojave villages. With much ingenuity he explained, placing five stones at certain distances apart to indicate so many marches, the last a long one. Then three or four water holes were represented and then a long channel, which he filled with water to show the course of Rio Colorado. With sticks he then built huts upon the stream to denote the position of the Mojaves, creating a Yampais map. Having kept the artist as long as they wished, the officers loaded him with presents—a blanket, a sheepskin, and a leg of mutton—and bade him depart in peace. "Through this whole scene," Whipple wrote, "this red man illustrated the characteristic stoicism of his race. Not for a moment did his countenance show a trace of emotion. Fear for his life, hope of escape, despair at being caught, gratitude for presents and freedom changed not a muscle of his features nor affected the quiet dignity of his deportment."[8]

Joined by the wagon train on February 1, the entire party started through Cactus Pass, and it was hard going. The wagons were lightened, and Tidball wrote "after some cutting and digging in the pass we descended through by letting the wagons down with ropes. All got through safely with the exception of 3 or 4 upsets." On February 2, another advance party set out, as Sherburne noted, "with the change of Lieut. Jones for Lieut. Tidball." Then Sherburne described how their coffee gave out and "we took to 'corn coffee' which we found a very good substitute." He claimed several of the mess who were not aware of the fact didn't recognize the change, which suggests that either they had been using very bad coffee or had found some very tasty corn. Only one ration of provisions was issued to the three messes in place of one and a half, which had formerly been issued. "We will undoubtedly be short of a great many things before reaching settlements," Sherburne added, "notwithstanding the precautions taken."[9]

Meanwhile, Whipple's exploration party moved southwest along the dry bed of a creek to its junction with a large sandy arroyo, which he presumed to be the Big Sandy, and then traveled south through the center of a wide valley, and after a march of six miles, encamped without having found water.[10]

No water was found, but a new cactus was discovered; *Fouquieria* abounded on the hill where they bivouacked. They also observed antelope, deer, rabbits, and partridges living on the rich grama grass. Wolves and coyotes were equally numerous and were preying upon their weaker neighbors. "The varied notes of their nightly serenades are replete with discord," Whipple wrote, "as if . . . they were possessed of evil spirits wailing & gnashing their teeth." Dr. Bigelow, the cactus lover, must have been in heaven. Another discovery was a new species of *Cactodendron* called *chug*. "It grows in extensive patches to the height of eight to ten feet; a confused mass of angular joints, whose sheathed spines at a distance glisten beautifully in the sun; but a near approach requires caution. The joints, about three inches in length, are so fragile that, for some distance around, the ground is covered with them; and the sharp barbed spines, now difficult to avoid, wound severely the feet of men and beasts."[11]

Nothing, however, would exceed the "famed *Cereus giganteus*," which was scattered upon the hills that bounded the valley. "I think," Whipple wrote, "it has never before been seen except in the vicinity of Rio Gila. The singular appearance of the tall columns, sometimes shooting out one or more branches, communicates a strange effect to the landscape." This remarkable plant, today known popularly as the saguaro cactus, inspired another drawing by Tidball. Reproduced as a woodcut entitled *Cereus Giganteus, on Bill Williams Fork,* it appears on page 101 of part 1, volume 3 of the *Reports*. Tidball's drawing in the archives of the Oklahoma Historical Society matches the woodcut in every detail, which depicts, rather whimsically, a large man astride a small mule alongside one of the giant cacti. The man, grasping a stick, is reaching upward as though trying to touch the top; the cactus appears to be about forty feet high.[12]

In his memoirs written many years later, Tidball still remembered with awe the giant cacti, and how everything in the country seemed to have thorns. "Nature appears to have vied with herself in the production of new varieties of vegetation on which to exercise ingenuity in developing thorns and prickles, and in her race of self-emulation seems to have far overrun the mark." The *Cereus giganteus* is the largest of all cacti, truly

Cereus Giganteus, on Bill Williams' Fork.

Cereus Giganteus, on Bill Williams' Fork. This remarkable plant
is today popularly known as the saguaro cactus.

a giant, growing to the height (measured) of fifty-five feet, often in one straight trunk, fluted like a Corinthian column. Generally it has one or more branches springing at right angles from the main stem for a few inches and then running up straight like the main stalk. The longitudinal flutes or ribs are studded with hard sharp thorns from three to four inches in length. So thick were those thorns, pointing in every direction, Tidball said, that it was impossible to touch with the finger the green glossy surface of the stem, which they guarded. Those huge vegetables spring from gravelly places and crevices in the rocks—from any place where it seems impossible for anything to obtain foothold or draw sustenance. "But their roots are so deep and strong," Tidball wrote, "that it is no easy matter—in fact very difficult to push them over, and when, with the aid of poles and strong arms this is effected, they come down with a heavy thud that shakes the ground like a miniature earthquake, so full are they of sap. From what source they draw this sap is a mystery not yet solved so far as I know."

Tidball continued to be entertained as well as amused by Dr. Bigelow's obsession with the prickly plants. "In a preceding page I mentioned the craze that our worthy botanist—Dr. Bigelow—had for cacti. When he saw these monsters his joy was ecstatic, but soon became mingled with regrets that he could not carry away a specimen in his pouch. The accompanying picture I drew at the time, endeavoring to portray in a faint way his frenzy of delight. He has left his mule and mounted the cacti and seated himself on the thorny spikes of its crest. At the foot of the plant are represented other varieties of this, his favorite plant—the *chug*, the *Opuntia*, the *mammillania*, and many others." The drawing, which could be described as a cartoon, has never before been reproduced. Entitled *Dr. Bigelow's Moment of Triumph*, it depicts the botanist seated on top of the giant cactus, waving his hat exultantly in the air.

Tidball found that the ground was everywhere covered with thorns and prickles to such an extent, it was with difficulty that they found free spaces to spread their blankets, and it was distressing to their mules to thread their way through thickets of such thorny shrubs. "It is no doubt in consequence of the thorniness of this country that so few wild animals inhabit it. Their lives would be miserable. Nothing but the hide of a rhinoceros would stand it." But Tidball said an exception was the beaver, which confining itself to the streams was not much exposed to the thorny surroundings. On the few streams that they found, they saw frequent

Dr. Bigelow's Moment of Triumph. Tidball drew this imagined scene in an attempt to show the doctor's frenzy of delight for his cacti.

signs of this animal. Bird life was likewise scarce. "Although the weather was so spring like no songsters cheered us on our way."

Despite his openly declared dislike for the thorny plants, Tidball took home a few samples of the wondrous *Cereus giganteus*. "Their growth is evidently very slow, and age very great from the fact that young ones are rarely to be found. I secured two, each about the size of a pint measure. These I brought home with me and presented one to Mrs. Mary Purtes of Franklin, St. Mary's Parish, Louisiana, where it survived but did not increase in size. The other, I presented to Professor Bailey, my former instructor in Chemistry, mineralogy, etc., at West Point. He presented it to his friend Delaney Kane of New York. It also lived but like the other did not increase in size, from which I conclude that the plant demands for its development the peculiarly parched arid climate of Arizona."[13]

The most important discovery, however, was not the giant cactus but the river whose existence Whipple had begun to question. At last he had found the elusive Bill Williams Fork, or more accurately, the Big Sandy River, an affluent of the Bill Williams Fork that turns south to join it. They passed along the broad valley, described by Whipple. "The valley itself, except where sand has buried the stream, presents a refreshing prospect of fertility. Willows, Alamos and large groves of mesquite, grow in such dense profusion as sometimes to render it difficult to find a passage through them. Beneath the trees, and bordering the water-courses, there is a crop of fresh grass, and occasionally a few spring flowers. Upon the hills, or among the ravines which pass through them, there are patches of grama grass for the mules." As David E. Conrad wrote: "The scientists found something new and interesting at every turn of the stream, and the beauty of the whole scene was further enhanced by the snow-covered mountains that served as scenic backdrops on either side."[14]

It was at this time that Tidball created what art historian Robert Taft described as "the most interesting of the Tidball drawings." Reproduced as a three-color lithograph facing page 102 of part 1, volume 3 of the *Reports*, it is entitled *Valley of Bill Williams Fork*, and is the fourth of five lithographs taken from a Tidball drawing. The scene is a broad valley, bordered by low deciduous trees, with scattered saguaro cacti dotting the valley floor and hillside. In the background is a steep cliff or mesa; in the foreground, bordering trees are reflected in the water. At the center, three distant covered wagons of the expedition are traversing the broad expanse of the valley. In his memoirs, Tidball apologizes for being unable to

Valley of Bill Williams Fork. This depiction of a broad valley bordered by trees was described by one leading authority on western art as the "most interesting" of Tidball's drawings made during the Whipple expedition.

depict the scene accurately. "The following sketch gives some idea of the valley of Bill Williams Fork, but fails to convey a full sense of its barrenness, and of the rugged character of the adjacent mountains. It is impossible to represent the thorniness of the landscape."[15]

After breakfast on February 5, they mounted and rode onward, following the stream in the valley, where they found many fresh beaver dams, enlarging the river and making crossing difficult. Here, the imaginative Möllhausen gives us an amusing essay on the sociology of the beaver community.

> In a beaver republic there are, it appears, two classes of works, namely the public ones which are necessary for the welfare of the whole community—such as the building of new and the repair of old dams, and the construction of the houses, which are built in stories, and so that the upper one rises above the surface of the water.
>
> On the first, the whole population, without distinction of sex or age, takes part, and their united strength will effect what at first would seem incredible. Overhanging trees, of more than a foot in diameter,

are skillfully gnawed off so far that they must break and fall in; and fresh relays of workers are then at hand, to gnaw away the branches and any part of the trunk that may remain attached to the shore, so that it may be easily floated down to its place of destination. Other laborers are there awaiting it, having gone on before with sticks, mud, and earth, in order to secure the floating logs without loss of time, and fresh materials are continually brought and constantly added and secured, till at length the dam rises like a wall above the water; and the clever little builders, creeping along the top, smooth it with their broad tails, and so render it more solid, at the same time that they improve its appearance.[16]

As they rode onward, on February 5 Whipple observed that sometimes the bed of the stream descended and occasionally rose to its banks or spurs of the hills, jutting at times nearly to the water. "We traveled nine miles and encamped in the midst of the pass which it cuts through the hills. The day has been charming, of delightful temperature and each step of the route has been replete with interest. The stream itself soon changed from gushing rills that for a space would fertilize and beautify the valley and then sink beneath an immense sheet of barren sand—to a cascade stream, clear, deep and rapid, quickly widening to a pretty river." The next day Whipple again extolled the surrounding beauty. "Numerous Pitahaya add to the picturesque effect of rugged hills, sprinkled with shrubs and green-barked acacias. Another beautiful addition to the scenery appeared today; groves of tall and branching yucca, with shining leaves, radiating like a wide-spread fan." Beauty is in the eye of the beholder, and all of this evaded Stanley, afflicted yet by melancholy and hypochondria. "Marched nine miles down the sandy bed of the creek today. Nothing but sand, deep, all the daylong, the neighboring hills being of the same. . . . Tired, disheartened and disgusted."[17]

On February 7, they threaded the valley of the river nearly south eight miles to a point where the stream turned westward, and where a river as wide as the one they had been following entered from the east. They had reached the point where the junction of the Santa Maria River and Big Sandy form Bill Williams River. The Santa Maria River, Whipple recorded, "rolled upon a wide and sandy bed, occasionally with fertile soil upon its banks. Rocks, volcanic, metamorphic, and red sandstone, were piled upon each side of the valley in fantastic shapes. Upon the right was

Artillery Peak. This unusual geological feature was named by
Marcou in honor of the branch of the army to which Tidball belonged.
Tidball sketched the peak, and so did Möllhausen; the woodcut probably
came from Möllhausen's drawing.

a volcanic cone called 'Artillery Peak.' " Möllhausen also took note of this
unusual formation. "[T]he old volcano, which for some trivial reason, has
received the name of Artillery Peak, looked majestic under the beautiful
illumination of the rising sun."[18]

Tidball provides a lengthier and more plausible explanation in his
memoirs. "Marcou did me the honor of naming a remarkable mountain
peak—*Artillery Peak*—for the branch of service to which I belonged.
This mountain is to the east of the present town of Prescott—the capital
of the territory. When we were there this part of Arizona was unknown to
the white man, and natural objects received names from us. The country
being of volcanic origin many of the mountains have a reddish bronze
hue suggestive of artillery—hence the name given by Marcou." Tidball
sketched this unusual geological feature, and a woodcut of the mountain
appears on page 103, part 1, volume 3 of the *Reports*, the fourth of nine
woodcuts for which he takes credit. In his memoirs, this woodcut is

pasted below the explanation of how the mountain got its name. In the lower left corner, he wrote "J. C. Tidball, Del." the latter abbreviation standing for "delineator"—the creator of the drawing on which the woodcut is based; following the title "Artillery Peak" he added, "Named so in compliment to me."[19]

They bivouacked that night two miles below the confluence of the two rivers. Whipple noted that much of the river was lost in sand, but a channel was still left, ten or twelve feet wide and a foot deep. Tidball, having grown up on a farm in Ohio, described it in a more practical way. "At this point it is a beautiful clear stream of a size sufficient to keep constantly turning a sawmill."[20]

The evening of February 8 found the party ten miles farther down the river, "doomed again," Whipple lamented, "to disappointment, encamped without a sight of the Colorado." First it was the Williams Fork that day after day had eluded Whipple. Now it was the mighty Colorado that always seemed to be over the next mountain, but never was.

During the day they found deserted huts, the remains of cooking fires, and pottery shards. Whipple ruminated on the habits and destiny of the wandering Indian tribes, after finding the pottery but no ruins of settlements. "Here permanent water, soil for irrigation and plenty of game would seem so inviting, but the land seems to have been given to the sons of Ishmael. Their habits are simple, their wants are few. The cereus giganteus, agave & mesquite supply them with fruit, their winged arrows with unerring aim furnish meat and clothing. They ask no favors of a foreign race. . . . Rather than be sleek and well fed dogs of a kind master, they prefer to remain prowling wolves to prey upon whites, chase rabbits & deer or even starve if need be."[21]

Tidball, who was with the main wagon train and who was of a more practical bent, had other things to worry about. "Traveled . . . south along and in the creek which, where it passes through the mountains forms a cañon through which it is exceedingly hard to get the wagons on account of the quick sands in which the mules sink over the tops of their backs. The teams finally giving out we were obliged to stop in the midst of the cañon. Not much grass." Sherburne described the quicksand as being so deep that "[t]he first wagon sunk to the wagon bed & the mules went down, nothing being visible of the two foremost but their heads." Stanley was "weary, disgusted and tired to despair."[22]

The next day Whipple decided to turn the exploratory party back and entered the following note in the *Reports*. "Having but two days rations we deemed it imprudent to proceed further toward Rio Colorado in advance of the train. Jose from a high mountain yesterday saw a great valley coming from N. W. and filled with smoke. This was probably our long sought river whose banks are covered with Indians." He estimated the hoped-for river to be fifteen miles distant. After backtracking for four miles they entered a narrow chasm, the precipitous walls of which grew higher as they proceeded. They finally despaired of being able to make an exit from its head and turned to ascend the mountain ridges; at sunset they reached their bivouac of February 7, where they decided to await the arrival of Lieutenant Ives and the main party.[23]

With the main wagon train on February 10, Tidball found hard traveling on account of the deep sand. "Many of the teams gave out and we were obliged to abandon one wagon." Again he had trouble with the recalcitrant Ives and again had to prod him. "Lieut. Ives with his party became thoroughly discouraged and stopped in the midst of a deep cañon; what he was going to do I don't know. I directed all not of his party to proceed next morning and if he could not follow to stay. We were too near out of provisions to stop, and as I had over 60 hungry mouths to fill I could not reconcile it with my duty to wait for him." Sherburne reported that Leroux, Campbell, and Bigelow arrived at the main party's camp for provisions to take back to the advance party, as they were "quite out." Stanley, unsurprisingly, did not paint a cheerful picture of the view from the campsite that night. "I here ascended, with much labor, one of the neighboring peaks. . . . I could see the valley of the Colorado stretching away to the south. Nothing can adequately convey an idea of the perfect desolation and gloom of the prospect from this elevation without having once seen it. The rugged and huge mountains of black metamorphic rock, perfectly destitute of vegetation of any kind—without a living creature to enliven the scene, forms a picture somber enough to gratify the fancy of the most woebegone despair."[24]

Two days later, as Tidball was still struggling to catch up with the exploration party, conditions had not improved. "On account of the entire exhaustion of the teams I was obliged to leave one of the wagons this morning. The difficulties will cause us to be on mule meat before we are through; we are now on half rations and 250 mi. from any settlement." With the advance party, Whipple described his day more lyrically. "A sky clear as crystal—except a few cumulus strata near the horizon—

greeted the rising sun. Earth is well moistened with the gentle rain of last night. The moon appeared at sunset and a stiff breeze from the west brought a hazy atmosphere." That night a note arrived from Lieutenant Ives suggesting abandoning one or more wagons. "In my reply the matter was submitted to his judgment," responded Whipple.[25]

Years later, in his memoirs, Tidball recalled the great yearning with which the men hoped to reach the Colorado River and beyond that the almost fabulous vegetable products of California, the vineyards and fruit orchards, and the great and fertile valleys, "all of which we knew from common report to exist in that land, made us, contrary to our better judgment, look forward to the Colorado river as the termination of our hardships." As barren and uninviting as might be the eastern or Arizona side, they unconsciously expected to look across to the California side and see a land flowing with milk and honey, but their progress toward this delightful bourne was necessarily slow. From every eminence their eyes were strained westward for a glimpse of that river and the promised land beyond. "As we trudged the rugged way down Bill Williams Fork the river appeared to recede from our approaches until we almost came to the belief that its existence was all a myth. Our provisions were about exhausted and visions of mule meat stimulated our longings to behold what our fancy had painted the California side to be."

At the main camp that night, Sherburne reported that Lieutenant Jones and White came in. "They say the Camp of Ex'n party is about 4½ miles from here." Then he added plaintively, "The Colorado no one knows where—*probable some where West.*"[26]

Chapter 8

The Mountain Spur Was a Confused Mass
of Serrated Crests

The days lagged away as the men of the 35th parallel railroad survey worked their way westward, still searching for the elusive Rio Colorado. On February 14, the day after the wagon train arrived, Whipple decided to unload some freight. "To facilitate our movements, as we are already reduced to half rations of flour, we decided to leave three of the wagons, and lighten the rest, by abandoning such things as could be most easily spared." He knew they were running out of time. Tidball tartly agreed. "Arrangements were made today to abandon 3 more of the wagons. A very sensible idea especially since all the mules are broken down and not able, in teams of 8 & 10, to drag along the wagons comparatively empty. A great sacrifice was made of trunks and large chests. Every young gentleman of the party of which there are any number as meteorologists, etc. have supplies of trunks, chests and carpet bags enough to freighter a steamboat." He always enjoyed playing the role of skeptic and debunker, but his diary reveals his serious exasperation at the lack of discipline among the civilian members of the corps. His ridiculing of the "young gentlemen" of the scientific corps and his disdain of the undisciplined ways of civilians were not unusual, however; they were then and are today typical of the military attitude.[1]

During his entire career Tidball would be stern and forceful yet respected by his men. We have seen how one historian attributed to his strict upbringing the "taciturnity, the sternness, and the austerity which sometimes unnerved his subordinates in later years and which successfully camouflaged a lively sense of humor from all but his most intimate associates." A subaltern who served in Captain Tidball's flying artillery battery during the Civil War gives us a similar portrait, the only contemporary description of Tidball during the war years. "Joining his battery in December 1862, as a second lieutenant, I was led to believe by some of my brother subalterns that our captain was very exacting, of choleric temperament and much of a martinet. . . . In due time I discovered that if duty was well performed, service with him was most agreeable. Behind the austere, rather reticent and dignified exterior, there existed a love of humor and an affability that only required circumstances to develop."

Tidball's spontaneous commentary recorded during his journey across the Southwest with Whipple resembles his contemporaneous writings describing events during the early, bleak days of the Civil War; his letters railed at politicians, abolitionists, profiteers, and incompetent officers. He was bitter and disconsolate, and his writings showed it. But in his more considered memoirs, which were written in the decade after his retirement, a different persona emerges. He has had a chance to reflect; although his observations remain acute, his opinions are tempered and his sometimes-camouflaged humor is much in evidence. In his memoirs, more than thirty years after the fact, he describes the civilian members of the Pacific railroad survey in gentle, even affectionate terms. Indeed, the only two members of the party about whom he expresses reservations are both army officers—Stanley and Ives, and his criticism of them is muted.[2]

On February 15 Whipple, Möllhausen, and Dr. Bigelow cut off onto an Indian trail that led through a pass among the hills. Soon they found themselves enclosed by high walls, nearly perpendicular. Leaving their mules, they climbed a water-worn and polished rock, about thirty feet high, and entered a basin, walled in by lofty precipices. At the upper end, a projecting cliff formed a cave. Whipple recorded his impressions in the official *Reports*. "Beneath flowed a little of water, which first filled a beautiful pool in the hollowed rock, and then trickling down into the valley, ran to the cascade below. Above the fountain the cave was covered with hieroglyphics, painted red, purple and white. . . . The secluded nook and the fountain of water may have thrown a charm around the place, causing the Indian medicine men or priests to select it for a retreat sacred to the ceremonies of their craft. Such are said to be the habits of Indian soothsayers; and there is a somber aspect about this spot suggestive of superstitious rites." But, his mind soaring, he confided a more romantic version to his journal, describing how the hollow of an immense rock of white quartz formed a fountain "at which Narcissus might have gazed with pleasure. Doubtless many a bronzed Adonis has here decked himself with feathered plumage from the last victim of his unerring arrow. His apron is bleached and his person tinted with the favorite red if for battle or black to charm his mistress. Strange fancy these savages have. A lover seeks to charm his love with a face painted a ghastly blue black."[3]

Whipple did not mention in his official report that they had started that morning, as Sherburne wrote, "leaving behind four wagons, mess tables, boxes—& a great deal of useless trash including *medicine, wagon covers,* etc." The next day Sherburne reported that they "left behind one of the escort wagons—leaving three survey wagons, one escort wagon & one Carretella, thus reducing our train from 15 to 5 & that within 30 miles of this place. Before leaving Camp, 'cached' three tents, a box of candles, can of oil, & a lot of extra harness." Time was running out, and food was growing short. And Whipple was plainly worried. "Night is gloomy. The remnant of our journey too looks a dark uncertainty like the close of the day." He was also sick. "Having been quite unwell for some days I now am unable to sit up and throw myself upon my blankets sleepless from pain." Stanley, as usual, was despondent and found the prospect of more days scrambling over the mountains gloomy beyond description. "The bottom of the canyon is sandy and the whole country entirely uninteresting. Everyone is thoroughly tired and disgusted." Tidball added his voice to the lugubrious chorus. "The rocky hills on either side are entirely destitute of vegetation [and] even the abominable cactus which for the last 200 mi. have literally covered the earth have disappeared so barren is the country."[4]

The next night, February 17, after following the river until it was swallowed by sand, they encamped on a spot of coarse grass without water. Whipple was still not feeling good physically, and with his spirits ebbing, he wrote: "A cold drizzling rain and a muddy ground are particularly disagreeable to one suffering with pain and a feverish thirst." The following day, lost and plagued by worry and doubt, his mental condition had not improved, especially when he was informed that Ives had computed their latitude to be about 34° 14′.

We therefore appear to be far south of the junction of this river with Rio Colorado, as indicated upon the map of Capt. Sitgreaves. I am troubled at this and doubtful how to proceed. We had hoped tomorrow to see the Big River of the West. . . . Day after day for the last week we have been anxiously looking for this Rubicon to pass, holding on to everything we were able to transport. . . . It is hard to give up a determination so long tenaciously adhered to, but the decrees of fate must be obeyed.

At this point the leader of the expedition seems to shift his thinking and commenced thanking providence for what had been done, instead of asking for help in the future.

And yet why should we complain? A kind providence has watched over and guided us safely through winters, snow & a trackless wild unknown to all. Thus far we have succeeded in the great object of our expedition. We have found a country truly favorable for the construction of a railway and what matters a wagon more or less? Thankful for all mercies which have been bountifully heaped upon us we would be unworthy of their continuance should we murmur at the first turn of fortune.

There is an unmistakable note of despair in this journal entry. Daunted by the prospect of the wearying days that spread out ahead, he sounds nearly defeated. He is sick, lost, and discouraged. He described in his journal how they would have presented gifts to the Indians if they had gotten to the Colorado, as if it were an elusive, ephemeral goal, perhaps never to be attained. It is as though he were saying, "We have already accomplished as much of our mission as we ever will, and if we never find the Colorado, and perish in the desert, we should nevertheless thank providence for leading us this far." It is as though he were giving up.[5]

Tidball had no time for such musings; his impatience with delay, and his pique at the unmilitary demeanor of some civilian members, continued to show in his scornful remarks.

Made an early start this morning. The old grannies of our party by an extraordinary exertion were ready to start by an hour after sunrise. . . . Another sacrifice of big trunks was made this morning to lighten the wagons. It is with rueful countenances that the young dandies of the party look upon such a destruction of their perfumery and other like attire so suitable for a trip of this kind. Another wagon was abandoned today. We are now with broken down mules 250 miles from relief and upon half rations and not sufficient of them to carry us through, saying nothing of the expense the government is incurring by such unnecessary delays.

Tidball's caustic reference to the "old grannies" was simply an expression of impatience at civilian laxity in contrast to his own disciplined life. Thirty years later, at the age of fifty-eight, Tidball, as aide-de-camp to General of the Army William Tecumseh Sherman, traveled by horseback from Fort Ellis, Montana, through Yellowstone Park and up to Missoula, a twenty-two-day segment of a much longer trip. The schedule set by the grizzled Sherman, who was sixty-two, is described in Tidball's journal: "Soon after six o'clock we resumed our journey. Six o'clock was the hour fixed by the General for starting, and was habitually adhered to throughout our marchings. Reveille was at four and breakfast at five." It was the army way of doing things.[6]

Whipple concealed his despair when he entered his account of the party's progress in the official report on February 19. "Two miles from camp we were in the narrowest part of the cañon, about four hundred yards wide. The stream became deeper, and about twelve feet broad. The cliffs upon either side were nearly perpendicular, varying from two hundred to four hundred feet in height, being composed of conglomerate, capped by a huge mass of basaltic trap, assuming various fantastic shapes." Tidball's sketch of this scene appears as a woodcut on page 109, part 1, volume 3 of the *Reports*. It is entitled *Cañon of Bill Williams Fork*, but unlike his earlier drawing of that river valley, when it was broad and spacious, this one depicts the wagon train and men on horseback approaching the narrow defile described by Whipple. Tidball described this unusual scenery in his memoirs.

> At intervals of every few miles these streams cañoned through mountains. These cañons, always rough and sometimes impassible, were picturesque from their high and rugged walls, the rocks of which are often variegated with beautiful colors. In these cañons the water ran freely, tumbling boisterously over beds of boulders; but in the valleys the water generally disappeared under a wide bed of sand. In the cañons drift weed, lodged upon the rocks, indicated that at times great floods occur.

The sketch, he added, was "intended to give some idea of these cañons."[7]

At about the same time, Tidball completed another sketch that he said

Cañon of Bill Williams Fork. Unlike his earlier rendering of the valley of
Bill Williams Fork, in this drawing, Tidball depicts the
narrowest part of the canyon.

is the basis for the woodcut entitled *Lava Bluffs on the Hawilhamook*,
appearing on page 50, part 4, volume 3 of the *Reports*; the woodcut is
attributed to Möllhausen. Tidball described the scene as follows: "The
valleys are frequently enclosed by vertical walls often a thousand or more
feet in height. These are of granite, lime and sandstone, but most frequently of lava as represented in the following sketch. This variety of
rocks sometimes occurs, one following another, most singularly all within
a distance of but a few miles, and without any break in the vertical
escarpment." On his copy of the woodcut pasted in his memoirs he
wrote, "J. C. Tidball, Del.," standing for "delineator." He also wrote
"Bill Williams Fork" after the printed title. Tidball made another sketch
at this time that he said is the basis for the woodcut appearing on page 51,
part 4, volume 3 of the *Reports*, which also is attributed to Möllhausen. It
is entitled *Banks of the Hawilhamook*, "Hawilhamook" being the Indian
name for the Bill Williams Fork. The woodcut is described in the narrative in the geological report: "The above sketch was taken about six miles
above the mouth of the stream, and serves to show the rugged and

desolate appearance of its rocky banks. In engraving the sketch, the peculiar characteristics of the different rock formations were lost, and the whole seem formed alike." Tidball did not comment on this illustration, merely noting on the copy in his memoirs that he was the "Delineator."[8]

Stanley, as expected, was also discouraged. "Never have I seen a landscape so bleak, dreary and one can almost say horrid, as this presents." But the next day the new morning opened with great promise, cloudless and calm, and things began to look up as Whipple recorded a momentous event in his journal. Continuing the survey westward, they followed the now wide valley of the river four miles where suddenly to their surprise they found themselves at its junction with the Rio Colorado. Finding excellent grass, they made a noon halt, allowing the mules to graze, while Tidball and Möllhausen "made sketches giving a faithful representation of this meeting of rivers."

The most difficult part of the terrain had been conquered. Whipple's decision to find Williams Fork and then to follow it all the way had proven sound, despite the dire predictions of his guides and the faulty information he had received from Sitgreaves. It was a personal triumph for the young commander, and it was fitting that the range of mountains lying near the mouth of Williams Fork became known as the Whipple Mountains. "The day has been remarkably fine," Whipple wrote in the *Reports*.[9]

Tidball and the others, it will be recalled, were expecting a land of milk and honey on the California side of the mighty Rio Colorado, after what seemed like an interminable journey across the barren, cactus-filled desert of Arizona. It was not to be. Tidball remembered their bitter disappointment as they looked down upon its tawny waters and across to the land of their fancy; it was like changing a pleasant dream to a nightmare. The far side of the river was but a continuation of the barrenness of the eastern side, and he said, "[W]e turned furtive glances towards our mules and mentally estimated their value as articles of diet. Nevertheless we derived comfort from the prospect. The landscape had this beauty to our eyes: that we had but the river to cross and then we would be upon the last stage of our journey. We had the further consolation of knowing that however bad it might be, it could be no worse than that over which we had been."

The next day, as he gazed out on the unfriendly landscape, Tidball was not in a mood to rejoice, and he regarded bringing wagons this far as folly.

We are now up to a bed or mountain of lava which runs down into the river making it almost impassible even for pack mules. And preparations are . . . [being made] for leaving the two remaining wagons, but the spring ambulance is to be carried over bad places by hand. The mules are now all broken down with the bad management of bringing along wagons and having to camp so much in consequence without grass. Although they have been brought to the Colorado, yet this route can never be traveled except by mules to any advantage.[10]

Tidball described the long looked-for scene where the two rivers converge. The Colorado, immediately after receiving Bill Williams Fork, entered a range of mountains, curiously pointed and serrated, and of a terra-cotta hue. The whole country around was of the same color. From this point the party followed up the river to find a more suitable crossing and within a short distance came up against a metamorphic spur of mountain, "with a repulsive serrated profile like a hackle," which came up to the very brink of the river. There appeared to be no natural passage for wagons through this obstruction, and all that remained, and which had been brought so far with such labor, was abandoned. "The *Jerky* was, however, retained," he recalled. "It was light and could be carried almost anywhere, and it would be a great triumph in the eyes of Whipple to get it through to the Pacific."

Whipple said he "concluded to abandon all the wagons except the light spring-carriage—almost indispensable for the conveyance of instruments." Sherburne gave the vehicle yet another name. "Went into Camp & made arrangements for abandoning the remaining two wagons. The carretella will be taken anyhow—as the instruments must be carried in it & the distance must be measured." The jerky, spring wagon, or carretella—whatever its name—was the sole surviving vehicle. Sherburne also placed some importance on bringing the wagons this far. "We have done what has never been done before, that is brought wagons to the Colorado by a central route. The rest of the route is not of so much importance as 'tis well known that a wagon road can be made from Mohave Creek to Los Angeles."[11]

The following day, February 22, Tidball recalled in his memoirs, was spent threading their way over a jagged spur toward gravel hills through which a devious track led to some fertile land upon the river. Then, after all the trouble taken to drag, lift, and coax the wagons this far to prove a point, Whipple confided to his journal, "The wagons this morning we abandon to their fate as well as a few things which will scarcely be needed upon the remainder of the trip and cannot be packed. All things that seem necessary to complete the survey seem yet to be intact. Even the carretella with . . . barometer etc. placed under the pilotage of Lt. Stanley is again dispatched upon the survey. It is carried over ground which I would give advice no one with loaded wagons to undertake." The same day Tidball, in his last known diary entry, estimated that they traveled about nine miles northwest, leaving the river for three or four miles, and then passed through the volcanic mountains, which were "exceedingly difficult to get over on account of the deep chasms and heaved up rocks & precipices." Then they found a large valley with fine grass. The previous night, Indians had visited them; they were very friendly and the next day came to camp in large numbers. "Many from the other side of the river upon seeing us plunged in and swam entirely naked wearing nothing but a breechcloth and are fine large fellows. They loaded themselves down with the plunder we left when abandoning the wagons, and a mule which I was obliged to shoot they cut up skin and all and carried off for a feast. But a few of them are armed. Those that are have small bows and long arrows which they shoot with impressive accuracy."

Every diarist commented on the large number of Indians that suddenly materialized. "Upon entering the ravine," Whipple wrote, "Indians sprang up on all sides; some armed with bows and arrows, others without weapons, and many carrying things that we had abandoned at the last camp. We now felt the advantage of having established friendly relations with them, for in the difficult passes they could seriously have annoyed us by interrupting the survey, if not our progress. They professed to be Chemehuèvis, a band of the great Pai-Ute nation."[12]

Tidball wrote that while threading their way through the ravines of the spur just mentioned, Indians sprang up on all sides. The natural color of their bodies—a brownish red—was so near that of the rocks they were among, it was difficult to distinguish one from the other, and they would in consequence "appear and disappear from our sight like tricks done by a prestidigitator." The men were entirely without clothing except a narrow breechcloth, which was drawn up between the legs with the ends through and over a cord around the waist. This breechcloth was often nothing but strips of bark, but mostly it consisted of a strip of cloth, a piece of some cast-off garment obtained from Fort Yuma, about 150 miles down the river. "Between are the lands, or rather rocks, of numerous bands through which all commercial relations with the Fort must pass. The Indian is as jealous as the white man of the right to trade across his territory. Everything that came to these Indians from Yuma had to pass through the hands of all intermediate bands with no doubt a profit in trade to each." He described the breechcloths as "mere strips no longer than the ribbon with which a lady ties her bonnet," but they served to the wearer every purpose of decency. In adjusting it on the string around the waist, the wearer always managed to have the longest end behind, where it hung down like a tail. "As the Indians ran leaping like wild animals from rock to rock, these tails bobbed up and down in the most bizarre manner. They wore nothing upon their feet to protect them from the rocks and from the ever-present thorns of the country. Their feet had become calloused and insensitive to rough usage."

They were a tall race, he said, the men unusually so, and as they walked along, their muscular and well-proportioned limbs, without covering, showed to great advantage. They had remarkably fine heads of hair, long, black, and glossy. In front it was cropped along the line of the eyebrows, so as to just cover the forehead. Behind, it fell in a superb mass over the shoulders and was trimmed so as to hang evenly at the girdle. Baldness was unknown among them, and very seldom were gray hairs seen. Vermin were destroyed by matting the hair with clay of a bluish white color, which became quite hard upon drying and killed the insects. The matted hair and mud were fashioned on top of the head into horns or "some other fantastical device and gives the wearer a truly quizzical appearance." This covering was worn for two or three days, when the head was subject to a thorough washing in the river and again appeared in the superb covering that nature had afforded.

When a young buck desires to become exquisitely dudish he paints his face in the manner of Indians, and stripes his body and limbs in various colors and patterns, using for this purpose pigments of ochre, clays and charcoal. . . . The women, when young, are good looking—considering their advantages, but as they grow old they generally run to obesity. Their dress consists of but one garment—a petticoat reaching from the waist to the knees. This is made of strips of bark hanging loosely from a cord at the waist. These petticoats are quite bunchy, and when dry make a rustling skirt-like sound as the wearer moves about. The squaws, as well as the bucks, are expert swimmers, crossing and recrossing the river as though it were but a street. In entering the water the squaw slides down feet first foremost and at the same time slips her petticoat up and fastens it in a roll on top of her head, where it keeps dry during the passage. All of this requires but a moment, and the squaw is in the water before the beholder fairly realizes what she is doing.[13]

Möllhausen described the camp's visitors as "very tall, finely-grown young men, whose powerful forms and perfect proportions we had a full opportunity of admiring, as, except a narrow white apron, they had not a particle of covering, and even their feet were bare."[14]

On the morning of February 23, the luxuriant grass upon which the mules had feasted, Tidball wrote, "had such an astonishing effect on their stomachs that . . . several of them were found dead, swelled tight as drums with legs stretched stiff in the air." That day, as they ascended the eastern edge of the beautiful valley of the Chemehuèvi Indians, they saw numerous villages and a belt of cultivated fields upon the opposite bank. Great numbers of the natives swam the river and brought loads of grain and vegetables. "The chief begged us to encamp again within the limits of his territory to enable his people to trade," Whipple wrote, "but, as we could not, the poor Indians were obliged to turn homewards with their heavy burdens." The chief alone accompanied them, and after traveling eleven or twelve miles, they encamped on the coarse but abundant grass of the valley. Waiting at this place was a Mojave chief, with his band of warriors, to welcome them to his country. "With eyes cast to the ground, and in silence, he submitted to the ceremony of an introduction. With apparent indifference he received the few presents that were offered, and then quietly watched the trading of his people. It was now evident why the Chemehuèvis would not follow us with their articles of traffic to camp. They feared to encroach upon the privileges of the Mojaves."[15]

Trade with the gathered Mojaves, as described by Whipple, commenced by the offer of a basket of maize for three strings of white porcelain beads. No sooner was the bargain concluded than the whole multitude crowded in to dispose of their produce at the same price. "Delighted at their bargains, they were exceedingly merry." But the acting quartermaster, not wishing to dispose of all the beads, hid a part and tried to induce them to trade for other things. They at first refused all offers and were about to leave when, after an explanation, the trade was restored, and calico, being established as currency, became as popular as beads had been. The white men purchased in a short time about six bushels of maize, three bushels of beans, and considerable wheat, besides squashes and peas. At sunset the happy Indians began to make arrangements for passing the night with the party, but all, except the chief and a few of his friends, were driven reluctantly from camp. "Some of them were considerably exasperated, but they went quietly enough and built their fires just beyond the line of sentinels. Those remaining did not once lie down during the whole night, but sat at the fire using wood at the cook's expense. Indians" Whipple observed, "always expect to be waited upon by the servants of white people."[16]

Unlike other members of the party, who all thought the Indians finely formed, graceful, friendly, and interesting, Stanley, who evidently never met an Indian he did not despise, predictably felt just the opposite.

A more degraded race of Indians does not, perhaps, exist. The men go naked, except the few rich ones who possess a few rags they have gotten from the Yuma below—and the old duds they have traded us out of. The women wear a kind of petticoat made of willow, giving them a kind of ostrich-like appearance as they shuffle along. They seem neither to hunt or fish, but depend upon the soil for their maintenance. They cultivate pumpkins, beans, corn, wheat, watermelons. Generally they are large and stalwart, the women extremely fat, and they put me much in mind of an old matron sow—only they exceed that animal in dirt and disgusting appearance.

The next day, Whipple wrote in his journal, "Our Indian friends seemed to have recovered from the annoyance of being turned from camp last night and [returned] as brisk and lively as before. The chief and his friend I employed to take the carretella around the mountains as they said it couldn't pass by the trail. This was true as the sequel will show." The survey party was taken by that route, and a group with the pack mules kept the old trail that led through ravines and over hills to avoid bluffs upon the riverbank. The path in some places passed through deep chasms and over precipices of porphyritic rocks. The mules tumbled headlong, became weary and dizzy, and four were left on the roadside. The party emerged from the hills, descended to the river, and was gladdened by a sight of the great valley of the Mojaves. Tidball, with a portion of the escort, was still in advance. "Again," Whipple observed, "we have experienced the advantage of having cultivated a kindly feeling with the natives. Our parties today have necessarily been scattered widely, and an attack by Indians would have proved disastrous to the expedition. But instead of impeding our operations, they have rendered good service, giving valuable information and faithful guidance."[17]

Tidball, ahead with the small advance party, did not progress far before encountering another mountain spur impinging precipitously upon the river. "It was, if possible," he said, "the worst yet. It was a confused mass of gorges, precipices, and serrated crests several thousand feet high. The same formation exists on the other side of the river, and the whole is now known to travelers upon the Atlantic and Pacific Railroad as the *Needles*—a very appropriate name." He took the trail through the precipices accompanied by Mr. Marcou and Mr. Möllhausen. "The day was clear and hot and a hard trudge we had of it." At length they got through, emerging on a gravelly plain that sloped to the bottomland of the river about eight miles beyond.

By this time Tidball must have been weary of clambering over the thorny, parched mountains of the Southwest. Whatever enthusiasm he may have had for this exploratory adventure had by now surely melted away. He had left behind his bride of a few months, and like his solders, whose enlistments were near expiration and who saw the trip as a free ticket to California, he undoubtedly saw his transcontinental passage as a way to be reunited with Mary—at least temporarily—as he would travel by sea to the East Coast before again being consigned to the hell hole of Fort Defiance. Perhaps they were nearing the end of the worst of mountain travel, but ahead lay the broad Colorado, followed by miles of waterless desert. And in between were the dangerous and unpredictable Mojaves.[18]

Chapter 9

Lieutenant Tidball Ordered the Soldiers
to Fix Their Bayonets

As Tidball worked his way over the precipices and through the gorges of
the mountain spur leading to Mojave Valley, he experienced a severe
problem with one of his pack animals. He liked to tell a story, and in his
memoirs he related what may be described as "The Saga of the Mule of
Total Depravity." The story began at Fort Defiance and ended as they
threaded their way over the jagged spur at a time when the weather
moderated and a thick crust formed on the snow, which made traveling
exceedingly difficult. "We took turns in breaking the trail, and here was
exhibited the original sin and total depravity of one of my mules, the like
of which is rarely seen in this much anathematized, but really patient,
long suffering and useful beast." The mule he spoke of would lie down in
the crusted snow with grunts and groans as though exhausted. It required the combined strength of several men to lift him up and push him
along. This he repeated every few rods, "evidently with a view to exciting
sympathy and having his burden lightened. This act alone would not
have constituted total depravity, but might have been taken as an excus-
able trick to shirk his work and throw his burden upon others. When man
does thus he is applauded for his shrewdness." The whole life of "this
brute," so far as Tidball was concerned, "had been one of depravity,"
even though he was a fine-looking large bay animal—"a veritable dude
among his kind."

On the morning when they were to leave Fort Defiance, the sixty-five
mules that he was to take had been put into a corral. Tidball had pre-

viously selected one for himself for riding, a fine, large gray mule that had been a favorite for hunting purposes. "My men had had considerable experience with mules and in fact knew each and all of this lot personally, and days before we were to start had settled among themselves what two each man was to have. Therefore when the time came for heading out there was no wrangling. Each man captured his two and led them out as naturally as though they had been marked for him." While this was going on, Tidball observed that the finest-looking animal of the lot was left untouched and flattered himself that the mule was being left for his pack animal, "that the men were showing their high estimation for the *Lieutenant* by leaving him the best of the lot, and I said to myself, what rare generosity, the likes of which I had never seen before! I was quite touched by this act of unselfish generosity upon the part of the men whom I was about to lead into the wilderness."

The men saddled their riding mules and secured their packs upon their pack mules, and at length the sergeant asked Tidball if the "Liftinant" would have his mule packed and called several men to assist him. As soon as this was done, the mule, with the others, was turned loose down the road they were to take. And here, Tidball related, the surly animal commenced an exhibition of his true character. "His head went down and his heels went up, and off he went at full speed, bucking, rearing and kicking. My frying pan and coffee pot, the only cooking utensils I had, beat a tattoo together on top of the pack. By some acrobatic feat he had torn a hole in my flour sack and a white cloud marked his crooked course as he darted hither and thither." Men on their mules tried in vain to arrest him, but this appeared only to stimulate his activity. After a while he got the pack turned from his back to his belly, and here he had it, "as pugilists would say, in *Coventry*." He tore it in front with his teeth and kicked it from behind with his heels. "Piece by piece of my outfit fell from the pack; at the same time did the scales fall from my eyes, until I could see through the unselfish generosity which had prompted the men to leave the finest of the lot for their lieutenant's pack."

Thinking to get even with the unmannerly hybrid, Tidball then had him packed with the boxes of ammunition. Each box weighed about one hundred pounds, and there were three of them, one on each side and one on top, "inelastic, rigid lumps that soon chafed sores in his accursed hide." These boxes were so secured with rawhide thongs as to be safe against his most accomplished efforts at bucking.

In these boxes he met his match, and I frequently thought I detected regret and contrition in his wicked eyes as he cast furtive glances at the soft and elastic packs borne by his companions. I thought I could perceive a mental calculation going on in his mulish head as he saw the other packs diminishing in weight by the daily consumption of the provisions, while his remained constantly the same and chafed deeper and deeper into his ribs. But the old Adam was so grounded in his nature that nothing changed him. He was an inventive genius, and he turned this talent to devising means to annoy others.

That of lying down in crusted snow was of the mildest type. His chief delight was to kick everything that came within his reach, and at this he was ambidextrous, striking out equally well with the right or left, or both. The dead weight of his boxes did not prevent him from making the most lofty reaches with his heels at anything that came within reach behind him. All places and all circumstances were alike to him for this, whether crossing a creek or creeping along the side of a precipice, and it was this total disregard of places that finally brought his wicked career to a long-delayed end. "Neither the weight of his load, nor the depth of his sores excited the least sympathy; for, by the blackness of his crimes, he had placed himself beyond the pale of forgiveness. But his load of ammunition was a precious one, especially as we were then nearing the Colorado where the Indians were known to be numerous, and might be hostile." Tidball said he was fearful that the mule's instinct for cussedness would lead him to discover this and that his genius for doing the greatest possible amount of harm would lead him to play a trick with this ammunition—their only supply. Their provisions had by this time become almost exhausted, so the pack animals had next to nothing to carry. "I therefore distributed the ammunition and that gave relief to this beast of the Apocalypse, and afforded him opportunity for renewed deviltry."

Soon after this they were winding down the ragged edge of a precipice that overlooked a horrible gulch of jagged rocks. "A touch from another mule behind caused the fiend to kick up. Perhaps forgetting for a moment that he was disencumbered of his load he made too great an effort and losing his balance pitched headlong into the yawning gulf below. A joyous breath of relief was drawn by each beholder; even the mules seemed to join in this. He had at last gone to *Davy Jones Locker*, and no one in the party would scruple to give a certificate of his death strong enough to

The Mule of Total Depravity. Tidball sketched his pack mule, which he said had a remarkable "instinct for cussedness."

satisfy the most skeptical Treasury accountant of his loss." His fall was witnessed by a group of Indians who through curiosity were following, bounding like catamounts from rock to rock, unencumbered by clothing except in the case of the women, who wore a sort of petticoat. These followed the fallen mule and by means of their teeth, nails, and sharp stones—for they had no other implements—dismembered him. They halted for the night on some level ground near the foot of the ridge over which they had just passed. "In a little while we saw an old fat squaw trotting along, bending under a reeking hindquarter of the unregretted mule; the leg projecting in front like a pump handle was wrapped about by her begrimed arms, while the unskinned, frayed and bloody flank hung down her back, and was plucked and gnawed at by a number of naked urchins running along behind. The hoof bobbed up and down with the trotting motion of the squaw as to proclaim that even in death it had not lost its kicking energy."

Tidball described his other mules as exceedingly well behaved and mannerly and said he lost only five out of sixty-five that he started with, a loss unprecedentedly small for a journey of that nature. From the start each man took a personal interest in the two that had been entrusted to him—one for riding and the other for his pack. The men would turn aside to give their animals a nibble at any chance bunch of grass among the rocks, and when water was scarce, would share it from their canteens. "I turned the mules over at San Diego in better condition than when I received them at Fort Defiance. Those that I lost (not counting him of *original sin*) were in consequence of lameness from worn out feet, made so by the constant grind over the sharp and gritty rocks."

Tidball illustrated this segment of his memoirs with several sketches of the mule, including one showing the mule kicking up his hind legs, one showing "the manner in which this wicked animal met his death," and one showing the Indian woman with a hind quarter of the mule on her back, accompanied by two naked urchins munching on pieces of the animal.[1]

As the survey party entered the valley of the Mojave toward the end of February, where they would soon find themselves surrounded by hundreds of Indians, Whipple certainly hoped that they would continue to experience the "advantage of having cultivated a kindly feeling with the natives." The Mojave tribe, which numbered about three thousand, lived along the lower reaches of the Colorado River—from south of the Grand Canyon to the country of the Chemehuèvis. The silt-laden Colorado overflowed its banks in the spring, swollen with the melting snows of the Rockies, and the receding waters left behind a deposit of rich silt on the floodplain. "In these alluvial sediments the Mohave planted their crops, which ripened rapidly in intense summer heat." Despite this apparently peaceful, agrarian tradition, the Mojave, who were known as "the most warlike of all the Yuman people," had a reputation for treachery and were "unpredictable in their reception of strangers." Less than three years earlier, when Captain Lorenzo Sitgreaves refused to trade with the Mojave and barred their entry to his camp, the soldiers found themselves the target of an unprovoked attack. Artist Richard Kern was tying up his bed at 4:30 one dark morning when he heard a member of the party shout, "Look out, they're . . . throwing arrows here. . . . I have one in my leg." The artist looked up to see feathered shafts "glistening in the firelight." The Sitgreaves party escaped without serious injury, but the incident illustrates the volatility of the Mojave tribe.[2]

While Whipple approached the valley of the Mojave—passing over smooth prairie country without encountering a hill—Tidball, with Möll-hausen, Marcou, and a portion of the escort, was clambering across the rough mountain spur. "Our toilsome path seemed as if it would never come to an end," recalled Möllhausen, "and when at last we thought we had reached level ground, we found that after a short time the path went up the rocks again, where the iron-shod hoofs of our weary mules rattled on the ground as they faintly toiled along, and then died away in the deep silence of the desert." Late in the afternoon they reached the plain, formed by the low banks of the Colorado, that was thickly populated with Mojave Indians.[3]

Tidball described the spectacle as "swarms of Indians" coming out to meet them. They had heard of the party's friendliness and of their cast-off clothing, and were hilarious with delight at seeing them. Only a few of them had ever seen white men before. But what excited their curiosity most were the mules. "They had never before seen mules, one of which, happening to give a most hideous bray, astonished the Indians into momentary panic." Up to this time the explorers had seen no signs of any domestic animal among them, and they greatly admired two athletic fellows, each on a pony, bounding up to meet them. The ponies were of California stock, large, fat, and sleek. They were without bridles, being controlled only by a twine of bark around the lower jaw. "The ponies were equally surprised at our outfit, and cavorted around us with distended nostrils. The tawny agile forms of their riders made them look like veritable centaurs."

Tidball had neglected, in the enumeration of the members of his outfit, to mention Cap, a pet dog of the soldiers. He was, or seemed to be, a cross between a collie and a Newfoundland. A good-looking dog, clean and good natured, he had faithfully accompanied the escort all the way from Fort Defiance. "He was as much a curiosity to the Mojaves as were the mules, and was greatly petted by the squaws. The soldiers soon observed this and he became a medium of commerce. Every day he was sold to a squaw, who would lead him off in tittering triumph; but the dog always returned, only to be sold again." A sketch in Tidball's memoirs entitled *Old Cap* shows a furry dog comfortably curled up on the ground. The sheep too, Tidball said, were a new inspiration to the Indians. They had seen pouched rats, sometimes rabbits, occasionally a coyote, and perhaps once in a while a deer, but had never before seen an animal clothed in wool. "In their mild climate the use of this covering was beyond their comprehension. The goats they could better understand. They looked upon them no doubt as cousins germane to the big-horn, which they were accustomed to see gazing down upon them from their mountain perches."[4]

After traveling over the eight miles of gravelly plain, Tidball's advance party descended to a wide range of rich alluvial soil, the bottomland of the Colorado, and bivouacked there for the night, about a mile from the river on a "beautiful sward of fresh green grass." There they had hoped the main party would join them, but they did not. Tidball described how the Indians came in groups, the women laden with baskets of wheat, beans, and other goods for trade with them. No money was exchanged; they did not know what money was. Only old clothes and blankets were used instead. The white men soon discovered that the Indians did not want such things for garments but only for breech rags, or perhaps to tie around the head. As soon as they got a garment or blanket, they tore it into strips suitable for their purposes. The members of the party then did likewise, making their stock in trade go much further. By this means each person hoped to lay in a supply of provisions sufficient for his journey to the nearest settlement on the Pacific, which at the smallest estimate was yet two weeks distant. The Indians had for sale a good deal of a coarse kind of flour that Tidball said they made by grinding the grain on "meta-tas," which were flat stones about the size of a washboard. On this the grain was ground by using another long stone shaped something like a rolling pin. The stones were selected for their hardness, and it was desirable that they should have a coarse grain or burr for taking hold of the grain. "The squaws, of course, did the grinding, squatting upon their knees behind the stone which sloped down in front. The motion was similar to that of a washerwoman at her tub. The breasts of the old squaws frequently hung low and were in their way when grinding. In such cases they were tied back over the shoulders with strings." Although the day had been hot, the evening was chilly and a campfire was comfortable. Marcou, Möllhausen, and Tidball had a small one around which their guests crowded to the great discomfort of the expedition members. The Indians took great offense at being invited to stand back, and all started to leave.[5]

Soon they were surrounded by hundreds of Indians, which concerned Möllhausen: "It was fortunate for us," the German said, "that they were not inclined to abuse our confidence, for as there were but twenty-seven of us, and of those scarcely the half in the camp together at one time. Had a skirmish taken place, we must have got the worst of it." But then the moment of danger suddenly arrived, described by the German artist. "[It] happened that when Lieutenant Fitzball, Mr. Marcou and I were standing near a group of these fine-looking fellows, and admiring their magnificent limbs, one of the young ones who stood near us thought proper to behave in an unbecoming manner, though, I believe, more for the love of fun than any other motive." Whatever the young Indian did, Tidball, who happened to have a small cane in his hand, was not amused, and the numeric odds did not deter him from disciplining the transgressor. He gave the young Indian a cut across his naked shoulders, provoking merely a laugh from the Indian, who seemed to take it as a joke. Möllhausen described what happened next.

But unluckily a wrinkled old woman, who had been looking on, flew into a furious passion, and in a croaking voice poured out upon us a whole torrent of what doubtless were curses and invectives, though of course we did not understand a word of them. Other women joined in chorus with the old witch, and we easily made out from their gestures that they were threatening us that a whole crowd of their warriors should come, and make us disappear from the face of the earth. We observed attentively, however, the Indians near us, and we did not see in them any signs of ill will; but they became more serious and reserved. By degrees, nevertheless, the men began to assemble round the scolding woman, and, not to be taken too much at a disadvantage, our soldiers received orders to send every Indian immediately out of the camp—and fix their bayonets.

Sending the Indians away seemed to make a still worse impression on the agitated crowd, but the party was camped in the middle of a meadow so that no Indian could approach within arrow-shot without at the same time becoming a mark for their rifles. A doubly vigilant watch was kept during the night, with sentinels pacing continually around the camp. "We slept with arms in our hands," Möllhausen remembered. Fortunately the night came on piercingly cold, and the Indians fled for refuge in their huts, and when they returned the following morning, "their blood was much cooled." All appeared to be forgotten, and they teased and knocked each other about with their usual playfulness.[6]

Tidball remembered the incident somewhat differently and described what happened after the Indians were told to stand back from the small campfire near which he, Marcou, and Möllhausen were warming themselves.

The bucks looked sullen and threatening, and the squaws were loud in their denunciation. Each one became a virago and seemed to try to outdo the rest in vehement utterance of, no doubt, the choicest Mojave billingsgate. They would move off a little way and then run back, stamping and gesticulating at us, to give vent to a little more wrath. Altogether this conduct was anything but ladylike. The men greatly outnumbered my party, and lest they might do us some injury during the night I beckoned back the chief or head man, and gave him to understand that while I could not have his whole band about our camp he was welcome to stay and that I would give him plenty to eat. This appeared to satisfy his people, and they departed.

The headman remained, with his two wives, and Tidball had a sheep killed for them. To be certain of him as a hostage, a strict watch was kept over him. He and his wives sat the entire night through by the fire roasting and eating the sheep. In the morning there was scarcely a vestige of it left; even the bones were gnawed as if by wild animals. "He turned out to be a pretty good fellow," Tidball remembered, "and next day guided us to their village, about ten miles further up the river. His feast of mutton did not agree with him and on the way, when he was seized with colicky pains, he would throw himself on the ground. One of his squaws would then get on his back with her knees and by jouncing and kneading him with her fists would temporarily relieve him of his pains. Our doctors could not prevail with him to take their medicine." At this place in his memoirs Tidball included several sketches, one delineating the head man as he sat eating the sheep, one showing a wife starting to cut up the sheep, and another depicting one of the wives astride the man, kneading his body.[7]

Meanwhile, Whipple and the main party described a wind from the north that had been blowing a gale the whole day, filling their eyes with sand. "Men & even mules seemed sometimes unable to stand before it. This added to the labor of driving the weary mules and replacing the often broken packs, and put the men in bad humor. A fight ensued—the first fight we have had on the trip—in which one was knocked down with a rifle and the other had his finger nearly bitten off. The night calmed the tempest within & without." Needless to say, this incident went unrecorded in the official report. Whipple also described misbehavior on the part of the Mojaves. At first he found them quiet and obedient, but then they became insolent. "One trod on Mr. Hutton's foot and laughed with his companions. Mr. Hutton returned the compliment, placing his boot upon the bare toed Indian and laughed in his turn. The Indian went off leaving his friends highly amused at his discomfiture." By the time Lieutenant Stanley heard of the incident in Tidball's camp, it had taken on the aspect of a melee. He wrote the next day that some of the Indians "had been very insolent to Lt. T's party and he had been compelled to thrash several before they would leave camp. We accordingly thought it expedient to wear our revolvers."[8]

On February 25, Whipple descended into the valley of the Mojave and joined Tidball's advance party. Indians soon gathered around them and informed the explorers that one of their great captains was coming to visit. A few hundred yards distant a long procession of warriors was seen approaching, headed by the chief and his interpreter. Whipple described how the latter with great formality introduced the distinguished dignitary of the Mojave Nation, "who returned our salutations with gravity becoming his rank." He then presented his credentials from Major Heintzelman, who stated that the bearer, Captain Francisco, had visited Fort Yuma with a party of warriors when upon an expedition against the Cocopas and had professed friendship, *but Heintzelman advised Americans not to trust Francisco*. "The parade and ceremony were not, upon this occasion, as vain and useless as might be supposed," Whipple wrote, "for without them we should have taken this great chief for the veriest beggar of the tribe. He was old, shriveled, ugly, and naked, except a strip of dirty cloth suspended by a cord around his loins, and an old black hat, bandless and torn, drawn down to his eyes. Judging from his half stupid, half ferocious look, one might suspect that there had been foul play towards the former owner of the hat."[9]

Whipple explained the object of their visit and asked the chief to provide a guide to conduct them to the intersection of the Mormon road with the Mojave River. The chief replied that all was well; none of his people would disturb their property, and they would give all the aid in their power. Whipple presented some gifts—tobacco, buttons, and earrings, which the chief distributed to his people. Then a blanket was given to the chief for himself. "This he spurned with his foot saying in his own language that he had plenty such things & wanted only some pieces for his own men. Taking the proffered scissors he cut the blanket into about 20 strips which he distributed." Then the trading commenced, and the scene suddenly changed from grave decorum to boisterous merriment. When the trading was concluded, the Indians ranged about camp in picturesque and merry groups, making the air ring with peals of laughter. Target firing and archery were then practiced—the survey party firing rifles and Colt pistols, and the Indians shooting arrows. Fortunately, the firearms were triumphant, and finally an old Indian, in despair at their want of success, "ran in hot haste and tore down the target." Whipple believed that the Mojaves were in as wild a state of nature as any tribe then within the limits of the United States' possessions. "They have not had sufficient intercourse with any civilized people to acquire a knowledge of their language or their vices. Leroux says that no white party has ever before passed them without encountering hostility."[10]

According to Tidball, "the tribe had never before had friendly intercourse with whites and were as near an aboriginal state of simplicity as it was possible to find Indians." They had no firearms of any description and at first scarcely comprehended the use of those the survey party had. They had a few bows and arrows. Their bows were very long, made roughly from cottonwood. In cultivating their wheat, they did not sow it broadcast but planted it in little hills. What little ground they had that was at all fit for cultivation was very fertile, and they appeared in their way to be skillful agriculturists. Although it was the last of February, they had watermelons, kept over from last year's crop, but Tidball could not ascertain their method of preserving them so long. "They were a jolly set of beings and had many games and sports."[11]

By the bank of the Colorado River, the party observed the scene described by David Stanley in his diary: "Perhaps a thousand naked savages—men, women and children—surrounded us all day and some of the scenes of the day were highly picturesque and interesting." Möllhausen described a game played by the men of the tribe:

Several of the men carried poles sixteen feet long in their hands, the use of which I could not make out, till I saw the brown forms leave the crowd two by two, to begin a game, which remained somewhat obscure to me, though I looked on at it for a long time. The two players placed themselves near one another, holding the poles high up, and one of them having in his hand a ring, made of strips of bast, of about four inches in diameter. Lowering the poles, both rushed forward, and at the same time the one who held the ring rolled it on before him, and both threw the poles, so that one fell right and another left of it, and arrested its course. Without stopping a moment, they then snatched up the ring, and the poles, and repeated the same movements back again, over the same spot, a piece of ground about forty feet long, and so on again and again.

It was this tranquil and picturesque scene—of the Mojaves at play and at work—that Tidball captured in his panoramic *Camp Scene in the Mojave Valley of the Rio Colorado,* a lithograph appearing opposite page 113 of part 1, volume 3 of the *Reports.*[12]

On February 26, with chief Francisco as guide, preceded and followed by great crowds of Indians, the party continued its survey up the magnificent valley of the Mojaves, passing wheat and cornfields, and rancherias and many granaries filled with corn, mesquite beans, and tortillas. The houses, constructed for durability and warmth, were built upon sandy soil, thirty or forty feet square. The sides, about two feet thick, were of wickerwork and straw; the roofs were thatched, covered with earth, and supported by a dozen cottonwood posts. Along the interior walls were ranged large earthen pots filled with stores of corn, beans, and flour for daily use.

Although all fifty of the illustrations in part 3, volume 3 of the *Reports,* "Report Upon the Indian Tribes," are summarily credited to Möllhausen, Tidball claims one of them as his—the woodcut depicting a Mojave dwelling appearing on page 24. It is as Whipple described the typical dwelling except, as the narrative in part 3 explains, "This particular house appears to run into a sand-bank, and is peculiar. Others are formed in the valley, with all their walls supported by posts." As the survey party passed the rancherias, at first only a small portion of the villagers seemed inclined to join them, but at length, Whipple said, their little train swelled to a grand army a mile in extent.[13]

Tidball said the Mojaves occupied both banks of the Colorado from near the confluence of Bill Williams Fork to the foot of the Grand Canyon, a distance of about 150 miles, but little of this distance contained land fit for cultivation. What there was, however, was rich alluvial bottom, which if collected into one body, Tidball said, "might make what in

Camp Scene in the Mojave Valley of the Rio Colorado. This tranquil and picturesque scene of the Mojaves at work and play depicts a few of the thousand Indians that surrounded the survey party during a tense night when violence was threatened.

old slavery times would have been called a '*fifty nigger plantation,*' i.e. a plantation requiring fifty able bodied Negroes to work it." The Mojaves had great skill at making a coarse kind of pottery, principally the large jars, which sometimes had a capacity of four or five barrels and which were as smooth, regular in contour, and thin as if they had been turned from a potter's wheel. Because they possessed no axes or similar implements for chopping, the posts and other timber of their habitats were burnt to the proper size. Since they had no bedding more than bunches of grass and rushes, they snuggled themselves together for warmth in the deep black sand of the floors of their dwellings. In very cold weather—cold for that locality—they heated up the sand with fires, which they extinguished and then snuggled up where it had been. With the exception of the two ponies Tidball had earlier observed, there were neither dogs, cats, nor other domestic animals about the premises. Whipple, Tidball said, had brought along a quantity of beads and other trinkets, and "also some bolts of gay colored calico and bleached muslin for trade which came in good play in securing provisions for the remainder of the

Mojave Dwelling. A typical Mojave dwelling sketched by Tidball; Möllhausen also sketched the same scene, and this woodcut could have come from either artist's drawing.

journey. When one of them received a strip of bleached muslin, the first thing he did was to rub it well with dirt. It then became suitable for his purposes."

> They were as a body, very honest towards us; but some of the lads evinced roguishness by occasionally picking up small articles about our camps. They were very dexterous at this. Seeing a knife or spoon or other small article on the ground, a lad would sidle round in apparently the most unconcerned manner, until he got his foot on it. Then, grasping it in his toes, he would lift it up behind, rubbing his legs together as if scratching himself, and then reaching his hand around, as if still scratching himself, would secrete the article in his breech rag or by some slight of hand get it up and under his hair out of sight.

Tidball included twelve sketches in his memoirs depicting the activities of the Mojaves, including a woman grinding on a metate in front of a dwelling; a bride and groom on their wedding tour, the bride with her wardrobe carefully bound up in a net of bark twine, and the groom's wardrobe "about his loins"; a group of Indians with their wares waiting to trade; and a boy picking up a fork with his toes. He also drew a humpback sucker, abundant in the river, which he said "constituted a very acceptable addition to the slender larder of the natives."[14]

As the warm and pleasant day drew to an end, the Indians brought bundles of green rushes and large quantities of corn and mesquite beans to their camp to be exchanged for shirts and pieces of red flannel. As a consequence, Whipple reported, "that night the mules fared sumptuously." Meanwhile, under the direction of Lieutenant Ives, preparations were made for crossing the river. An old and much-worn India rubber pontoon, brought from New Mexico, was inflated, and the body of the spring wagon fastened upon it. Whipple was delighted with the result. "The vessel was then launched, and sat upon the water like a swan. The Indians were greatly disappointed, for they had hoped to ferry us across themselves, and be well paid for it. They all left camp at dark." But Whipple still feared treachery on the part of the Mojaves: "Some think this deviation from previous custom looks ominous." But the night passed uneventfully, and the next day they set about crossing the wide Colorado. It was February 27, and in Sherburne's words, "one of the most memorable days of our trip & at the same time most amusing & interesting."[15]

Tidball had vivid memories of the momentous crossing. The river at this point was about 500 yards wide, divided in the middle by a sandbar island. Having no axes, his men set to work burning off drift logs to the proper length for a raft, then secured them together with willow withes. Untying the ropes and straps from their packsaddles, the men made a line sufficiently long for hauling the raft back and forth across the channels. The channel to the island was not difficult to cross; in fact, it was almost totally fordable. But the far channel was deep and swift, and coming down from the snowy mountains of Utah and Colorado, it was very cold. Several of the men attempted to swim it, but the weight of the line prevented them from making the opposite bank. "Presently some bucks came floating by on a balsa made of tulé rushes. These rushes were bound in long fascines which being lashed together the whole made a buoyant raft. The bucks very kindly carried our rope to the opposite bank, and then we were all right. The few traps that we had were soon landed safely on the soil of California."

Tidball recalled that Whipple's India rubber pontoon, unswanlike, proved leaky. His bellows likewise "proved asthmatic," and the pontoons had to be inflated by lungpower. "This was great sport for the Indians who vied with each other in blowing. The top, or body of the *Jerky* was lashed to the pontoon cylinders, thus giving it quite a gondola-like appearance. But it was top heavy and unsteady and about every other trip turned bottom upwards." In this way many things were lost and others damaged, but fortunately neither the records nor the collections were among the things lost. Their mules swam across without difficulty, and the few sheep and goats that they had remaining also took to the water without trouble. The goats got over very well, but the fleece of the sheep held water, and their small feet affording but feeble propelling power against the strong current, they were carried down against the rope of the pontoon, and becoming entangled in it, several of them were drowned. Those that were drowned had seized the rope in their teeth and held fast even after death.[16]

During the excitement attending the crossing, an Indian messenger advised them that another great chief was about to pay a visit. Whipple described the approach of the dignitary, lance in hand and appareled in official robes. The latter consisted of a blanket thrown gracefully around him and a magnificent headdress of black plumage covering his head and shoulders and hanging down his back in a streamer, nearly to the ground. His pace was slow, his eyes cast downward, and his whole demeanor expressive of a formal solemnity. Upon his right hand was the interpreter, upon his left a boy acting as page, and following was a long procession of his warriors, attended by a crowd of men, women, and children. Having arrived within fifty yards, Whipple said, he beckoned his people to sit down upon the ground, while with interpreter and page he presented himself before the white men. Taking from the boy a paper, he offered one of the stereotyped credentials given by Major Heintzelman at Fort Yuma. "That having been pronounced 'a-hot-ka' (good), he took a seat upon the blanket spread for him, and smoked with us the pipe of peace. This done," Whipple continued, "we made the usual explanations of the object of the expedition; the wishes of our great Captain, the President of the United States; and the benefits that would result to them from opening a highway for emigrants, or a railroad, and thus creating a market for the produce of their fertile valley." The chief replied by a long and vehement speech in which he expressed his satisfaction at the prospect of establishing a system of trade with the whites whereby their nakedness would be clothed and their comforts be increased. He promised not only that the mules and other property of the explorers would be sacred in their sight but also that the Indians would afford them every assistance in their power to accomplish the objects of our mission. The gifts were by now exhausted, but when the Indians were told that the party was too poor to buy their goods, Whipple said they expressed no disappointment. "Merry as crickets and free from care," Whipple wrote in his private journal, "they wandered from fire to fire laughing, joking with all, curious but not meddlesome, trying with capital imitative tongue to learn our language & to teach their own."[17]

Whipple's characterization of the chief's eagerness to cover his people's nakedness with clothes is dubious, as none of them had ever expressed an interest in a garment more than a few inches wide; nor could the chief begin to comprehend how "establishing a system of trade with the Whites" would affect his people. And surely Whipple, of all people, who so often reflected on the innocence of the "noble savage" and confided to his diary so many times his concern over the ultimate fate of the Native American as that race collided with the onrushing white civilization, must have had misgivings. He of all people must have understood, even as he was delivering the formulaic message from his "Great Captain," the president of the United States, extolling the benefits that would soon be bestowed upon the Mojaves when modern commerce came to them, that the way of life known to the Mojaves was doomed. This handsome, lighthearted, and self sufficient people, "merry as crickets," without the slightest understanding of what lay in store for them once rails of steel penetrated their idyllic homeland, would soon sacrifice to a form of progress their carefree way of life. Despite Whipple's lofty aspirations, the tribe would be confined to reservations comprising only a part of the fertile paradise of the Mojave Valley, and a century would pass before they received just compensation for their lands.[18]

Chapter 10

The Clothes of the Murdered Mexican
Were Riddled with Arrows

The day after crossing the Colorado, members of the party paused to dry out their soaked gear. "The whole camp was laid out with books, papers, & articles of clothing drying in the sun," Sherburne remembered. He also recorded the issuance of the last allotment of food rations—seven and a half days' rations for fifteen days. "Lieut. Tidball uncorked two bottles of brandy tonight, in honor of our arrival in California," wrote Sherburne. " 'Brandy Clear' & 'toddies' flourished in abundance." The stern boyhood teachings of strict Presbyterianism were left far behind as Tidball celebrated the long-awaited river crossing. The party had pitched their camp not far from some dwellings of Indians who, according to Möllhausen, "passed the day with us, and towards evening, as they crouched about our fires, afforded us a great deal of amusement."[1]

That evening, according to Möllhausen, he and Tidball both remembered some conjuring tricks of their boyish days and, presumably fortified with a few toddies, performed them with great success. The crowning marvel, Möllhausen remembered, was when the lieutenant, "showing them one of his front teeth, which happened to be a false one, and kept in by means of a spring, pretended to swallow it, and opened his mouth to show them the empty place, at which they gazed with much surprise. But when, laying one hand over his mouth, and the other on his throat, he managed to replace the tooth, and displayed once more a perfect set, their surprise at such supernatural powers almost amounted to terror." They then called all the other Indians in the camp before the conjurers and entreated the lieutenant to repeat this incredible conjuration, "which he did again and again, every eye fixed the while upon his mouth." At last one sagacious old warrior came up to him and gave Tidball to understand that he wished him to perform the feat with one of his other teeth, which of course he declined to do, and the faith of the Indians in the white man's magical power was somewhat shaken by his refusal.

Whipple also described this amusing incident in his unpublished diary but understandably did not include it in the published *Reports*. Tidball and his magical dentures made an indelible impression on the Indians. In 1857–58, Lieutenant Ives returned to the West to explore the Colorado River. When he encountered the Mojaves, they were "inquisitive to learn something about the man who could carry his teeth in his hand."[2]

Guided by the subchief Cairook, who had successfully conducted them around the mountain spur to the Colorado Valley, the party started westward on March 2. Whipple could look back on his peaceful encounter with the Mojave people as an outstanding success, which he attributed to having cultivated a kindly feeling with the natives. "Our policy has been to treat them as reasonable beings; asking only what was right and submitting to no wrong." Stanley, who did not like and did not trust Indians, felt differently, attributing the lack of hostility to a nearby military presence. "They have behaved quite well during our stay among them, with the exception of a little stealing, which seems to be a necessary evil when Indians are allowed to come into camp. . . . It is gratifying to think, however, that ours is the first party of whites that ever passed through this country that the Indians did not use their greatest exertions to exterminate. We may thank the establishment of the post at the mouth of the Gila for our friendly reception."[3]

The day was cold, with flying clouds and wind from the northwest. Cairook, the guide, shivered under the piercing blasts until a dragoon overcoat was furnished to cover his naked body, after which he walked proudly ahead of the train. Many of his companions followed them the whole day, and they seemed to regret the Americans' departure. Whipple expounded his formula for getting along with the heretofore hostile Indians, whom he believed were inherently good; the Mojave were peaceful people as long as they were treated justly, he thought. "They saw that we were strong, fearing them not, but yet doing them justice, paying damages for wheat fields accidentally trampled by our mules and in all cases treating them as reasonable human beings & honest men. The effect has been to make them pleased with themselves and with us. Instead of annoying us as they might during the crossing of the river, for trifling rewards they aided us greatly." Instead of being moody and reserved like many of their race, keeping the explorers in suspense as to whether they might be planning to overwhelm them with numbers and take possession of their property, "they were in word and action frank and full in demonstrations of friendship." Although vigilance was not relaxed, Whipple said the party slept as free from care in the midst of a thousand savage warriors as they could have done in any city of the union. "In the accomplishment of this result," Whipple concluded, "great praise was due to the officers of the escort, and to the good conduct of the soldiers under their command."[4]

Tidball, looking ahead, contemplated the next leg of their journey. "From the Colorado to the Pacific, over the route we had to travel, is a little over three hundred miles. Although we found the country nothing like so rugged as that we had been over, we discovered that we had to traverse five formidable ranges of mountains and a good deal of sandy desert before reaching the shores of the Pacific. Some of the Mojaves knew the country as far as to the Mormon trail which leads from San Bernardino, where the Mormons had a settlement, to Salt Lake City, distant about 150 miles from the Colorado." The Indians warned them that this part of their route was scarce of water, most of which was in small springs among the mountains, difficult to find; consequently, Tidball took two of them as guides, who proved trusty and exceedingly useful. "Without them it is difficult to see how we could have gotten through without great suffering." Even Leroux's instinct or skill at finding water would have been of little use. The springs trickled out from crevices in rocks and gave no outward signs of their existence—"no bushes, no grass, no nothing to catch the eye." Until they struck the Mojave River—more properly creek—grass was very scarce. "But our mules, seemingly inspired by the prospects of the green meadows of the Pacific, managed to nibble out a scanty existence. Fuel was also very scarce; at times none at all, not even greasewood. The yucca, a Spanish bayonet-like bush, was the only thing that thrived in these deserts. It grew to the dimensions of a good-sized tree, and the dead trunks gave us a tolerable supply of fuel. Although the days were hot the nights, as nights always are in desert regions, were cool, and a little fire felt very comfortable." At this place in his memoirs, Tidball attached a woodcut taken from page 121, part 1, volume 3 of the *Reports*, probably from a sketch by Möllhausen. It depicts a good-sized bushlike tree, and standing in front of it is a large buck deer. In a note written along the side of the picture, Tidball comments, "The deer is mere fancy," an example of the German artist's tendency to embellish his sketches with imagined wildlife.[5]

Whipple was not able to stop thinking and writing about Indians—their relationship with the white man and their future. Although a kindly, well-intentioned man, possessing noble, if utopian ideals, he was a victim of his own woolly thinking, at times sounding foolishly idealistic in the thoughts he confided to his private journal.

It is surprising that a nation of savages heretofore supposed steeped in ignorance, should now seem so to thirst for the blessings of civilization. Government surely will aid them. Their fertile valley, their fine fields and their homes will not be wrested from them to satisfy the cupidity of adventurers. The true American race shall not be wiped from the face of the earth. The red man may at last find justice from the hand of the stranger. When civilization & refinement have developed the powers of body and mind which the creator has bountifully bestowed upon these, his untutored children, they may stand as proudly erect in the halls of congress as now they do upon their native soil.

But the fertile valley, the fine fields, and the homes of the Mojaves *were* wrested from them; they did *not* find justice at the hand of the stranger. As we have seen, one hundred years after Whipple recorded his aspirations for "this nation of savages," the Mojaves petitioned the United States government for wrongfully appropriating their land without due compensation—and won. In the official report, however, Whipple limited his observations to the mundane business of continuing the survey—always, the survey continued. On March 3, they camped by a flowing stream with good grass and took full sets of magnetic and astronomical observations.[6]

On March 5, as the morning broke with a few clouds and light wind, forty mules proved to be missing—either strayed or stolen—but search parties brought them back. Whipple joined Tidball in teasing the young members of the scientific corps. "As several disconsolate young gentlemen, deploring their hard fate, had exchanged top boots & spurs for sandals and were about to pace the route to California, the sight of the lost found turned our morning into joy." It was here, having been told by the Indian guides that the few springs along the route would not provide a supply of water sufficient for the entire train at once, that Whipple divided the party into three divisions. Tidball said, "Having the best outfit of mules and being entirely unencumbered with instruments, records or collections, I was in best condition to take the lead, and by more lengthy marches gain distance in advance of the following parties."[7]

Sherburne reported that, accordingly, "Lieut. T. and company started tonight about 5 intending to travel till 12 & obtain good water. He was uncertain whether he would lay by for us or not, as he is very anxious to reach settlements. His men are out of meat, & have nothing but a short ration of flour, pork & beans. He took an Indian for guide & left one for us, although the latter appeared unwilling to stay, saying there were too many Pahutahs [Paiutes] round for so small a party."[8]

"On arriving at Lt. Ives' camp," Whipple wrote, "we found that Lt. Titbald had gone on two miles to better water, and the gentlemen were walking post. Our Indians had persuaded them of danger from Paiutes, a party of whom seemed near. Their campfire was last night seen. The messrs. White, Sherburne, Möllhausen & Campbell were ranged in a row sleeping under the canopy of heaven. Tired ourselves we too sought the luxury of sleep." Whipple wrote in the *Reports* that for an emigrant road "it is probably the best route yet discovered across this western desert." Again Tidball disagreed with Whipple; his acerbic note in his copy of the *Reports* was: "I pity the other emigrants."[9]

Tidball's party now approached the valley of the Mojave, described by him as "a typical desert, almost destitute of water, abounding in drifting sands, bitter waters, siroccos and all." In descending into the basin through the gorges of the mountains, they encountered large quantities of drifting sand, which the wind had carried up to the tops of the spurs, projecting into the basin. "The following sketch," he continued,

so far as showing configuration, is a good representation of that part of the Basin where we struck it. It fails however, to convey a just idea of the utter barrenness of the country. The broken character of the mountains, together with their sharp, ragged outlines, renders the scenery highly peculiar. The effect is heightened by the purity of the air and deep coloring which distant mountains assume and change each hour of the day. The absence of vegetation, the nakedness of the rocks, and the prevailing sandy-brown color of the whole surface, affords a strange contrast to the green fields and forests of the Atlantic States.

Here Tidball is referring to his drawing *Valley of the Mojave*, which appears as a woodcut on page 53, part 4, volume 3 of the *Reports*. It depicts men walking beside mules pulling a carretella as they approach a rugged trail leading through the mountains to a vast valley beyond. Although the illustration is entitled *Valley of the Mojave*, in the *Reports* it is described as the valley of the Soda Lake, and as being within the Great Basin. This is the last artistic contribution to the *Pacific Railroad Reports* claimed by Tidball, bringing the total to fourteen—nine woodcuts and five lithographs—although several illustrations Tidball thought were based on his sketches probably should be attributed to Möllhausen. Unbeknownst to Tidball, his artistic work on this expedition would soon lead to a choice assignment that would rescue him from the rigors of service in a frontier garrison.[10]

In the varied and illustrious military career that lay ahead of him, John Tidball would achieve distinction not as an artist but as a warrior and military educator. But to the end of his life he was proud of his artistic ability, and he alluded several times in his memoirs to his days at West Point, when he excelled in his drawing class. Although his natural artistic aptitude is manifest in his drawings, his talent was sharpened by the instruction received at the academy from his mentor Robert Weir, whose influence can be seen especially in the proficiency of his landscapes. Under Weir, a distinguished American painter whose mural *Embarkation of the Pilgrims* is one of four historical paintings in the rotunda of the Capitol at Washington, Tidball remembered that he practiced a large amount of instrumental drawing—problems in descriptive geometry and in shades, shadows, and linear perspective—paving way to the more advanced course in engineering. "Having a natural aptitude in this direction all of those things were mere recreation to me." Alluding to his days at West Point, he remembered that to most cadets drawing was a bore, and to many an intense bore, but with him it was not so. "Fortunately I had a fondness for it, and, although developing but slowly, came within an ace of the head of my class, a circumstance highly gratifying to me, not alone because it helped me in general standing, but because it warmed up

Valley of the Mojave. Tidball wrote that his sketch, which actually depicts the valley of Soda Lake, part of the Great Basin, failed to convey "the utter barrenness of the country."

in me a little vanity which had lain dormant ever since, when as a mere lad, I had painted with the crude paints and brushes of a country wagon-maker's shop, a gingerbread sign for an old cake woman. So natural and life-like was it, it attracted flies by its counterfeit sweetness."

Tidball never attempted to progress as an artist. He devoted his retirement years to writing and initiating a family genealogy, but he never entirely lost his interest in drawing. He remembered with fondness how his family spent their summer vacations in the mountains at some quiet place where he and his daughters "could enjoy out of door sketching; for they had from an early period evinced great aptitude and fondness for drawing."[11]

It was just sundown, Tidball recalled, when he and his twenty-five men entered the Great Basin and observed along the farther side of what appeared to be a lake, what in the obscurity seemed to be a row of campfires. "For a few minutes we thought these might be the fires of some other party exploring from the westward, and we were joyful at the prospect of meeting friends and probably obtaining news from the inside world. We had now been over three months thus cut off. Our hopes, however, vanished with the last rays of the sun." What they saw were reflections from what they afterward discovered to be white saline incrustations on the far side of Soda Lake, a name that they gave to the dry bed of a lake about ten miles wide, covered with efflorescent salts, probably sulfates of soda. The next morning, before it became too hot, they crossed it. The salty incrustation was solid enough for the men, but the mules broke through into a soft bottom beneath. "Traveling was thus excessively distressing to them, especially as they had been practically out of water for the last three days. When we reached the western margin of this lake we halted, and as there were no signs of water from many miles ahead we dug holes in the sand at the edge of the incrustation. Here we obtained a brackish water which even the thirsty mules rejected."[12]

Whipple followed, arriving at the lake on March 9, where he too found highly alkaline water, "effervescing with acids like Rochelle Powders." Their Mojave guide again expressed a desire for Americans to come and trade with his people, "giving them clothing and knives," causing Whipple to conclude, "It would seem as if these simple people were really pleased with the first dawning of civilization. They feel the want of comfortable clothing, and perceive some of the advantages of trade." But he confided private doubts to his diary. He was becoming ever more foggily mystical and seemed unsure that his "untutored children" would someday be standing shoulder to shoulder with the white man in the halls of Congress. "This valley is destined to flourish. Wigwams give place to shops, lodges to hotels. What then become of our red brethren that have already extended the right hand of fellowship? Shall they be thrown overboard to float to the misty land of material? Or shall we take him upon the railway & bring back from that eastern land the unknown object of their faith and establish the house of truth among Mojaves forever."[13]

Amidst these lofty thoughts, he slogged on with his survey party. "One weary mule was today left by the roadside," Whipple wrote, "and will probably make a good meal for the hungry Pai-Utes, who are watching our movements. Many tracks, a few hours' old, have been noticed proceeding from the hills to the valley." When they prepared to start out on March 11, the head packer for the escort reported that one of his Mexican herders had been left behind yesterday, alone and unarmed, in charge of two tired mules and that he had not yet made his appearance.

Whipple was pessimistic. "Defenseless, and with animals to tempt the cupidity of Indians, who in considerable numbers are evidently watching us, there could scarcely be a doubt of the fate of this poor man." A party of twenty-four was quickly assembled to search for the missing herder.[14]

In advance, Tidball pressed forward under a full moon, clear and bright, hoping to find water at the base of the mountains they were approaching. Their track was over deep, loose sand dunes and was excessively heavy traveling. The mules having been so long without water, the men, "out of compassion for them," made their way on foot. A trudge of about twelve miles brought them to spurs of the mountain where they halted for a few minutes' rest. "While thus resting," Tidball continued, "the mules sniffing the air, strayed ahead. The men who went after them soon sent back a whoop of delight. The mules had sniffed out water, and water in abundance. It was a large stream, tumbling over a gravelly bed, and into it the mules thrust their noses up to their eyes, and each drank a draught such as only thirsty mules can drink. This was the end of our march for that night. We lay down and slept to the sweet sound of the purling stream."

The stream, as he afterward found, proved to be the Mojave River, and this was the mouth of it, where it lost itself in the sand of the basin. Soda Lake, which received it, had no outlet but was a "veritable *sink*." In wet weather it was a shallow sheet of water, with an elevation of 1,100 feet above sea level. The ridge of mountains from which the Mojave emerged was not very large, but beyond it were still many miles—about seventy—of sandy desert, broken here and there by other small ridges through each of which the river made its way in a canyon. Tidball had taken with him a Mojave guide whose name was Irrataba, although Tidball referred to him as "Arrataba." The general course that he took was up to the guide, but they frequently left the river to avoid canyons or to cut off large bends. Occasionally the river disappeared in the sands, but the farther up they traveled, the larger it became, until it was a stream quite formidable to ford. It was fringed with cottonwood and willows, with frequent spots of fertile bottom grass for the mules. "Arrataba was an excellent guide," Tidball remembered, "and thinking to make the journey more easy for him, I mounted him on a mule. This was a new sensation to him. After riding twelve or fifteen miles he dismounted but was so stiff from the unaccustomed exercise that he could not at first stand. He did not try riding again, but skipped along on foot. My old gray mule became so accustomed to following at his heels that it was difficult to prevent him from doing so when he turned aside a few steps for any purpose."

Light sands heightened the brightness of the moonlit nights, and they took advantage of it to make some night marches, which were particularly lonely. The mules made no noise as they trudged through the sand, and scarcely a word was spoken by the men. "Even the irrepressible Jackson, the songster among the soldiers," Tidball said, "did not strike up his favorite '*Corporal Casey.*' Around us in every direction were long sloping sand hills, with ghostly yuccas standing here and there, in the moonlight, weird and uncanny. An unwritten tradition locates this as the trysting place of the demons of the mountains with the witches of the desert, from whence sprang the Pai-Utes, the most degraded of all Indians."

At length they reached the Mormon trail, a well-beaten road. Here Tidball parted with "the faithful Arrataba," giving him two or three blankets and what few old clothes he could spare. The men also contributed bountifully in the same manner, and he had so much more than he could possibly carry that Tidball gave him a mule. "When he met the rear parties he disposed of the mule for more blankets and clothing, saying that he could readily *cache* the blankets, etc. and return for them with his friends from the Colorado, but that it would be impossible for him to elude the Pai-Utes on his way back with the mule in charge. Sound reasoning for an Indian, or for anyone else." Tidball included in his memoirs a sketch of his faithful guide, of whom he was obviously fond. It is entitled "Arrataba Resting Himself," and depicts a nearly naked Mojave, squatting with a cigar in his hand, exhaling a cloud of smoke.[15]

In his memoirs Tidball does not refer to, and may not have known of, Irrataba's subsequent illustrious career. He served as a guide for Lieutenant J. C. Ives in 1857–58, and shortly afterward was involved in an attack on a wagon train of California-bound settlers and later in a skirmish with a detachment of soldiers from Fort Tejon. Several Mojave leaders were arrested, including the chief, Cairook, who was shot and killed while attempting to escape from prison at Fort Yuma; after his death Irrataba became the recognized chief of the Mojave in the eyes of the white men. The highlight of Irrataba's life was his trip to the eastern United States. His white friends sent him to the east to visit President Lincoln and see the power of the Union army, then engaged in the Civil War. When asked of his impressions, he is said to have replied. "Irrataba heap see 'em Mericanos; Mericanos too much talk, too much eat, too much drink; no

Arrataba scratching himself.

Irrataba. Tidball had high regard for his guide, Irrataba, whom he referred to as "Arrataba" and who went on to become chief of the Mojaves.

work, no raise pumpkins, corn, water melons. All time walk, talk, drink—no good." The purpose of sending him east was to enhance his value to the Americans by showing him the strength of the whites. "For a short time this was no doubt true, but in the long run it boomeranged and Irrataba, because he told the truth of what he had seen, was disbelieved by his own people and was accordingly discredited as a leader." He died at his home near La Paz in May 1874.[16]

The day the herder went missing, Sherburne said they met Tidball's Indian guide returning with a "quantity of blankets, coats, etc.—also a note from Lieut. T. giving us the distance to road and accounts of plenty of grass and water." Tidball was also careful to mention in his note that he had given the things to the Indian as a reward for his faithfulness in showing him the road. "He (Lieut. T.) started this a. m. for settlements. He will be there probably as soon as one week from today. Our flour & meal gives out tonight. Salt gone two days ago. Until we get in, will have to live on beans, mutton without salt, & cornmeal coffee without sugar. What a meal for an epicure! As a substitute for tobacco, which gave out 'long, long, ago' we use tealeaves, corn grounds & dried willow leaves."[17]

On March 12, mournful tidings were brought of Torrivio, the lost herder. The search party went back about six miles and tracked a party of Indians driving two mules. They came on a hiding place that the Paiutes had occupied several hours previously and found the remains of a mule on which the Indians had feasted. In a few moments they came into the Paiute camp, from which it was evident that fifteen or twenty had just fled in haste. A fire was burning, and on it were large pieces of mule meat that had only just begun to roast. In their flight they dropped cooking utensils, baskets, clothing, and even their bows and arrows. "The clothes of the murdered Mexican were also found, literally riddled by arrows, and stiff with hardened blood." A party in ambush had probably killed him as he was riding his mules along the ravine. A long and laborious search failed to turn up the body. Torrivio, it will be recalled, was the peon whose freedom Whipple had purchased for fifteen or twenty dollars at Covero in mid-November; he did not live to enjoy his freedom nor to be reunited with his wife and five children.[18]

Everyone was feeling the pinch of short rations. "Our provisions are now beginning to fail," wrote Whipple. "Upon the Colorado full rations were issued to the 15th inst and corn, beans and meal & pumpkins purchased from Indians were furnished to each man in camp, soldiers & all, as much as they wished to carry. But on a trip like ours men are blessed with such extraordinary appetites that it is probable if not restrained they would consume double rations. Luxuries such as sugar & coffee none of us have seen for many a day." On March 13 they struck the Mormon road. Whipple described how on the next day they encountered their first white men in months, a small party of two Mormons with a pack train on their way from San Bernardino to Salt Lake City. "They were athletic, well mounted on fat mules and looked able to whip forty Pai-Utes." Inquiring for news, Whipple learned the melancholy fate of Captain Gunnison. "Young, talented and enterprising this excellent officer has been cut off from life when his moral worth and usefulness were just beginning to be appreciated. We were told that while he was employed upon the survey of Sevier River, a party of twelve Indians fell upon them and four only escaped. It is to be hoped that these murderous Pai-Utes will be thoroughly chastised."

The two Mormons professed to have no fears of the Paiutes because, they said, the Indians were at peace with the Mormons, a response that drew a sharp rebuke from Whipple. "Although it may be in accordance with an old system of the Mexican government, it is a new feature in ours, for one State or Territory to be at peace with a band of Indians known to be hostile to, or at war with the rest. For many years it has been the practice of the Apaches, who reside upon the frontiers of Chihuahua and Sonora, when meditating an attack upon one, to make peace with the other. . . . But the practice should not be permitted within our limits."[19]

Thirty years later when Tidball accompanied General-in-Chief William Tecumseh Sherman on a tour of the West, they passed the town of Gunnison, which was, in Tidball's words "named after Captain Gunnison, of the Army, who, while exploring this region in 1853, was foully murdered, some say by Indians and others say by Mormons." While modern accounts of the murder of Captain J. W. Gunnison and seven of his companions dutifully report stories that the Latter-day Saints, or Mormons, carried out the massacre, historians now dismiss these accusations as lacking in credibility. Tidball's remark, however, is indicative of the lingering suspicion that the Mormons were somehow implicated, if not by participating in the event itself, by their failure to zealously apprehend and prosecute the perpetrators. At the time the impact was serious. Historian Durwood Ball went so far as to say, "The aftermath of the Gunnison killings cut any remaining strands between the army and Mormons. In the army's opinion, the . . . atrocity was a Mormon-Indian enterprise plotted and unleashed by the Saints' hierarchy." Uncharitable sentiments were to be discerned even some years after the army's intervention in Utah. When Fort Douglas was established in 1862 by General Patrick Conner, who was convinced that the Latter-day Saints constituted "a community of traitors, murderers, fanatics and whores," he located the post on a plateau east of the city "within a cannon shot of the Mormon community."[20]

The survivors of the Gunnison massacre had escaped, leaving behind their camp equipment, instruments and records, and their extra horses. Four days later a party of Mormons reached the spot and set about to collect from the Indians all the equipment and horses that could be located. "The Gunnison murder brought down upon the Mormons a flood of criticism. The murdered men were employees, and, some of them, officers of the United States Government. The offending Indians belonged to the one tribe in Utah that maintained friendly relations with the Mormons. There was this serious question: Since the Mormons could find the killers, to recover from them all stolen records, instrument, and other items of equipment, why had they not taken action to punish them?"

Because of the friendly relations between the Paiutes and the Mormons, which Whipple had so sharply condemned, no action was taken until two years later, when Colonel E. J. Steptoe arrived in Utah with a detachment of soldiers. The Indians were apprehended and brought to trial in federal court. The judge explicitly instructed the Mormon jurors that they must either acquit the defendants or return a verdict of premeditated murder. Much to the judge's astonishment, the jury found the three Indians guilty of manslaughter. Inexplicably, the judge did not declare a mistrial but sentenced the defendants to the maximum three years in prison. They later escaped, not at all being "thoroughly chastised" as Whipple had hoped.[21]

Miles ahead, Tidball was out of the wilderness and nearly out of provisions. He was following a known path but had not yet left all hardship behind. The Mormon trail continued to lead up the Mojave but finally left it and struck across a gradually ascending plain to a depression in the Sierra Nevada, distant twenty miles—a gravelly plain without water and little on it except an occasional yucca. The depression was the Cajon Pass, and beyond it about twenty-five miles was the Mormon settlement of San Bernardino. On either side of the pass, the mountains were covered with snow, and when they reached the crest, they were met by a furious wind that brought dust, gravel, and snow into their faces. The descent from the crest for about a thousand feet was at an angle of about 45 degrees. "It was quite dark when I reached the bottom of this descent, and not knowing how much farther it was to water I halted for the night, and found shelter from the keen winds among the small trees that grew there in abundance. For the last twenty-four hours we had been entirely out of provisions. But the men, knowing that the next day would bring us to plenty, preferred hunger to mule meat."

The next morning dawned clear and beautiful, and being both hungry and thirsty, they made an early start, which the "extreme meagerness" of their camp outfit simplified. Their route lay down the canyon still descending at a steep grade. They had not gone more than two or three miles when they came to a beautiful mountain stream flowing rapidly among clean granite boulders. At the same time they saw a huge flock of sheep browsing among the trees that lined the canyon. They looked in vain for a herdsman. "Our hunger was equal to that necessity which knows no law, and we laid violent hands upon many of the lambs. We halted, unsaddled, and, in biblical language, builded unto ourselves an alter whereon we sacrificed and feasted. To us the feast was as a feast of Lucullus." After this they proceeded on down the canyon. Sycamores, maples, and other trees that had been familiar to them in the east greeted their delighted eyes, and in a little while they emerged from the canyon onto an open undulating plain, covered with the most luxuriant vegetation. "Only those who have seen southern California in the springtime can fully appreciate the loveliness of these pastures. Looking over the green plains immediately in front of us, to a distance of about fifteen miles was the Mormon settlement of San Bernardino."[22]

Constrained by the survey route he was supposed to follow, Whipple came behind, but he was now making compromises. On March 15, with provisions nearly exhausted, he was powerless to examine the passes through the Sierras to the Tulare Valley. "Lieut. Jones, with the escort, has been already obliged, on this account, to push ahead for the settlements. Therefore we propose to follow him and proceed by the shorter route through the Cajon, continuing to take notes and make sketches of the route we traverse." Stanley went with Jones; for the first time, Whipple was the only soldier in the survey party.

He found the river valley alluring, filled with rich soil, abundant trees and grass, and sweet and transparent water. "Doubtless within a few years the valley will be filled with a large Mormon population. It is a connecting link in their great chain uniting San Bernardino with Salt Lake City and as their road passes through it they probably look upon it as their own already. They are also waiting patiently for the time when they shall be called to occupy the great valley of Rio Grande. One may depend upon it. The Creator has designed some great object to be accomplished through the wonderful working of the singular Mormon creed."[23]

By March 16, Tidball had already arrived at San Bernardino, but the lieutenant had not forgotten his comrades. Sherburne reported that he sent back a Mormon trader "loaded with flour, pork, coffee, sugar, tobacco, pipes & other little sundries" to meet them. The trader also brought two dozen eggs that he sold for a dollar a dozen, and "a keg of indifferent whiskey at six dollars per gallon." Sherburne bought a small piece of butter that tasted delightful. Whipple was less pleased. "Upon arriving at our camp ground, we found a Mormon from San Bernardino come out to meet us with a load of provisions for sale. He professed to be one of the Saints, but nevertheless charged most exorbitant prices for his sugar, flour and coffee. He also smuggled in a keg of whiskey; but as none of the men have money, it is likely to return untouched." That turned out not to be the case, according to Möllhausen. "The trader was strictly enjoined not to sell brandy, as there were many among our men who did not know how to keep within bounds. . . . The trader promised to obey the injunction, but there were nevertheless in a short time several drunken men found in the camp, who gave a great deal of trouble. One of them, and he, my own servant, had to be kept out of mischief, by having his hands tied to the bent-down branch of a tree, so that when it recovered its position, the culprit could only just touch the ground with the tips of his toes, and he was left there till he recovered his senses."[24]

The fieldwork for the survey was nearly over, but John Tidball had more stories to tell. He would continue to record his reminisces of his experiences at San Bernardino and other locations as he made his way to the Pacific, describing some of the local personalities he met while preparing to depart for the East Coast.

Chapter 11

I Will Not Have to Go Back to That Miserable Place

As his little band of frazzled soldiers approached the Mormon settlement of San Bernardino, Tidball thought the distant houses "looked like veritable palaces." Beyond a fringe of trees and a meandering creek, on rising ground, were emerald fields of wheat and barley.

> Between us and the town the plain was variegated with wildflowers intermingled with the fresh greenness of the grass. The flowers were in large masses, often acres in extent, red in one place, yellow in another, orange in still another, and so on, all blending with the green grass into the most perfect harmony. In the abstract this prospect was most magnificent. I have since been there and know that the impression of it did not arise from the contrast with the barren waste through which we had been so long traveling. It was simply gorgeous, pure and simple. Herds of cattle were grazing over this plain attended by native Californians who, swinging their riétas, galloped hither and thither. The sky was of the deepest blue with here and there a cumulus cloud. This was truly a realization of what our fancy had pictured California to be.

About sundown they reached the Mormon settlement, where Tidball procured provisions for his men. "The lambs upon which we had feasted had allayed hunger but did not compensate for coffee—the soldier's great solace—the absence of which we had sorely felt for a long while. The men soon supplied themselves with tobacco, another luxury—more properly necessity—they had been out of also for a long while." Having made preparation for the night he then went in search of "*one square meal.*"

This, upon inquiry, he found at the private house of a Mormon, there being no public eating-house in the place.[1]

The original settlement had consisted of cabins enclosed in a stockade, but by the time Tidball arrived, it had grown far beyond its original boundaries. He saw frame houses and adobe houses as well as tents and found that many families lived in canvas-covered wagon bodies placed on the ground and with their wheels removed. "Some of the people appeared happy," he wrote, "while others seemed squalid and wretched." He found Jews among them with their stores but "no Gentiles," employing the Mormon term for non-Mormons. It rained heavily during the first night in the settlement, and he awoke wet and cold. While the men made their coffee and prepared to start, he returned to the same place for breakfast where he had had dinner.

A good wood fire soon made me comfortable while I had an agreeable chat with the woman who was preparing breakfast. I was curious about Mormon customs and she answered my questions with feminine volubility. Her husband sat by in dejected silence grinding coffee in a mill between his knees. She was evidently boss absolute of the house. In reply to one of my questions she said it was true that many of the Mormons had each several wives, to which I remarked that I saw only her about the house. At which, straightening up her buxom form, and giving a warning glance at her husband, she replied: "No, and I guess there will not be any other as long as I live."

This scene was captured in a drawing in his memoirs depicting a bearded man dejectedly looking down at a coffee mill as he turns the crank. Standing above him, arms akimbo, is a stout, stern-looking woman who clearly is in charge.[2]

Meanwhile Whipple, due to a constant succession of showers, awoke on March 18 to find his camp equipage nearly as wet as when it was gathered up from the water of the Rio Colorado. "The once goodly tents, now shaved down to shreds to diminish the weight to be transported, afforded little protection from the incessant rain. The poor mules, with curved back, and four feet drawn into a bunch, looked the picture of discomfort, as with ill grace they submitted to the galling packs." Descending along the steep and rocky bed of Cajon Creek, after six miles they encountered a spur that followed the right bank of the creek and separated it from a smaller ravine called El Puerto de los Negros. Then they left the road Tidball had followed leading to San Bernardino and to the military post at Jarupa and instead turned westward along the base of the mountain chain toward Los Angeles. After leaving the base of the mountains, they entered a great grassy plain replete with herds of horses and cattle grazing on an "immense sheet of tall and luxuriant grass" variegated with an abundance of bright flowers.[3]

After a march of twenty miles, Whipple and the survey party arrived at the rancho of Cucamonga and encamped by a pretty stream that watered it near the house of Señor Leon V. Prudhomme. The next day, March 19, they rested for a day to give the herders time to round up some strayed mules. In Prudhomme's storehouse they found many barrels of wine, manufactured from his vineyards. Months of deprivation had evidently not dulled Whipple's expert palate. He said the wine "was new, and not pleasant to our taste." They were more interested in the hedges formed of huge cacti, growing twelve to fifteen feet in height, the leaves or joints of which were a foot and a half in diameter. The next day they saw another superb estate, Rancho de China. After traveling twenty-four miles more they encamped on the bank of the stream of San Gabriel opposite the town of El Monte.[4]

Twelve miles from the Mormon settlement was Rancho del Jarupa, where on March 16 Tidball found a company of the Second Infantry under Captain Christopher Lovell. Rancho del Jarupa was about forty miles east of Los Angeles and about one hundred eighty miles north of San Diego. One of many old Spanish California ranches, it was, Tidball thought, "one of the finest in this part of the country." He then described how before the War of the Rebellion, all of Southern California was a vast grazing country, divided under the old Spanish laws into ranches of many square miles in extent—about the ordinary size of counties in the older states. "There the proprietor—Don Somebody—lived with his retainers or peons, lord of all he surveyed. The great fertility of this country, its all-the-year-round spring-like climate, and particularly its adaptability to the production of wine, oranges and other tropical fruits, attracted a more enterprising population, to whom the old Spanish class soon gave way. The newcomers married the daughters and thus came in possession of some of the land; they gambled with the fathers and brothers until soon they had what was left." The ranches were divided into farms of a size suitable for vineyards and orange groves and other profitable husbandry. Railroads soon followed, bringing more population, attracted thither by the equable climate and speculative prospects of the country. Then, instead of being a range for herds of horses and cattle and flocks of sheep, it had become a sea of vines and orange and lemon groves, with long vistas of the waving eucalyptus shading the highways. Towns took the places of the ranches, and the old adobe pueblos of the indolent Spaniards grew into cities. In this somewhat subjective history lesson, it is easy to discern the bias of Tidball, who was raised on a hardscrabble farm in Ohio and had little time for those who enjoyed what he perceived to be the easy life of a landed lord.[5]

In a few days Lieutenants Jones and Stanley, who, like Tidball, had to go to San Diego to turn over their men and public property, joined him at Jarupa. "From Jarupa to San Diego we found the journey to be a pic-nic excursion compared with what we had on the east side of the Sierra Nevada. The country was diversified with the hills and plains, all green with wild oats, then just bursting into head." At San Diego Tidball found two companies of artillery—"Magruder's of the 1st and Burtons's of the 3rd." Although he fails to further identify these two officers, they would have been John Bankhead Magruder and Henry S. Burton, both West Pointers, classes of 1830 and 1839, respectively, and both to become well-known Civil War artillerists, although on different sides of that conflict. Magruder, a veteran of the Mexican War, would become famous as "Prince John" Magruder, a title given to him, Tidball said, "in consequence of his grandiose pretensions and his general qualities of affectation." Style and elegance were his strong points. Tidball remembered him as a fine-looking man, even at the time he knew him a few years later at Fort Leavenworth, when he was in his fifties, and "somewhat florid in countenance and rubicund of nose from dissipation." But his neatly shaven face and the manner in which he wore his moustache curled up on either side of his nose "gave him the distinguished air of an Austrian Grand Duke." Burton was more staid; he also had served in the Mexican War and had been a professor at West Point before his service in California.[6]

Two artillery companies were quartered in the old mission about eight miles from the "rickety old Spanish town of San Diego." Where the present city of San Diego now stands was a small establishment called "by way of flattery" a quartermaster's depot, under the command of Lieutenant Eddy, identified by Tidball as "afterwards Colonel Eddy of the Quartermaster Department." That would have been Asher Robbins Eddy, graduate of West Point, class of 1844. To him Tidball turned over his mules. Also stationed at San Diego was Lieutenant George Horatio Derby, West Point class of 1846, of the topographical engineers, "or as he styled it, *Hypothetical* Engineers." It was at that time that Derby was writing under the name of John Phoenix those funny letters published in the *San Diego Herald* "that made that otherwise insignificant sheet so popular." These stories as refined literature were, Tidball remarked, "generally very much *off color*; but after being benzined and disinfected, they were collected into book form under the name of *Phoenixania*, the witty sayings from which are now often quoted by those who know nothing of their origin."[7]

Derby was one of California's first humorists. As with many celebrities, fictitious stories sprouted about him.

> One dealt with the reason for his transfer West. Headquarters assigned him, so the tale goes, to survey the Tombigbee River "to see how far up it runs." Lt. Derby supposedly responded in great detail how he had studied the river and its adjoining topography. He even interviewed travelers along the river's banks in Alabama and Mississippi. "My conclusion," he wrote, "is that the Tombigbee River does not run up, but down." Secretary of War Jefferson Davis, never known for his sense of humor, reportedly was not amused. Soon the lieutenant was sweating with General Bennett Riley and his men exploring the Sacramento and San Joaquin valleys. Then on to even hotter terrain—Fort Yuma in California's Imperial County, just across the border from Yuma, Arizona. His "exile" there didn't diminish his penchant for practical jokes and witticisms. "One of our Fort Yuma men died," Derby would tell newcomers, "and unfortunately went to hell. He wasn't there one day before he telegraphed for blankets."[8]

In 1855, after the publication of the preliminary reports on the Pacific railroad surveys, Derby unleashed his mordant humor on Whipple and the other survey leaders by writing a burlesque of their reports in a California magazine. As John Phoenix, chief astronomer and engineer, he described a reconnaissance, "with eight scientists and 184 laborers, from the heart of San Francisco to the Mission Dolores (a distance of two miles) 'with a view to ascertaining the practicability of connecting these points with a railroad.' Derby included farcical details about the simplest matters and satirized the scientific pedantry that frequently marked the genuine reports."[9]

Despite his penchant for not taking life seriously, Derby had graduated high in the class of 1846 at West Point, two years before Tidball. During the Mexican War he was wounded at Cerro Gordo and was brevetted for gallant and meritorious conduct in that battle. He was promoted to first lieutenant in 1855, and captain in 1860. He died in 1861. Tidball knew Derby at West Point and remembered him well. He had occupied a seat at the same table with him and Tidball recalled that he had listened to Derby's jokes for one long year. "He was always original and sparkling, but even this cloys with time. In caricature he was equally facile. His passion for joking and ridicule was so irresistible that he spared neither friend nor foe."[10]

On March 21, some one hundred twenty miles to the north of Tidball, Whipple and the survey party crossed the little river of San Gabriel and entered the town of El Monte, east of the present Alhambra. Each spot of 160 acres, for miles in all directions, appeared to be ditched around, hedged, and cultivated. They heard "the cheerful sounds of American voices, of the blacksmith's hammer, and the merry laughter of children trudging to school." It was very odd, Whipple thought, "as if a New England village had by some magic sprung up upon the Pacific." Next they passed by the mission of San Gabriel, and then, from a slight eminence, looked down on the valley and city of Los Angeles. They entered the city and found dismal-looking lanes, along which were scattered piles of adobe houses with the intervening spaces lined with mud walls and cactus hedges. But as they proceeded toward the plaza, they thought the somber character of the place was brightened by the appearance of American improvements and indications of business activity, and they noticed hotels, cafes, barbers' signs, and a long array of "flaunting shops." "The buildings, which were formerly of one story, with a broad piazza in front," were being replaced by houses erected in a more modern style, "and many white tents in the suburbs mark the spots where new comers design to build. The population is said to be 3,000," said Whipple, "and is rapidly increasing."[11]

Whipple pitched camp on the point of a ridge overlooking the city. It must have been with a great sense of fulfillment, as well as relief—but also with an inescapable feeling of regret—that the great adventure was over, when Whipple wrote, "As we were now within the limits of operations of the 'Coast Survey,' and an almost unbroken plain is said to lead from Los Angeles to San Pedro, we determined to disband the party, and proceed with all possible dispatch to Washington; there to make known the results of our explorations." The miles traveled from Fort Smith to Los Angeles—some easy, many hard—were 1,845.27. As there was no officer of the government in Los Angeles to whom the United States property could be turned over, Whipple decided to sell it and posted a notice that a public sale would take place at the plaza on the next day. That night, for the last time, Whipple recorded in the official report, "astronomical observations were taken for the determination of latitude and longitude."[12]

Möllhausen described how the civilian exploration corps assembled for the last time in a little coffee room near the post office. The whole party was there with the exception of the officers who had gone to San Diego and "our good Dr. Bigelow, who, being a zealous Catholic, could not prevail on himself to leave Los Angeles without paying a visit to the mission of San Gabriel, eight miles off." With the joy of their return was mingled some feeling of melancholy, as they clinked their glasses for the last time with the companions they were leaving behind, and wished them success in their undertaking. "The parting was painful to them, for when we were gone they would not have a single friend near to take an interest in their welfare; but the enterprising spirit of the Americans, and their incessant brooding over the question of how to obtain an independent position in society, allows little room for feelings of this kind, and it seems to them, as it is in fact, a mere matter of course, that when men have to follow various vocations they cannot always remain together."[13]

The next morning the dense fog soon dispersed and they were favored, Whipple wrote, "with a bright and beautiful day, such as are said to render the climate of Los Angeles the most delightful of California." At ten the auction commenced; the sale being forced, prices were low, but Whipple was pleased that some of the mules, even after all they had been through, brought upwards of one hundred dollars each. They brought the sale to a conclusion quickly in order to rush to San Pedro to meet a steamer for San Francisco. At four in the afternoon, the stagecoach left. Still, Whipple could not refrain from collecting data. "The odometer was attached to a wheel, to measure the distance; and with a prismatic compass and sketchbook, we hoped to make a hasty reconnaissance of the country passed over." They finally arrived at San Pedro about midnight. On March 24, on a bright and clear morning, Whipple compulsively continued to survey everything he saw and fretted because their reconnaissance the previous day "was interrupted by the darkness." But he was able to report, "The distance measured by odometer was nearly twenty-five miles and the course, approximately obtained, was a few degrees west of south, to San Pedro." The survey finally was put behind them as the steamer from San Diego arrived, and Whipple wrote his last entry in the official report: "Excepting Mr. White and Mr. Sherburne, who, delighted with the beauty of the country, preferred to remain in Los Angeles, all the officers of the party took passage for San Francisco, en route to Washington."[14]

Tidball was naturally relieved and pleased to be in San Diego, the terminus of his overland journey. "I have since congratulated myself," he wrote, "upon having had the opportunity of making it. Besides affording me the opportunity of seeing and studying so much of this heretofore undescribed country and of participating in its exploration for one of the great railroad routes to the Pacific, it gave me experience that has been of the greatest benefit throughout my military career," although he did not specify the manner in which that benefit accrued to him. After an agreeable delay of a few days with his fellow officers at San Diego, he took passage for San Francisco and there took lodgings at the Tahoma House, then one of the principal hotels of the city, described by him as a "rambling, rickety, baboon-frame building characteristic of the early structures of that remarkable city." Buildings of magnificent architecture and of great commercial importance, he noted at the time he wrote his memoirs, now occupy its site on the corner of Sansome and California.[15]

Tidball's stay in San Francisco was short but sufficient to afford him an opportunity to observe the "building of a city" then only five years old. One great feature of the operation described by Tidball was the forest of piling extending from about what was then Sansome Street far out into the bay. The huge sand hills, where later stood the fairest and most important portion of the city, afforded ample material for filling in the piling and making street after street where only a few months earlier vessels of the heaviest draught rode at anchor. In some instances these vessels were caught, surrounded, and built in with the newly made land. "Everything was moving," he remembered, "with a rush; all were busy. The population was composed of the young, active and enterprising. The feeble, old and sluggish had not yet found lodgment there. Piles of gold, in coin, in slugs, or in dust abounded on the tables. The betting was high and reckless." The chief gambling places were around the plaza and were magnificent with music and gaudy decorations. It seemed to the young lieutenant that everyone patronized those places, either as participants or as beholders. Women were comparatively scarce. They had been left behind in the wild rush to the golden state—and society had not to any great degree settled down into houses and families. Hotels and boarding houses took their place. "The Chinese were a great curiosity to me," he said, "their mode of living, of dressing and of working; everything about them in fact was strange and novel, and I was greatly interested in studying them. I greatly regretted that time did not admit of my visiting the mining regions or of extending my sight seeing beyond the city."[16]

Whipple with his party—all except Marcou—had sailed for the East Coast previous to Tidball's arrival in the bay city. Marcou had remained to visit the mining regions and the "*Big Trees*"—Yosemite had not yet been discovered. By happenstance Tidball was thus allowed to cultivate further his friendship with the renowned geologist, a relationship that would prove important to his future career. "In his companionship about the city he was as delightful as when we were among the cacti of Arizona. He soon made acquaintances among the large French element of the city, and we frequented together the cafés where they resorted." Here Tidball met Count Bul-Bon (Count de Raousset-Bolubon), then drumming up recruits for a filibustering expedition against Nicaragua. He was in these enterprises with that "prince of filibusters" Walker, who had but a short time previous to this failed in his expedition to Sonora, Mexico, and "had his neck spared from the just indignation of the Mexicans by the kindly intervention of the United States authorities." His expedition to Nicaragua also came to grief, although for a time he held possession of the country and proclaimed himself generalissimo and emperor. Righteous retribution subsequently overtook him when engaged in another of his expeditions—this time against Honduras. "This was the epoch when filibustering was very popular among a certain class in the United States," Tidball wrote, and was acquiesced in by the government, apparently through want of backbone. "Count Bul-Bon proposed to me to join their filibustering projects, holding out brilliant inducements so far as words went. They styled themselves patriots, but I failed to comprehend the patriotism. I never afterwards heard of Bul-Bon. He probably soon afterwards met his death in one of their ill-stared expeditions."[17]

It was at this time that Tidball encountered a man who would come to be known as one of the greatest soldiers ever to fight for his country, and whom he would come to know intimately when, late in his career, he became aide-de-camp to the general-in-chief. It was twenty-six years before that when he saw William Tecumseh Sherman on the streets of San Francisco. "I met General Sherman here for the first time. He was then a banker in San Francisco, and I met him and was introduced to him by a brother officer. He was hurrying, in his accustomed way, across Montgomery Street with a package of banking business papers in his hand." He was in too great a hurry for more than a moment's chat with his "old-time chum," the officer Tidball was with; but that moment was sufficient for Sherman to say much and make a lasting impression on Tidball of his energy and alertness. "Many years afterwards when our official relationship brought us together, I had ample opportunity of verifying my first impressions, and the pleasure of knowing that they were correct."

In order to return to his post at Fort Defiance via the Isthmus of Panama and New York, and then again over the plains, Tidball needed to get an order to take a ship to New York from General John Ellis Wool, then in command of the Department of California. The general, who had the reputation of being somewhat fierce to youngsters, was very polite to Tidball. "In fact," Tidball remembered, "he was in exceedingly high spirits; for someone had just proposed that he should be brought forward as a presidential candidate. To which, as was so frequent with him, he replied that he could not think of such a thing unless it were forced upon him; but if forced he would feel it his duty to serve his country in that capacity if called upon to do so by his patriotic countrymen." He readily gave Tidball the necessary order to rejoin his proper station, and the young lieutenant took the steamer in the middle of April for Panama.[18]

On the trip to Panama there were about a thousand passengers of all classes, and the ship was full but not overcrowded. Many of the passengers were mining engineers or agents for mines returning with bags of specimens as "baits for capitalists." Lieutenant Stanley and Marcou were his stateroommates; they were as comfortable as the heat would permit, as they sailed southward. The Panama railroad was, at this time, completed from the eastern side only about halfway across the isthmus, leaving about twenty-five miles to be traversed by mule. The fare tickets included this transfer from ocean to ocean, and the passengers had "to stick to the back of a mule over a very rough mule path," which, for Tidball, considering what he had just been through, should have been easy. A delay in procuring mules required them to stay overnight in

Panama, "occupying beds—if beds they could be called, in which others before us had sweltered through many a tropical night." For a short while after leaving the city, the road was good, the morning fresh and delightful, and it seemed as though they were starting on a picnic excursion.

But soon they entered tangled forests, impenetrable except by the narrow trail they were following. The country soon became hilly and mountainous and, as it was the rainy season, the clouds gathered and poured down not as rain but as torrents. The sun came out momentarily so hot as to boil them in their wet clothing. The constant traveling back and forth of the mules had worn the narrow path over the hills into deep defiles filled with mud, and, Tidball remarked, "altogether it was anything but a pic-nic journey. Women who braved the journey in those days mounted their mules straddlewise like Indian squaws, and refined ladies had, for the time being, to cast aside their hoop skirts and delicacy. At Gorgana—a place, not a town—the terminus of the railroad, we met the steamer load of passengers from the Atlantic side on their way to California. So many mules, so many people drenched and sweltering, with little or no shelter, much less accommodation, made the scene resemble a routed army. The night we spent here is not to be forgotten."[19]

"The little railroad was begun in 1850, with the idea that it could be finished in two years. It was finished five years later, and at a cost of $8,000,000, six times beyond anyone's estimate." It was the world's first transcontinental railroad, forty-seven miles long. It was also the world's most expensive line to build on a per-mile basis, and also to travel on; a one-way ticket cost twenty-five dollars in gold. Its construction was also expensive in human life. Six thousand lives may have been lost to cholera, yellow fever, and dysentery. John Tidball and his fellow travelers were fortunate to escape the terrible scourges against which there was no known protection or any known cure. The worst year had been the previous year, 1852, when cholera swept across the isthmus: "of the American technicians then employed—some fifty engineers, surveyors, draftsmen—all but two died." When a large military detachment of several hundred men, along with their dependents, made the crossing that year, 150 men, women, and children died. "The horrors of the road in the rainy season are beyond description," wrote the young officer in charge, Captain Ulysses S. Grant.[20]

The next day, after a few hours' ride on the railroad, Tidball boarded the steamer that was to carry him to New York. Unfortunately, the baggage was left behind, apparently a common occurrence, and a steamer crowded with passengers in a tropical climate with nothing but the wet and reeking clothes with which they crossed the isthmus was, Tidball remembered, "anything but luxury." The usual passage of eight days, however, brought them "delighted and happy" to New York. Tidball at once left for Newport, Rhode Island, to join his wife, who had made this her residence, awaiting his return from his long wanderings. They had not yet been married quite a year.[21]

Whipple too had arrived in New York, on April 25, where, he wrote, the health officer put them in "quarantine on account of two cases of small pox on board." The next day, however, he was in the city at French's Hotel. His party was met by their families, and a round of entertainment followed—"dinner at Delmonico's, visits to the Crystal Palace and the current plays—which lasted for two weeks. Reluctantly, the companions of eleven months who had crossed a continent and returned together now said goodbye. Whipple and several others proceeded to Washington—and the considerable task of writing their reports."[22]

Whipple was back, and the survey was over, but he faced a stiff task. Even during his family reunion, the conscientious Whipple must have been preoccupied with how he would proceed with collating and verifying the massive amount of data he had collected and how he would organize and write the final report for Congress. He arrived in Washington on May 6, 1854, to commence work, and he and his scientists beavered away for months on their reports. Lieutenant Ives, Dr. Bigelow, Albert Campbell, Dr. Kennerly, and Jules Marcou started working either at their homes or in the capital. Möllhausen spent a few months touching up his drawings before returning to Germany. Congress published the preliminary survey reports in 1855, and Whipple complained that he had been "obliged" to complete his report for the secretary of war by July 31, 1854, even though some of the other commanders "took their own time." As a result, the "hastily, crudely and imperfectly" prepared report was full of the "grossest" typographical errors. Whipple's construction cost estimate was nearly $162 million, an astronomical sum far higher than the estimates given by the other commanders, a sum he later corrected.[23]

Although Tidball had no further responsibilities with the survey, he too was preoccupied with what lay ahead. He was faced with the prospect of joining his company at the dreaded post of Fort Defiance; the wagon train would leave in a month's time, and he and his wife would be crossing the torrid desert of the Southwest in the scorching sun. But his first priority was a reunion with Mary. In Newport "we met after a year's separation, many months of which were without hearing from each other. . . . I obtained from the War Dept. permission to delay proceeding to New Mexico until the fall train. This gave us several months during which we went to Carlisle Pa., a pleasant and economical place to live. Mary had determined again not to be separated from me, when it was in her power to be with me; accordingly preparations were made for her to accompany me to New Mexico."[24]

About the middle of September, John and Mary finally "hauled out" from Fort Leavenworth and, taking the Old Santa Fe Trail, started their "long and toilsome journey to New Mexico." The party was comparatively small, consisting of only about one hundred enlisted men and eight officers; the four married officers had their own private ambulances and mules. Major Grier of the dragoons, an experienced plainsman, was their commanding officer. He was, as the well-known song went, the same "Old Billy Grier the Buena commandante" who "lived down in Albuquerque in a doba shanty," and well did he merit the title of "*Buena commandante*," Tidball remembered. But the weather was exceedingly hot and dry; no rain having fallen for several months, it was with difficulty that the party obtained water, and what they did find was in holes in the creeks—stagnant and green.[25]

Early on the morning of the sixth day out, they were overtaken by a courier from Leavenworth bringing delayed mail and "a dispatch announcing the massacre of Lt. Grattan and party on the plains not far distant from their line of march." The dispatch also informed the party, for the purpose of putting them on their guard, that the Indians were becoming troublesome all around. But what proved of more importance than hostile Indians was a telegraph from the War Department read to them by the commanding officer, directing Tidball to report in Washington for duty on the Coast Survey. At first he and Mary thought it was a joke, but to their great surprise it was a cheerful reality, as unexpected as it was delightful, at which Mary gave "a war whoop of delight." It relieved them "from the wearisome journey to that most remote of all posts—Fort Defiance—and from an indefinite stay in that God Forsaken country, and again from the wearisome journey returning from it. It would bring us back to civilization and me to congenial pursuits." He was greatly mystified by being ordered to the Coast Survey and couldn't imagine how it came about that he was selected. Subsequently he learned that it was through his friend Professor Marcou. "A kindred feeling of science brought him and Professor Bache, the superintendent of the Coast Survey together, and Marcou took occasion to mention me with great praise."

It took but a few minutes for John and his wife to prepare to retrace their steps to Leavenworth. With a hasty goodbye they parted from their friends, "they continuing their winding way across the plains, and we, more fortunate, returning upon the trail we had just passed over." His assignment to the Coast Survey commenced on September 6, 1854, and would last just over five years. Several years after he began his new assignment, he wrote his father, "My company has been ordered in from New Mexico so that I will not have to return to that miserable country."[26]

Meanwhile, Whipple had finished his report. In a summary of the 35th parallel survey, Secretary Davis complimented Whipple "for the completion of the work in all its parts, the full and exact observations which he made for the determination of longitudes and latitudes, and the wide range of scientific research which he instituted into all the collateral branches connected with the question which his exploration was designed to solve." Whipple was not complimented, however, on his engineering estimates; the evaluation by Captain A. A. Humphreys and Lieutenant G. K. Warren emphasized that the "description of the topographical features of the route is not sufficiently minute to enable one to form a satisfactory opinion of the difficulties of the ground to be encountered, and consequently of the probable cost of the formation of the road bed." All of this leaves the impression that Whipple's report was thought to be more valuable for its artistic, ethnological, zoological, geological, and botanical data than for any information describing the feasibility of building a railroad along the route. The preliminary estimate was qualified with a note that it was "thought to be largely in excess," and in conclusion the evaluation found that all the estimates would "doubtless be found to contain many errors"; and that the same amount of error will probably be found in each of the other estimates, and therefore the "actual expense will thus preserve the same proportion." No matter how the estimate would be adjusted, however, the erroneous impression that this was an expensive route, perhaps prohibitively so, was a lasting one.[27]

When the results of the Pacific surveys were compiled, revealing that not one but several practicable routes existed, the high-ranking officers of the topographical engineers, and Jefferson Davis himself, may have been surprised. Ever since the Mexican War, the topographical engineers had focused their attention on the Southwest. Both Emory and Abert had become convinced that the national destiny was linked to the construction of a railroad along the 32d parallel to California, the southernmost route. To southern political leaders the annexation of Texas and the acquisition of vast lands from Mexico foreshadowed an opportunity for the South to expand slavery to the Pacific.

William H. Goetzmann concludes, "Jefferson Davis was in a unique position to appreciate fully the value of the extensive army surveys in the Southwest. He had served on the Senate Committee for Military Affairs from 1848 to 1851, and in 1853 he was appointed Secretary of War. . . . Because he knew well the views of the Topographical Corps on the feasibility of the Southern route, it was easy for Davis to be positive that his section possessed the key to Manifest Destiny in the West."[28]

When Captain Humphreys submitted his final report, he clearly favored the 32d parallel route; Davis's identical conclusion was predictable—he confidently declared that "the route of the 32nd parallel is, of those surveyed, the most practicable and economical route for a railroad from the Mississippi to the Pacific Ocean." Goetzmann attributes Davis's failure to make the surveys serve the whole country "to a certain rigidity of mind, an inability to appreciate the nature of existing reality. His attention was too narrowly confined to the scientific findings of earlier years, and hence upon the good fortune of his own section. This caused him, as it did most Southerners, to look upon the railroad surveys as a ritual that had to be undergone before the rest of the country could perceive the scientific advisability of the 32nd parallel route."[29]

The 35th parallel route was found to be "extremely favorable in all respects" except for Whipple's unfortunate and perhaps fatally astronomical cost estimate. Even when the costs were reduced to $94,720,000, it was not as cheap as the 32d parallel route, but it had an advantage in more accessible timber and water, and an easy connection with San Francisco. Davis was accused of failing to serve the interests of the whole nation, and even betraying the South because of his inflexible failure to see that the 35th parallel route had the best chance of satisfying the diverse political and factional groups.[30]

Whipple's labors in Washington involved not only attempting to justify the 35th parallel as the best transcontinental railroad route, but in overseeing the completion of the parts of the report that had little or nothing to do with railroad building. Dr. Bigelow contributed the botanical report; botanists were still praising his collection decades later. Dr. Kennerly's zoological collection, gathered with Möllhausen's help, was examined by scientists at the Smithsonian Institution along with collections from the other railroad surveys. Zoological studies of all the collections, lavishly illustrated, filled three volumes of the published *Reports*. Jules Marcou's geological report, however, was immediately embroiled in controversy when the volatile Frenchman claimed poor health and went to France to recuperate. The final report was written by W. P. Blake, geologist in the office of Pacific Railroad Exploration and Surveys, who promptly undermined Marcou's preliminary report. Although each one of the surveys was to produce a report on Indian tribes, Whipple alone came up with a lengthy ethnological report, written with the assistance of Thomas Ewbank, of whom we shall hear more later, and Professor William W. Turner. Whipple's report on Indians was the source of an 1858 article in *Harper's New Monthly Magazine* entitled "The Tribes of the Thirty-Fifth Parallel," adorned with woodcuts from the report, depicting Indians from most of the tribes encountered by the explorers. The majesty of the western landscape and the exotica of Indian life contributed by Whipple's artists—Möllhausen, Campbell, and Tidball— also attracted attention.[31]

The reports generated by the surveys, which were published by the federal government between 1855 and 1861 in a twelve volume work entitled *Reports of Explorations and Surveys to Ascertain the Most Practicable and Economic Route for a Railroad from the Mississippi River to the Pacific Ocean*, comprise an encyclopedic compendium of western geography, geology, botany, zoology, archeology, and ethnology, lavishly illustrated with drawings, woodcuts, and color plates. Although the surveys themselves ultimately required a congressional appropriation of only $455,000, publication of this monumental work cost more than twice as much—$1 million. The pictorial value was recognized immediately; even before the entire set was issued, the profusely illustrated *Reports* attracted wide attention. Early in 1859, Senator James Harlan of Iowa urged his colleagues to use the "immense mass of information" in the *Reports* to reach an enlightened decision on a transcontinental railroad route. Then, speaking down to his fellow legislators, he said:

But lest some Senators and members of Congress might not be able to read and comprehend them, they have been illustrated. Every unusual swell of land, every unexpected or unanticipated gorge in the mountains has been displayed in a beautiful picture. Every bird that flies in the air over that immense region, and every beast that traverses the plains and the mountains, every fish that swims in its lakes and rivers, every reptile that crawls, every insect that buzzes in the summer breeze, has been displayed in the highest style of art, and in the most brilliant colors.[32]

Were the Pacific railroad surveys a success? Was it worthwhile to spend hundreds of thousands of dollars to send hundreds of men out to span the continent, to endure hardship, privation, and death? It is not an easy question to answer. William H. Goetzmann declared the Pacific railroad surveys a failure: "Controversy resumed where it had left off, with little hope of ever producing a transcontinental railroad. Science and politics had had their chance, but the Corps in its professional pride and the Secretary in his sectional prejudice had ignored reality. In the end, though nature had offered the alternatives and science had revealed them, it was still the passions of men that governed their relevance to the course of national progress." The first transcontinental railroad would not be completed until 1869, at Promontory Point, Utah, far north of the 32d and the 35th parallels.[33]

Goetzmann was right in declaring the surveys a failure, but only in the narrowest sense in that they did not provide an easy political or technical answer to the interminable question of where the transcontinental railroad should be built, an answer that it was unrealistic to expect in the first place. The success was the published *Reports,* which bestowed upon the country a rich artistic and scientific legacy, the enduring value of which surpasses the worth of the engineering data so painstakingly compiled by Whipple and his fellow engineers. That legacy was the work of the botanists, zoologists, geologists, and the eleven artists who traveled in the field with the exploring parties, braving dangers from the Indians and "the hardships of a hard land." Speaking of the artists, William H. and William N. Goetzmann wrote, "Theirs was one of the great epic adventures and contributions to knowledge of the nineteenth century in America, and they have yet to receive their due."[34]

That arduous winter of 1853–54, Tidball and his fellow artists of the

35th parallel survey, looking upon a land that was empty, virgin, and devoid of history and sentiment, brought it to life and captured for all generations the picturesque landscape of the Southwest—scenes that are preserved today in the illustrations of the *Pacific Railroad Reports*. It is this story that is a success—the story of how the heroism of these artists, "by vanquishing physical obstacles enroute to a destination," did indeed become a "tour de force" in American frontier art.[35]

Epilogue

Whipple had finished his work on the final edition of the *Reports* during the summer following Tidball's assignment to the Coast Survey. On June 30, 1855, he sent it to Secretary Davis, and in his transmittal letter he complimented the military contingent of the survey party. "The officers of the escort to the expedition were 1st Lieutenant John M. Jones, 7th Infantry; Lieutenant J. C. Tidball, 1st Artillery; and Lieutenant D. S. Stanley, 2d Dragoons. Each, in his appropriate sphere, contributed greatly toward the success of our operations. The quiet and peaceful manner in which we passed through the various tribes of Indians, usually hostile toward Americans, is a proof of the sound discretion of those officers, and the good discipline of the men composing their command." When the final reports were published, Whipple sent a copy of volume 3 to Tidball with his compliments, the copy in which Tidball vigorously disagreed with Whipple in many instances by making humorously disparaging marginal comments.[1]

On July 1, 1855, Whipple was promoted to captain and ordered to Detroit, where he supervised lighthouses and worked at the channels through the St. Clair flats and St. Mary's River, opening the Great Lakes to navigation by larger ships. When the Civil War started, Whipple was at Bull Run, serving as Irvin McDowell's chief topographical engineer. Promoted to major in the engineers in September 1861, he received an appointment as brigadier general of volunteers in April 1862 and commanded a brigade and then a division in the defenses of Washington. In December 1862 he went into battle for the first time, leading a division at Fredericksburg. At the battle of Chancellorsville, his division suffered more than a thousand casualties. During this battle, on May 4, 1863, while near a battery directing construction of earthworks, Whipple was mortally wounded by a Confederate sharpshooter. The bullet passed through his belt and stomach and came out the small of his back close to the spinal column. He was taken to Washington but never regained consciousness. He died of peritonitis on May 7, 1863. Just prior to his death, President Abraham Lincoln, who attended his funeral, commissioned him major general, volunteers. When a military post was established near Prescott, Arizona, in October 1863, it was named Fort Whipple in his honor. It is still there, now a Veterans Administration Medical Center.[2]

At the moment when Amiel Whipple was cut down by a sniper's bullet in the debacle at Chancellorsville, he was poised to solidify his reputation as a combat commander. Despite his propensity to indulge in the kind of woolly musings he confided to his personal journal while leading the 35th parallel railroad expedition—hesitation, disappointment bordering on despair, and idealistic reveries—there is every reason to believe that this dependable soldier, who was not lacking in courage and intelligence, would have become a gallant and effective wartime leader of men. After his flights of metaphysical fancy, he always glided back to ground. Had he lived, Whipple likely would have emerged at the end of the war an esteemed officer, and could have looked forward to a distinguished career serving out his years in the elite engineer corps.

He was an idealist, and when he died a soldier's death, his idealism was undisturbed by a history he would never know. His lofty aspirations for the American Indians were never diminished by living to observe his Mojaves, once "merry as crickets"—as John Tidball would say thirty years after the survey party crossed the Rio Colorado—now idle, unemployed, attired in white man's clothing, loitering around a depot on a railroad line his survey had helped create.

Heinrich Balduin Möllhausen, adventurous and ambitious, pursued his career in the museums of Europe and the Rocky Mountain wilderness of North America. Upon his return from the Whipple expedition, he wrote and prepared for publication his diary of the trip, but before it was published, he was off on another expedition, this time with Lieutenant Joseph Ives to explore the Colorado River basin in 1857. Building on the success of the publication of his diary, he wrote an account of his second trip and entered a life of writing. Between 1860 and 1905, he produced some thirty-nine novels and became, at least for twenty years, Germany's most popular novelist. He enjoyed posing for photographers, fully bearded, dressed in fringed buckskin and holding a long rifle. His writings were set on the frontier of North America after the style of James Fenimore Cooper, and he became popularly known as the "German Cooper." He died in 1905.[3]

Of the five West Pointers, the career of Joseph Christmas Ives was the most unusual. He led an expedition to explore the Colorado River in 1857–1858, accompanied by Möllhausen, then served as engineer and architect of the Washington National Monument. Ives was a native New Yorker, but when the war broke out, he defected because of his southern wife, and during the latter part of the war served as an aide-de-camp to President Jefferson Davis with the rank of Colonel. Ives and his wife had been intimate friends of the Davises before the war, and "the Ives house was one of the few private homes in which Jefferson Davis ever appeared. It was sometimes called 'a detached segment of the White House,' for the Iveses continually entertained foreign guests and various dignitaries for the President." After the war, Ives returned to New York, where he died in 1868. His youngest son was a lawyer who moved to Arizona, returning to the scene of his father's early explorations.[4]

Like so many antebellum West Pointers, Stanley and Jones each attained the rank of general and served their respective causes gallantly. Jones resigned his captaincy when the war broke out, and was wounded as a Confederate brigadier general during the assault of Culp's Hill at Gettysburg. He was again wounded during operations on the Rappahannock, and during the Battle of the Wilderness, he was killed while attempting to rally his brigade. Stanley was a major general of volunteers by 1862 and saw action in a number of battles while serving in the Army of the Cumberland. For meritorious service at the battle of Franklin, Tennessee, where he was severely wounded, he received the Congressional Medal of Honor. He retired from active service in 1892, and died in 1902.[5]

Poor John Sherburne, the bright cheerful young man of the 35th parallel survey, who so loved fandangos and "toddies and brandy clear," failed at everything he tried, not the least at being a soldier. His military records comprise a litany of nervous breakdowns, bad debts, pleadings for mercy, litigation, and finally, in John Tidball's words, being "benzined" from the service. He was commissioned a second lieutenant in the infantry in June 1856, a rank he held until the war started, when he was promoted to first lieutenant. In October 1861 he was made captain in the Nineteenth Infantry regiment, and in July 1862 was promoted to major in the adjutant general's department. He applied to go into the field and was appointed colonel of volunteers (Eleventh New York Cavalry) in March 1864. For about three months he was chief of cavalry, Department of the Gulf, and then things started to go downhill. He said that he "lost his health by exposure" and resigned his commission, but he was certified as "suffering from extensive nervous prostration" in November 1864 and sent to New Orleans for treatment. In 1869 Congress began enacting reorganization statutes designed to thin out the oversized wartime army, and Sherburne was called before a board of officers for the examination of officers "unfit for service." His principal problem was impecuniousness—which may have had its root cause in excessive use of alcohol—and his principal accuser was one Ann Brower, who ran a boarding house in Morristown, Pennsylvania, where he and his family resided after the war, and who claimed he owed her $416; several merchants also filed claims. Perhaps the most serious charge was a claim by the quartermaster general that Sherburne failed to properly account for furniture and other government property. Sherburne wrote long pleading letters in his defense, claiming illness and advancing various other excuses, as well as promising to pay the money owed, but to no avail. The board reported that "Major John P. Sherburne, Ass't Adjt. Genl, is unfit for the service by reason of disregard of his pecuniary obligations, to the discredit of the Army: and also for the reason that he has not uniformly well performed the duties of his office and the board does therefore recommend that he be mustered out of the service." He was discharged December 28, 1870, and died ten years later at the age of forty-eight.[6]

During his first year with the Coast Survey, Tidball received a note from Henry R. Schoolcraft, L.L.D., a prominent explorer, geologist, and ethnologist, who was compiling for the government an account of the North American Indian tribes. Captain Seth Eastman had been with him a number of years illustrating his work. "Eastman," Tidball wrote, "had been relieved from duty with Mr. Schoolcraft, and the latter had heard that I had some skill in drawing and wanted me to continue the unfinished work of Eastman. The handsome compensation to a lieutenant living in Washington with a family was not to be ignored, so I undertook the work." Everything went well, Tidball remembered, until one day

when Schoolcraft informed him that Thomas Ewbank had some archeo-
logical specimens "despoiled" from ancient graves of Central America,
consisting of mummified heads of Indians with grins and matted hair,
and other artifacts which he wanted drawn. Ewbank, it will be recalled,
had collaborated with Whipple in the preparation of the report on Indian
tribes.[7]

Tidball filled his room with these sepulchral objects and remembered
how a maid entered the room while he had one of the grinning heads
before him on a table, and was "frightened into kicking hysterics and left
the premises as a place filled with evil spirits." Tidball made a number of
drawings, thinking that there was a kind of partnership between Schoolcraft and Ewbank, and was greatly surprised when one day he received a
"savage" note from Schoolcraft telling him that he had done great wrong
by giving the drawings to Ewbank. "I made no reply to this note, and thus
my otherwise very pleasant acquaintance with this distinguished gentleman ended. This incident taught me what I so frequently observed
afterward—that between scientific men there is apt to be great jealousy,
and sometimes-sharp practice. In this instance Schoolcraft wanted to get
ahead of Ewbank by making use of the specimens of the latter, who in
turn wanted to forestall the former by earlier publication, and I became
the victim to misplaced confidence. I was not much of a victim after all,
for I dropped them both to their own jealousies."[8]

Tidball's artistic career was not yet quite over; in August 1855, he was
assigned to take charge of the Coast Survey drawing division. Perhaps the
most exciting thing that happened during his tenure in that position was
that for a short period James McNeill Whistler, who subsequently became an artist of worldwide fame, was employed in his division as a
draughtsman. On January 15, 1859, Tidball's wife died of consumption,
leaving him a widower ten days short of his thirty-fourth birthday, with
two infant sons to care for. When his application to be returned to his
company was granted in the fall of 1859, he sent his sons to live with his
father in Ohio.[9]

He had no sooner arrived at Fort Monroe than his company was
ordered to Harper's Ferry to assist in putting down John Brown's rebellion. By the time he arrived, the short-lived insurrection was over, but
he stayed on long enough to become acquainted with his commanding
officer, Robert E. Lee. He returned to Fort Monroe and stayed there until
the next summer, when he went to Fort Leavenworth to join Battery A,

Second U.S. Artillery, the battery he would take into battle in less than a year, and which he would cover with glory. The time for training was nearly over, and history was about to catch up with John Tidball. On January 8, 1861, he departed Fort Leavenworth for Washington, D.C., commanding the first regular artillery unit to arrive in the nation's capital that year.

It was an anxious time in Washington, and in March 1861 he received a different kind of assignment. It was believed that a plot was afoot to assassinate Abraham Lincoln. Side streets along the line of march of the presidential procession were guarded, and selected marksmen closely watched houses known to be infested by rebel sympathizers; the procession was so formed that the incoming president was constantly surrounded by reliable regular troops. Tidball stationed his light battery at the corner of Capitol and B Streets. "Here with an ample supply of canister at hand we stood ready at a moment's notice to debouch in any direction." Finally the procession arrived, and from the mighty throng that occupied the open space in front of the eastern portico of the Capitol, there came to the officers and men on guard the sound of applause, announcing that the new president had presented himself to take the oath of office. "This was the supreme moment of anxiety," remembered Tidball. Presently all was still, and then he heard the sound of Mr. Lincoln's voice as he delivered his inaugural address. The new government was peacefully installed.[10]

A month later, on April 6, Tidball marched his battery to the foot of Canal Street in New York and boarded the steamship *Atlantic*, bound for Fort Pickens in Pensacola Harbor where the Confederates under Braxton Bragg were threatening. Six days later the Confederate Army attacked Fort Sumter. He soon took his battery back to the East Coast, arriving in New York on July 14 and in Washington the following night. "Here we received information that McDowell's army was already on the move in quest of the enemy then supposed to be somewhere near Centreville about twenty miles from Washington. A note from McDowell informed us to join him at once or we would miss the fight." The Battle of Bull Run, the first of the war, was about to be fought.[11]

In 1861, after the Battle of Bull Run, John Tidball, now a captain, mounted all his cannoneers and organized a horse artillery battery that "became celebrated in the annals of the Army of the Potomac" because of its ability to direct rapid and witheringly accurate fire against the enemy.

Officers of Battery A, Second Artillery. This photo, which was taken in the vicinity of Fair Oaks, Virginia, June 1862, by James Gibson, shows from left: Lieutenant Robert Clarke, Captain John C. Tidball, Lieutenant William N. Dennison, and Lieutenant Alexander C. M. Pennington.

Early in the war he fought at Yorktown, Williamsburg, Mechanicsville, and Gaines Mill, where he won a brevet for gallant and meritorious services. A legacy left by Tidball to generations of future American servicemen is the custom of sounding taps at graveside. On withdrawing from the Peninsula in August 1862, Tidball's battery was serving with the rear guard and, on reaching Harrison's Landing, one of his cannoneers died and was buried there. Not wishing to stir up the enemy by firing three rounds from his guns, which was then the practice, Tidball substituted the sounding of "Taps," or "lights out." It has been the custom at military funerals ever since. A month later, at the battle of Antietam, he was brevetted lieutenant colonel for gallant and meritorious services.[12]

In the Gettysburg campaign, Tidball commanded a horse artillery brigade, including his old unit, Battery A, Second U.S. Artillery, which he said, "had the honor of firing the opening gun of this sanguinary momentous battle." Impatient with the torpid rate of advancement in the regular artillery, in August 1863 he accepted an appointment as colonel of the New York Heavy Artillery. In March 1864 he was placed in command of the II Corps Artillery in the Army of the Potomac, and directed the guns of that corps in the battles of the Wilderness, Spotsylvania, North Anna, and Cold Harbor. He was brevetted brigadier general on August 1, 1864, and later brevetted major general, volunteers, for gallant and meritorious services in the Petersburg campaign, where he commanded the IX Corps Artillery. Ulysses Grant praised General Tidball for effectively deploying at Fort Stedman a large number of pieces of artillery "so as to sweep the narrow space of ground between the lines very thoroughly."[13]

After the war, Tidball reverted to his regular rank of captain and began gradually working his way back up through the ranks. While fulfilling various peacetime assignments, including commandant of the Military District of Alaska at Sitka in 1870, he authored the "voluminous and exhaustive" *Manual of Heavy Artillery*, which was adopted as a textbook at the U.S. Military Academy. On July 1881 he was appointed aide-de-camp to General-in-Chief William Tecumseh Sherman, whom he accompanied on a ten-thousand-mile journey through the western United States and Canada. In his memoirs, Tidball recalled the memorable crossing of the Colorado many years before when, thirty years later, he returned to the scene at almost the identical spot and traveled over the river on a pile bridge. "In 1883 I passed over this railroad—then just opened to travel—and distinctly recognized the place. There is a station there and a small settlement. (Chiefly Mormons I was told). Around this station were Mojaves, idle, listless and loafing. There were among them some whom no doubt I had seen as children thirty years before."

He then reflected on the many great events that had transpired in the world since Whipple and his men had crossed the mighty Colorado. "The Crimean War, then just commenced, was fought to an end. Other European wars—notably the Franco-Prussian—had also taken place, greatly changing the map and rule of the continent. Napoleon with the connivance of some of his neighboring monarchs had seized upon what they deemed an auspicious moment to set up a monarchy on the western continent, and had established Maximillian as emperor of Mexico" who was deserted by his supporters and "soon met the fate he from his bloody tyranny so justly deserved."

Ocean cables had been put into successful operation and four lines of railroad to the Pacific had been constructed. "But, greatest of all, the war for the preservation of the Union had been successfully fought. Slavery had been abolished—swept away by the rebellion that its advocates instituted for its extension. The population of the United States had more than doubled itself. In the midst of all this progress, this band of aborigines had but marked time. The only change that I could see wrought by the railroad traversing their country was that now the bucks covered themselves with calico shirts, whereas before they did not."[14]

The creator's untutored children, as Whipple had optimistically fantasized thirty years before, would not be standing "as proudly erect in the halls of congress as now they do upon their native soil." Instead, as John Tidball sadly observed, they were listlessly loafing around a railroad station, located on the route he and Whipple had helped to chart.

Tidball kept the official journal of Sherman's western trip, which was published as part of the *Report of the Secretary of War*. In it he remarked, with humor, on crossing the Cañon Diablo by rail. Whipple, it will be recalled, on a cold December day thirty years earlier, just two days after John Tidball joined his party, could not cross this precipitous chasm and in disgust gave it its ominous name. "It has a depth of 210 feet and an average width of about the same." Tidball wrote in 1883, and added in a humorous aside, "It has irregular sides of solid rocks, many of which about the bridge are ornamented with patent medicine and other like signs painted in letters so conspicuous that even the Navajos cannot fail to comprehend the virtues of the articles advertised. This suggests that perhaps many of the Indian inscriptions that so bother ethnologists are nothing but trade signs recommending superior tomahawks, arrowheads, and other fabrics of Indian manufacture."[15]

The law mandated retirement at age sixty-four, and on January 25, 1889, the clock struck midnight for John Tidball. When he retired he was in command of the artillery school at Fort Monroe, where Tidball Street today still traverses the post. After the war his reputation as a military educator grew until he stood alone as the most prominent writer and commentator on artillery matters. He died May 15, 1906, at the age of eighty-one, remembered by veterans of the War of the Rebellion for his "intrepidity, self-possession and coolness under fire." At West Point, where his long and distinguished military career had begun, John Caldwell Tidball, the last surviving member of the class of 1848, was laid to rest to the sweet, sad notes of "Taps," as had been the cannoneer he buried at Harrison's Landing forty-four years earlier.[16]

Notes

Abbreviations of Works Frequently Cited in the Notes

APS   Grant Foreman, ed. *A Pathfinder in the Southwest.*

IT   John C. Tidball. "Itinerary."

JCTP   John Caldwell Tidball Papers.

MD   Heinrich Balduin Möllhausen. *Diary of a Journey from the Mississippi to the Coasts of the Pacific.*

RES   *Reports of Explorations and Surveys, 1855–1860.*

SD   David S. Stanley. "Diary of D. S. Stanley, United States, 2d Dragoons, of a March from Fort Smith, Arkansas to San Diego, California, made in 1853."

TD   Tidball, John C. "John C. Tidball en route for California."

TICC   Mary McDougall Gordon, ed. *Through Indian Country to California: John P. Sherburne's Diary of the Whipple Expedition, 1853–1854.*

WJ   Amiel W. Whipple Journal.

Preface

1. Eugene C. Tidball, *No Disgrace to My Country.*

Chapter 1. Glory Grabber or Reliable Wheelhorse?

1. Bergon, ed., *Journals of Lewis and Clark,* ix–x; Goetzmann, *Exploration and Empire,* chapters 1–11; Goetzmann, *Army Exploration,* 263–74; Tate, *Frontier Army,* 3–28. Frémont's expeditions made few contributions to science. Although his exploits may have lured thousands of Americans to the West, they were largely symbolic, with a political purpose—a rallying point of Manifest Destiny, a "supreme gesture." His second to last trip, in 1848, was a debacle. In the San Juan Mountains of Colorado in December, he encountered snow ten feet deep and temperatures of 20 below zero. Ten of his men froze or starved to death. Yet, as a recent biographer wrote, "By forcing Americans—even those

who would never visit the region—to reimagine the American West, he also compelled them to reimagine America itself—to conceive of their nation, for the first time, as a sea-to-sea empire." Chaffin, *Pathfinder,* xxix.

Well into the next century, the armed forces continued to lead America's exploration efforts. In 1925 a naval officer, Rear Adm. Richard E. Byrd, made the first flight over the North Pole and continued probing the largely unknown Antarctic through the 1930s. In 1969 humans achieved the long-awaited goal of landing on the moon. Manning *Apollo II* were Edwin Aldrich Jr., Lt. Col. Michael Collins of the air force, and Neil A. Armstrong, a navy veteran. *Funk and Wagnalls New World Encyclopedia.*

2. Goetzmann, *Exploration and Empire,* 265, 270–71. John James Abert graduated from the fledgling U.S. Military Academy in 1811 and was appointed head of the Topographical Bureau in 1829. Due mainly to Abert's influence, in 1838 a separate Corps of Topographical Engineers was established. Abert's continuing emphasis on exploration as a means of contributing to scientific knowledge was a reflection of his role in the emerging scientific community. He was a friend of John James Audubon, and a founder of the National Institution for the Promotion of Science. He retired in 1861 and died in 1863. Garraty and Carnes, eds., *American National Biography,* 42–43.

3. Goetzmann, *Exploration and Empire,* 271–72; Goetzmann, *Army Exploration,* 213–16.

4. *APS,* 15. John Mcrae Washington, whose father was a second cousin of George Washington, graduated from West Point in 1817. In the Mexican War he performed gallantly in the Battle of Buena Vista and was brevetted a lieutenant colonel for gallant and meritorious service. After the war he served as civil and military governor of Santa Fe. In 1853 he embarked with the Third Artillery on the steamer *San Francisco* for transportation to the West Coast; in a violent storm, he, with three other officers and 178 men, was washed overboard and drowned. Malone, *Dictionary of American Biography,* 19:528–29.

5. Goetzmann, *Army Exploration,* 243; A. Wallace, "Across Arizona to the Big Colorado," 325–26.

6. Ibid., 326–27, 330, 352, 357, 359–64; Childs, Jr., ed., *Register of Graduates,* 257; Hubbell and Geary, *Biographical Dictionary,* 392; JCTP, "Genealogy," 84–85.

7. Pierce, *Message from the President of the United States to the Two Houses of Congress,* 8; Goetzmann, *Army Exploration,* 296–98.

8. Goetzmann, *Exploration and Empire,* 265, 281; Goetzmann, *Army Exploration,* 262–63, 273–74.

9. Goetzmann, *Army Exploration,* 262, 274–77; U.S. Department of War, *Report of the Secretary of War,* 1853, 21, 59–60, Goetzmann, *Exploration and Empire,* 281.

10. Goetzmann, *Army Exploration,* 278; Malone, *Dictionary of American Biography,* 17:612–13; Richards, *Isaac I. Stevens,* 94–99. For an account of the Stevens expedition, see Eugene C. Tidball, "In the Footsteps of Lewis and Clark: The Northern Route of the 1853 Pacific Railroad Survey."

11. Goetzmann, *Army Exploration,* 283–85; Mumey, "John Williams Gunnison," 19–21; Childs, Jr., ed., *Register of Graduates,* 267.

12. Goetzmann, *Army Exploration,* 289–91; Hubbell and Geary, *Biographical Dictionary,* 410.

13. *APS*, 7; *TICC*, 8; Malone, *Dictionary of American Biography*, 20:66–67; Stoddard, "Amiel Weeks Whipple," 226–27. There was another Pacific railway survey, unauthorized and privately financed, led by none other than the redoubtable John C. Frémont, at the instigation of his father-in-law, Senator Thomas Hart Benton, who championed the central route because of the political advantage of having the railroad originate in Missouri. Frémont's fifth and last expedition, like his fourth, was undertaken to demonstrate the feasibility of Senator Benton's proposed "central," or 38th parallel, railroad route to the Pacific. "Frémont's purpose was to prove that the southern Rockies could be crossed in winter, that they did not pose an insurmountable barrier for the proposed transcontinental railroad. Like the fourth expedition, his fifth expedition floundered in the mountains and left a legacy of death and suffering." Stegmaier and Miller, *James F. Milligan*, 76–77.

14. Goetzmann, *Army Exploration*, 153–61.

15. Childs, Jr., ed., *Register of Graduates*, 268; Scharf, "Amiel Whipple and the Boundary Survey," 20–23.

16. Scharf, "Amiel Whipple and the Boundary Survey," 23–28.

17. Engstrand and Ward, "Rancho Guajome," 250–83; McKanna, Jr., "An Old Town Gunfight," 258–73. Cave Johnson Couts was born at his family's ancestral home near Springfield, Tennessee, in 1821 and received an appointment to West Point in 1838 through his uncle Cave Johnson, later James Polk's secretary of the treasury. On April 5, 1851, Couts married Ysidora Bandini; among the wedding presents was a 2,219-acre ranch of land known as Rancho Guajome. He resigned from the army in 1851. Couts was a man of influence in his community and served as a county judge, but he was a man with a violent temper. Twice he was indicted for whipping two Indians with a rawhide *reata*— one of whom died of his injuries, but the charges were dropped. On February 6, 1865, in Old Town San Diego he shot and killed a former employee. He was indicted for murder but acquitted. When Couts died in 1874 at the age of fifty-three, he controlled almost 20,000 acres.

18. Scharf, "Amiel Whipple and the Boundary Survey," 29–30.

19. Goetzmann, *Army Exploration*, 167–84; *APS*, 7–9; *TICC*, 8; Wright and Shirk, "The Journal of Lieutenant A. W. Whipple," 236–38.

20. Norris, Milligan, and Faulk, *William H. Emory*, 155–56; E. S. Wallace, *The Great Reconnaissance*, 41.

Chapter 2. The Ultimate Destination Is India

1. Nevins, *Ordeal of the Union*, 1:545–46.

2. Ibid., 1:550–59, 2:194.

3. Ibid., 2:89, 92

4. Conrad, "Whipple Expedition in Arizona," 148–49.

5. WJ, April 27, 1853; Goetzmann, *Army Exploration*, 267; *TICC*, 7. In 1861, at the outbreak of the Civil War, Emory was still in the West—in command of the troops in the Indian Territory. Convinced he could not hold the forts with the territory in a state of insurrection, he withdrew to Fort Leavenworth and was the only officer on the frontier to bring an entire command out of the South without the loss of a man. In 1862 he was promoted to brigadier general and assigned to command a cavalry brigade in the Army of

the Potomac. From 1862 to 1864 he commanded a division in Louisiana and later commanded the XIX Corps under Philip H. Sheridan. He retired a brigadier general in 1876 after forty-three years of service and died in 1887. Malone, *Dictionary of American Biography*, 6: 153–54; Hubbell and Geary, *Biographical Dictionary*, 165–66.

6. WJ, April 27, 1853; *RES*, Intro., 3:1–2.

7. Goetzmann, *Army Exploration*, 275.

8. *TICC*, 10–11.

9. *APS*, 9; *TICC*, 11–15; U.S. Military Academy Cadet Application Papers, 1805–1866. Sherburne's cadet application file does not contain his actual letter of application and therefore may be incomplete.

10. *TICC*, 15.

11. MD, Intro., v–viii; *TICC*, 15–16.

12. *TICC*, 16–17. Unfortunately, Whipple did not leave personal descriptions of the members of his party—with one exception. More than a month after the expedition left Fort Smith, he included in his journal this profile of Marcou. "Jules Marcou, geologist to this expedition, a gentleman of 30 yrs., tall, of finely chiseled features and of elegant manners, was a son of La Belle France. He was educated at the Polytechnic school & entered the army but soon resigned to be appointed geologist upon a military expedition to Algiers. . . . He married a lady of Boston and became half American. . . . He published in Boston a geological map of the U.S. and elements of geology with practical hints from observations. When he recd. my appt. to this expedition, he refused an offer to accompany an exploring party to New Granada with Salary $500 per month and all expenses paid. I pay him but $100 per month." WJ, August 28, 1853.

13. Goetzmann, *Army Exploration*, 305; *RES*, Intro., 3:3.

14. *TICC*, 19–20; Stanley, *Personal Memoirs, 27;* Childs, Jr., ed., *Register of Graduates*, 266, 276.

15. *APS*, 10–12.

16. Conrad, "Whipple Expedition in Arizona," 150. *Carretella* is the Spanish word for a small two-wheeled cart not much bigger than a wheelbarrow; Whipple spelled the word "carretela." Sketches of the mule-drawn carts, however, show that they resembled the longer two-wheeled carts known in Spanish as *carretas*. Whipple bought two in Fort Smith, one for himself and one to carry the delicate scientific instruments and the surveying equipment. *TICC*, 36, n. 2.

17. *RES*, Intro., 3:1–2; *TICC*, 19.

18. *TICC*, 21–22.

19. *APS*, 18; Goetzmann, *Exploration and Empire*, 265; MD, 1:11. Peter Fritzell, who wrote the introduction to a new edition of Möllhausen's *Diary*, claims that the German made no pretense of accuracy or objectivity in writing his *Diary*. "It is not a daily record of personal observations and experiences . . . rather it is a piece of romantic monism presenting a literary picture of the American Southwest." MD, Intro., v–viii. This characterization is vigorously contested by Professor David Miller, who has studied and written extensively about Möllhausen, and who maintains that the German artist's writings are "accurate in every detail." Professor Miller said that he has carefully examined Möllhausen's account of his travels in 1851 with Duke Paul Wilhelm von Wurttemburg

along the Oregon Trail and also obtained a copy of Duke Paul's manuscript diary, which he translated into English. His conclusion: "Basically the duke substantiates Möllhausen's account of his 1851 adventure in every detail." Miller adds, "Fritzell was no historian, and for the most part had no idea what he was talking about in his assertions set forth in his introduction." Letter from Miller to the author, December 14, 2001.

20. Miller, "A Prussian on the Plains," 177–80.

21. *TICC*, 23; WJ, July 15, 1853; *APS*, 18–19.

22. B. Tidball (comp.) *The Tidball Family History*, 244; Returns from Second U.S. Artillery Regiment, January 1851–December 1860; Morrison Jr., ed., "Getting Through West Point," 305; JCTP, "Getting Through West Point," 59–64. Tidball, not a man to forget injury, was relentless in his pursuit of his erstwhile tormentor. Fifteen years later, while en route home for a summer vacation from West Point, he tracked him down in New Castle, Pennsylvania, vowing to thrash him. But when he found the man who brutally beat him on that distant Sunday afternoon to be senile and helpless, he left him sitting on his porch unharmed.

23. JCTP, "Getting Through West Point," 147–48. Although the president was much more approachable in that era—Tidball would twice meet the chief executive in a receiving line, once Lincoln, and later, Garfield—this was a private interview and unusual for the audacity Tidball displayed in personally challenging one of the president's policies. Despite Tidball's passionate plea, Polk went ahead with his plans. Quaife, ed., *The Diary of James K. Polk*, 30–33.

24. J. C. Tidball (JCT), "Mary Hunt Davis," 5–7. This fifteen-page typescript copy of an original manuscript in possession of Gordon Blaker of Augusta, Georgia, is an elegy Tidball wrote at the time of Mary's death, describing in intensely personal terms their courtship, marriage, and Mary's illness and death. I am grateful to Mr. Blaker for giving me a copy of this typescript, which was acquired from a descendant of John Tidball.

25. JCT, "Mary Hunt Davis," 8–11.

26. JCTP, "Genealogy," 83–84.

27. IT, 12–15; Returns from Fort Defiance, New Mexico, September 1851–April 1861. John Garland had been commissioned a first lieutenant in 1813. He was decorated for gallant conduct in the Mexican War and promoted to colonel in the Eighth Infantry in 1849. He died in 1861. Heitman, *Historical Register*, 447. Edwin Sumner was commissioned in the Regular Army in 1819. He served with distinction in the Mexican War, winning two brevets, and then he functioned as acting governor while serving as military commandant of the New Mexico region in 1852. During the Civil War, he remained the very incarnation of the crusty, Indian-fighting cavalry colonel but was ill suited for high command. He died in 1863. Hubbell and Geary, *Biographical Dictionary*, 517–18. Joseph Mansfield graduated from West Point in 1822 and won three brevets in the Mexican War. During the Civil War, he took command of the XII Corps during the Antietam campaign and was wounded on September 17, 1862. Had he lived he undoubtedly would have proved a splendid corps commander, but he died the next day. Hubbell and Geary, *Biographical Dictionary*, 339–40. David Meriwether was born in Virginia in 1800 but grew up in Kentucky, where he served thirteen terms in the legislature. As Tidball correctly remembered, Meriwether was appointed to the U.S. Senate to fill the vacancy

left by the death of Henry Clay, serving in that position from July to September 1852. After serving as governor of the New Mexico Territory from 1853 to 1857, he returned to Kentucky. Although he had earlier defended slavery, he supported the Union during the Civil War. He died in 1893. McMullin and Walker, *Biographical Directory*, 237–38.

28. *APS*, 27–28; MD, 1:28; WJ, July 15, 1853.

Chapter 3. Across the Ocean Prairie

1. *APS*, 29.

2. MD, 1:34; *APS*, 33–35. The Choctaw are the largest Muskhogean tribe in North America. Along with the Cherokees, Chickasaws, Creeks, and Seminoles, they were one of the "five civilized tribes," for they adopted white culture more rapidly than other tribes. The first white man to encounter them, Hernando de Soto, fought a fierce battle with the Choctaw in 1540. The Indians, although defeated, terrorized the Spanish. Between 1783 and 1830 the Choctaw signed a series of eight treaties that gave away most of their land and provided for the removal of the tribe to Oklahoma. American Indian Publishers, *Dictionary of Indian Tribes*, 2:5–7.

3. *APS*, 37–40; SD, July 25; *TICC*, 39.

4. *APS*, 40–42; MD, 1:53.

5. *APS*, 43; SD, July 31, August 1, August 3, August 4, August 7.

6. *APS*, 47–48.

7. Bergon, ed., *Journals of Lewis and Clark*, 243; *RES*, 1:308–9 and 12:124; Utley, *The Lance and the Shield*, 7, quoting James R. Walker, *Lakota Society*, ed. Raymond J. De-Mallie, 57.

8. *APS*, 44–45, 49–50; WJ, August 11, 1853.

9. *APS*, 51–56; SD, August 12. Captain Marcy arrived with his command at a place near present-day Bryars, in eastern Oklahoma, in August 1850, and erected a number of log houses. The post was later relocated twenty-five or thirty miles southwest to what was later Fort Arbuckle. When the old post, Camp Arbuckle, was abandoned, it was occupied by the Delawares. *APS*, 55, n. 27.

10. *APS*, 57–59; WJ, August 19, 1853; MD, 1:94.

11. WJ, August 19, 1853; Waldman, *Who Was Who in Native American History*, 65–66. Chisholm married the daughter of fellow trader James Edward and had thirteen children; he eventually operated three trading posts in Indian Territory. After the Civil War he drove a wagonload of goods from his Kansas post through Indian Territory to the Red River country of Texas to trade with the local tribes. He returned with a wagonload of buffalo hides, cutting ruts in the prairie, which became the famous Chisholm Trail. He died in 1868.

12. *APS*, 59–62; SD, August 20; *TICC*, 63.

13. *APS*, 62–67.

14. SD, August 23; WJ, August 30, 1853; *TICC*, 65, 67, 75; *APS*, 72; MD, 1:114; *RES*, part 3, 3:27.

15. *TICC*, 80; *APS*, 77–78; SD, September 7.

16. Coffman, *The Old Army*, 42; Records of United States Army Continental Commands, 1821–1920.

17. *APS,* 80–85; WJ, September 8–10, 1853; *TICC,* 85; Conrad, "Whipple Expedition in Arizona," 151. The Kiowas at one time lived at the sources of the Yellowstone and Missouri Rivers in present-day Montana but migrated southward. Gaining horses, slaves, and guns from the Spanish, the tribe evolved into a completely nomadic lifestyle of predation, pillage, and warfare until they became one of the most feared of the Plains tribes. They made a lasting peace with the Comanches, Kiowa-Apaches, Southern Cheyennes, and Arapahos. After they fell upon a wagon train and killed most of the teamsters in 1871, William Tecumseh Sherman arrested two of the leaders. They were tried and condemned to death, but the sentence was commuted, and two years later they were paroled. It took military conquest to place the Kiowas and their confederates on the reservations. At Fort Sill the last of the hostiles was brought in by 1875. American Indian Publishers, *Dictionary of Indian Tribes,* 2:367–73.

18. Morris, *El Llano Estacado,* 284. "Interestingly, Möllhausen soon appropriated these columns for his later surrealistic chromolithograph, 'Sandstone Formation in the Prairie Northwest of Texas.' This appealing illustration was a zoologically tarted-up version of his geological etching. This image had a prominent place in his book, *Diary of a Journey,* and Möllhausen romanticized the classical-looking columns with flourishes of half menacing buffalo and distant antelope. The animation of the landscape gave a different impression, however. In comparing these two illustrations, it seems clear that Möllhausen made his etching exotic, compounding science with art in order to animate a landscape and excite the nineteenth-century sensibility." Möllhausen's "faithful but lifeless" illustration appears on page 18, part 4, vol. 3 of the *Reports.*

19. Morris, *El Llano Estacado,* 288–89; *APS,* 89; WJ, September 17, 1853. Whipple's description of the spectacular sunrise is recorded in the official report on September 16, but in his personal journal on September 17. As is the case with many of the drawings published in the *Reports,* there is some confusion about *Bluffs of the Llano Sunrise (one hour before sunrise, Sept. 17),* which appears on page 23, part 4, vol. 3 of the *Reports.* In his essay, "Whipples's Ocean Prairie," Morris gives Whipple credit for sketching "this magnificent predawn sunrise," citing his source as Center for American History, University of Texas at Austin. In the list of illustrations for part 4, vol. 3 of the *Reports,* however, H. B. Möllhausen is credited with the drawing.

20. *APS,* 89–90; SD, September 17; Conrad, "Whipple Expedition on the Great Plains," 62.

21. WJ, September 20, 1853.

22. *APS,* 99; Conrad, "Whipple Expedition on the Great Plains," 65.

23. *APS,* 99–100.

24. *TICC,* 103; SD, September 27; MD, 1:313–15.

25. *APS,* 102, 105, 111.

Chapter 4. Twenty-Five Wild, Daring-Looking Fellows Join the Expedition

1. WJ, October 17, 1853; Conrad, "Whipple Expedition in Arizona," 152.

2. *APS,* 113–16; Conrad, "Whipple Expedition in Arizona," 152–53. Upon his return to Albuquerque from Isleta, Whipple declared that the newspaper account of Aubry's discovery of a new wagon route was "absurd." "Very shortly afterwards Richard Weightman,

editor of *Amigo del Páis,* appeared in camp, apologized for the inaccuracies in the story, and published a retraction. This infuriated Aubry and a feud developed which later ended in a knife-pistol fight in La Fonda Hotel in Santa Fe, in which Weightman killed Aubry with his Bowie knife." Conrad, "Whipple Expedition in Arizona," 153, n. 15. The author has used the correct spelling of Aubry's name; Whipple, Conrad, and Foreman all misspelled Aubry as "Aubrey." See Chaput, *Francois X. Aubry.* Foreman and Conrad also mistakenly refer to Joseph Rutherford Walker as Joseph Reddeford Walker. The mistake may have originally occurred when an 1876 obituary was published in which the deceased was referred to as Joseph Reddeford Walker. Bil Gilbert, Walker's biographer, surmises that "very likely the writer heard the name from a family member, then spelled it phonetically and incorrectly"—an easy error to make because of the Scotch-Irish southern accent of Walker's family. Gilbert, *Westering Man,* 299.

3. WJ, October 11, 1853; Conrad, "Whipple Expedition in Arizona," 153.

4. WJ, October 11, October 17, 1853.

5. *APS,* 116–18; *TICC,* 119, n. 27; WJ, October 27, 1853; SD, November 10.

6. *APS,* 122–23.

7. Ibid., 123; MD, 2:57.

8. *APS,* 125–28; *TICC,* 126; SD, November 15. Stanley refers to the town as "Cuvera," and Sherburne, as "Cubero." According to Grant Foreman, Cubero is a station on the Santa Fe Railroad a few miles west of Laguna. The old Mexican town of Covero seen by Whipple was in the northeastern part of Valencia County, northwest of Cubero, nearly north of Acoma.

9. *APS,* 129–35; SD, November 18. "Long a Spanish landmark, known as *El Morro* because it reminded early explorers of a Moorish Castle, the mesa (now a national monument) was named Inscription Rock in 1849 by Lt. James Simpson. The oldest Spanish name was apparently carved in 1605." *TICC,* 127, n. 4.

10. *APS,* 137–41; *TICC,* 128.

11. MD, 2:93; Conrad, "Whipple Expedition in Arizona," 155–56; *APS,* 147.

12. Conrad, "Whipple Expedition in Arizona," 156; *APS,* 152.

13. Conrad, "Whipple Expedition in Arizona," 156–57; *APS,* 153; WJ, December 4, 1853. We have seen how Tidball crossed the plains from Fort Leavenworth to Fort Defiance. How he got from Fort Moultrie to Leavenworth is another story, too long to be told here, except for one entertaining vignette. "At Montgomery [Alabama] I had to wait a day or so for a steamer, and to while away the time I made myself a spectator for a short time at the statehouse. This was the first time that I had heard Southern chivalry blow off in full blast. They commenced by asserting that each southern man was able to thrash two Yankees, but ended in being fully persuaded that he could thrash at least five. It was amusing, but at the same time disgusting to think that any part of our country could have so considerable a body of braggarts." Tidball was, and would remain always, a staunch Union man. IT, 11.

14. Mangiante, "History of Fort Defiance," 4–5, 9–11, 14–15, 52. U.S. Department of War, *Report of the Secretary of War,* 1851, 10–11. The fort was an active post for fewer than ten years; in spite of the unsettled conditions in the area, all troops were removed from Fort Defiance on April 25, 1861. The year after McCall's message, Secretary of War

C. M. Conrad made the absurdly optimistic statement: "In New Mexico the depredations of the Indians have been entirely arrested. The Navajos and the Apaches, the two most formidable tribes in all that region, have been completely overawed, and manifest every desire to be at peace with the whites." U.S. Department of War, *Report of the Secretary of War*, 1852, 3. It was not until sixteen years later, in mid-1868, that William Tecumseh Sherman removed the Navajos from the Bosque Redondo Reservation and sent them back to their homeland, after which peace ensued. See Thompson, *The Army and the Navajo*.

15. IT, 16.

16. Ibid., 17–20. Tidball fondly remembered Sergeant McLellan, who at the time Tidball wrote his memoirs was a major in the Tenth Cavalry. "He was promoted from the ranks at the outbreak of the rebellion and proved himself a most gallant officer and reliable man." He was commissioned second lieutenant in 1861 and was brevetted twice for gallantry in the Civil War; he retired in 1893. Heitman, *Historical Register*, 676.

17. IT, 19–21.

18. *APS*, 160.

19. SD, December 12; WJ, December 12, 1853.

20. MD, 2:129.

21. JCTP, "Genealogy," 85; IT, 21a–22.

22. Ball, *Army Regulars*, xiv, 78, 85.

23. E. C. Tidball, *No Disgrace*, 23.

24. Shelby Foote quoted in Burns, 1990.

Chapter 5. A Continuous Succession of Mountain Ranges Lay in Our Path

1. IT, 23–24; "Report on the Botany of the Expedition," *RES*, part 5, 4:11; Kearney and Peebles, *Arizona Flora*. After writing his botanical report for Lieutenant Whipple in 1854, Bigelow resumed his medical practice in Ohio. He later became professor of botany and pharmacy at the Detroit Medical College and in 1868 was appointed surgeon to the Marine Hospital in Detroit. He died in 1878. *TICC*, 248.

2. IT, 24–26b. Marcou's geological findings related to the Whipple expedition were severely criticized in the United States, but his reputation in Europe remained high. He became professor of paleontology at the University of Zurich, and later was the geologist for Harvard's Museum of Comparative Zoology. He served as the geologist with a survey of southwestern Nevada in 1875 and late in life wrote a two-volume biography of Louis Agassiz. He died in 1878 at the age of 74. *TICC*, 258–59. Dr. Kennerly "joined the final phase of the United States and Mexico Boundary Survey under Major William H. Emory in 1854 and 1855. In 1857 he received an appointment as surgeon and naturalist for the United States and Great Britain survey of the northwest boundary." He died in 1861 on board ship while returning to the United States from Canada. *TICC*, 257. Campbell served with Lieutenant John G. Parke's survey in 1854, and in 1857 became general superintendent of the newly established Pacific Wagon Roads Office in Washington. The rebellion did not sweep Campbell away as Tidball surmised, but rather rewarded him. In 1861 he joined the Confederate Army as a major and chief of the topographical bureau.

After the Civil War, he was the chief engineer for a number of railroads. He died in 1899. *TICC*, 250. The entry in Granger's *Arizona Names* simply states, "Albert H. Campbell, topographer for Whipple's expedition of 1853–1854, located this potential railroad pass at the west end of the Rio Puerco, on the south face of the Dutton Plateau. Whipple named it in his honor" (112).

3. IT, 27–27b. Baron Karl Friedrich Hieronymus Münchhausen (1720–1797) was a German hunter, soldier, and supposed teller of absurdly exaggerated stories. Professor David H. Miller, who has written extensively about Möllhausen, says that actually it was Möllhausen's wife who may have been a love child of the famous geographer. Letter from Miller to author, February 27, 2001.

4. IT, 27b–29. During the Civil War Garner served on Confederate General Braxton Bragg's staff. In 1863 he became chief of staff of the Department of the Gulf in Mobile, Alabama. *TICC*, 252–53. John Sherburne was mustered out of the army in 1870. Sherburne's military records reveal what Tidball meant by being "benzined out." By 1870 benzine was being used to clean clothing, and the army boards that made the "reduction in force" were jokingly referred to as "Benzine Boards." After he was ejected from the army, he became an inspector in the San Francisco Custom House. *TICC*, 241–43. See the epilogue for more on Sherburne's military career.

5. IT, 30–33. Leroux returned to Taos after arriving in Los Angeles with the Whipple expedition, by traveling along the Virgin River and retracing the Whipple route from the Little Colorado to Albuquerque. He acted as guide for several government explorations in the West before he died in Taos in 1861. *TICC*, 258.

6. IT, 34a–35. The unusual modifier "buskering" used by Tidball tells us quite a lot about his opinion of Savedra. The Oxford English dictionary defines "busker"—one who "busks"—as an itinerant entertainer or musician, one whose "avocation is strictly peripatetic."

7. IT, 36–37.

8. *APS,* 162–64; IT, 37a.

9. Taft, *Artists and Illustrators,* 27. Tidball probably did not have his sketch in his possession when he wrote his memoirs, however, so he could not definitely have ascertained or remembered whether the lithograph was a close representation of his drawing. But he thought it was. The question is complicated because of the number of different versions of the scene appearing in the published *Reports.* A Möllhausen watercolor of San Francisco Mountain closely resembles the Sinclair lithograph attributed to Möllhausen. But the unattributed Sarony lithograph published in some copies of the *Reports,* that Tidball claims was based on his drawing, is similar but yet quite different in several respects from the view portrayed in the Sinclair lithograph and the Möllhausen drawing. Many lithographs when compared to original drawings reflect liberties taken by the lithographers—changes in detail and the like; the same thing could have happened in this case, but the dissimilarities between the Möllhausen watercolor and the unattributed Sarony lithograph published in the *Reports* are radical. To further complicate the question of attribution, a lithograph depicting San Francisco Mountain attributed to Möllhausen by Sarony that Major and Knapp published in some copies of the *Reports,* is identical to the unattributed lithograph published by Sarony and Company. Although we can never know for sure, it is possible that one lithograph was taken from a Möllhausen drawing, and one from a Tidball drawing.

San Francisco Mountain is described in Barnes's "Arizona Place Names" as "an eroded volcano with serrated rim in Tps. 22, 23 N., R. 7 E. . . . Known locally as the San Francisco Peaks, because of a number of prominent peaks on its rim." The name is one of the oldest in the state, dating probably back to 1540. Barnes, *University of Arizona Bulletin,* 383.

In his memoirs, Tidball described traveling through this country many years later. "Thirty years, almost to a month, after the time when I took this sketch, I passed this same spot, traveling luxuriantly in a car upon the road, then just opened, the route for which we were then so laboriously exploring. Fain would I have turned aside and drank from the waters of Leroux' Spring to his memory. The railroad had already wrought great changes in this locality. Settlements had sprung up and the meadow like openings before mentioned had been converted into farms. Sawmills were busy transforming the huge pines into lumber, which was carried by the same road to the valley of the Rio Grande and assisted in building up Albuquerque and other towns, then of booming tendency. Large quantities of this lumber, principally railroad ties, were transported to the interior of Mexico, and assisted in linking the Republics together." He also recalled the great chasm they had encountered. "This Cañon Diablo is one of the great curiosities along the route of the Atlantic and Pacific Railroad which now crosses it. It is spanned by a single truss of iron, which viewed from the bottom of the cañon appears above like a tissue of spider webs." IT, 37a–38.

10. IT, 33–34a, 36–37. Leroux Spring is about seven miles northwest of present-day Flagstaff. Conrad, "The Whipple Expedition in Arizona," 162.

11. *APS,* 167; SD, December 19; vol. 3 of the *Reports,* annotated by JCT, 80. Tidball's marginal notes cover the period from December 18, 1853, six days after he joined the party, to March 11, 1854, when he and his men struck out for the Pacific on their own. The marginalia tend to identify perceived inaccuracies in the printed report; as one familiar with Tidball's writing style would expect, the comments are terse and tart. This volume, which is in the Special Collections, University of Arizona Library, Tucson, is inscribed on the inside cover, "Jno. C. Tidball," and below, "With the Respects of A. W. Whipple, Capt. U.S. Top'l Engineers." Many of the illustrations have been cut out and pasted in "Itinerary," Tidball's memoir of the expedition.

12. *APS,* 170–71; *TICC,* 150–51; Vol. 3 of the *Reports,* annotated by JCT, 82; SD, December 24.

13. *APS,* 173; Vol. 3 of the *Reports,* annotated by JCT, 82; WJ, December 27, 1853.

14. *APS,* 174; Conrad, "The Whipple Expedition in Arizona," 164–65.

15. WJ, December 28, 1853.

16. SD, December 28.

17. IT, 38–39; *TICC,* 153–54.

18. *TICC,* 154; SD, December 30; *APS,* 176.

19. IT, 47–51.

Chapter 6. The Artist as Hero of His Own Journey

1. IT, 52–52a.

2. *APS,* 177; Vol. 3 of the *Reports,* annotated by JCT, 84. Although Tidball gave no

reason for his opinion of the impermanence of New Year's Spring, he was probably correct. Recently Professor Andrew Wallace described his extensive search for New Year's Spring in an interesting and persuasive report, at the conclusion of which he announces that he has found the location of the site. Wallace found "a perfectly round hold in the prairie, brimming with melted snow," in wintertime, just as Whipple did, but the modern stock tank does not appear to be spring fed. The impermanence of the spring is no reason, however, to throw cold water on Professor Wallace's important discovery. A. Wallace, "Where Was New Year's Spring?".

3. *APS*, 177–78; IT, 52a (reverse side). Mr. Harley G. Shaw of Hillsboro, New Mexico, has conducted a detailed reconnaissance of the vicinity of the January 1 sketch and was kind enough to provide me with a photograph of Granite Mountain taken from a hill near Williams, Arizona. Mr. Shaw writes, "This hill shows up as Signal Hill on current maps. The similarity of the skyline in the photograph to Tidball's sketch to me seems striking. It is even more striking when you can see the real thing without the haze that photographs inevitably record. The idea that Whipple was confused about exactly what Tidball had sketched is supported by the fact that his hand written diary for that day said that the sketch was of Bill Williams Mountain. Apparently he changed his mind when he was preparing the itinerary for the official publication." Letter from Shaw to the author, September 22, 2001. Indeed, as Mr. Shaw contends, his photograph resembles the view portrayed by Tidball and bears no resemblance to either Pichaco Mountain or Mount Floyd (Sierra de la Laja).

4. Novak, *Nature and Culture*, 18, 137.

5. Goetzmann and Goetzmann, *West of the Imagination*, 13, 36–38, 43–44, 48, 58–66.

6. Ibid., 102–3.

7. Novak, *Nature and Culture*, 144. The eleven artists were John C. Tidball, Albert Campbell, Richard H. Kern, James G. Cooper, John M. Stanley, John Y. Young, Gustav Sohon, F. W. von Egloffstein, H. B. Möllhausen, W. P. Blake, and Charles Koppel. The names and spellings of the artists' names vary slightly, depending on the source. One writer in particular had trouble with John C. Tidball, referring to him in one book as "Henry" and in another as "Joseph." The above list is from Taft, *Artists and Illustrators*, 8. The organization of volume 3 of Whipple's report reflects the preoccupation with art as opposed to science. Several of Tidball's drawings of spectacular geological formations appear in part 4, "Report on the Geology of the Route," and would have been of great interest to a structural geologist. But others depicting bluffs, canyons, and mountains of equal interest can be found in part 2, "Report of Topographical Features," while most of them, including all of the lithographs, appear in part 1, "Itinerary." When Whipple organized the report, he apparently intended to appeal to the aesthetic sense of the nontechnical reader as well as to the scientist and dispersed illustrations throughout the report accordingly.

8. Goetzmann and Goetzmann, *West of the Imagination*, 104–7, 110; Novak, *Nature and Culture*, 141.

9. Goetzmann and Goetzmann, *West of the Imagination*, 36–38; Dippie, "Government Patronage," 49; Taft, *Artists and Illustrators*, 13; Richards, *Isaac I. Stevens*, 143.

10. Eugene C. Tidball, "In the Footsteps of Lewis and Clark," 150, 154; Taft, *Artists and Illustrators*, 276; Nicandri, *Gustav Sohon's Views*, 8, 31.

11. Taft, *Artists and Illustrators*, 264, n. 17; Goetzmann and Goetzmann, *West of the Imagination*, 110; IT, 27; Huseman, *Wild River, Timeless Canyons*, 23, 24, 28, 73, n. 59.

12. Goetzmann, *Army Exploration*, 332; *RES*, part 3, volume 3, "Report on the Indian Tribes," 27, 31–32; Dawdy, *Artists of the American West*, 231.

13. Miller, "A Prussian on the Plains," 176–77.

14. Taft, *Artists and Illustrators*, 27–29, 255–56, n. 13; Novak, *Nature and Culture*, 289, n. 5.

15. *APS*, 179. Grant Foreman describes Whipple's reconnaissance as a loop that took him first southwest from New Year's Spring, probably over the site of Williams to a point southwest of and near Bill Williams Mountain, then east of the site of Ash Fork northwest and north to the head of Partridge Creek, and then southeast back to New Year's Spring.

16. TD, January 3.

17. *TICC*, 159; *APS*, 181–82.

18. *APS*, 182; *TICC*, 160; SD, January 6; MD, 2:170.

19. WJ, January 8, 1854; *APS*, 185.

20. *APS*, 186–87.

21. MD, 2:172; WJ, January 12, 1854.

22. *APS*, 187–88; *TICC*, 162–63.

23. WJ, January 14, 1854.

24. *APS*, 189; Vol. 3 of the *Reports*, annotated by JCT, 90; *TICC*, 163–64.

25. *APS*, 191–2; *TICC*, 164.

26. WJ, January 18, 1854; *APS*, 192; Vol. 3 of the *Reports*, annotated by JCT, 91.

27. TD, January 19; WJ, January 19, 1854.

28. WJ, January 19, 1854.

29. "Report on the Topographical Features and Character of the Country," *RES*, part 2, 3:35–36.

30. *APS*, 194; Vol. 3 of the *Reports*, annotated by JCT, 92; SD, January 22; *TICC*, 165–66.

31. MD, 2:194.

32. SD, January 23; *TICC*, 166; WJ, January 23, 1854. Mr. Campbell discovered the ruins of an Indian fort that commanded a view of the pass. Whipple wrote, "From a fancy founded on the evident antiquity of these ruins, we have given the name of Aztec Pass to this place." "The passage between Juniper Mountain and Santa Maria Mountain still bears Whipple's name of Aztec Pass. It is ten miles west of Juniper Post Office." *APS*, 199, n. 1.

33. Gemini Peak (the Twins) is about four miles west of Baca Grant. *APS*, 199; *TICC*, 167.

Chapter 7. We Will Be on Mule Meat before We Are Through

1. *APS*, 201; Vol. 3 of the *Reports*, annotated by JCT, 95. Aquarius Range, thus named by Whipple because of the rainfall, is on the east side of Mohave County in Townships 1 and 12 North.

2. WJ, January 26, 1854.

3. TD, January 26, January 27; WJ, January 26, 1854; IT, 52c. The scholar who denied

Möllhausen's responsibility for the sketch wrote, "To credit the composition to Möllhausen is incorrect because he was not present to make the original sketch. Whipple had still not found Bill Williams' Fork, and on January 25, he had organized another exploring party, which included Tidball, but not Möllhausen." Huseman, "Romanticism and the Scientific Aesthetic," 159. I have examined two lithographs of this scene, one attributed to Tidball and one to Möllhausen; they are similar, but not identical, probably due to the fact that two different engravers worked from Tidball's drawing. Tidball's identification of Bigelow examining his "favorite cactus," information which has just recently come to light, is further evidence that the lithograph is based on Tidball's drawing, not Möllhausen's.

4. WD, January 28, 1854; *APS*, 202–4; TD, January 28; IT, 52b. These lithographs are printed in two or three colors on heavy paper; many in black and brown, some in black and green; in still others a third color, blue, has been added. The lithography was either a two-plate or three-plate printing process, and was all handwork. Evidently because of the large number of plates required, different firms occasionally lithographed the same illustration; as a result, slight differences occurred. Taft points out that sometimes the various color plates failed to register exactly in the successive printings. Impressions from the same stone vary also, depending on the number of impressions made and on the amount of ink present at each impression. And, as noted earlier, the crediting of illustrations to the original artist occasionally differs on the different printings, all of which adds to the difficulty of properly identifying the lithographs and artists. The lithography was done by A. Hoen Company (Baltimore), J. Bien (New York), Sarony and Company, or Sarony, Major and Knapp (New York), and T. Sinclair (Philadelphia). Taft, *Artists and Illustrators*, 7.

5. WJ, January 29, 1854.

6. *APS*, 205; A. Wallace, "Across Arizona to the Big Colorado," 352–53.

7. *APS*, 205; Conrad, "Whipple Expedition in Arizona," 170.

8. WJ, January 31, 1854.

9. TD, February 1; *TICC*, 173.

10. *APS*, 211.

11. WJ, February 3. The *Fouquieria*, as described by Whipple, "is a singular shrub, with many thorny stalks shooting from the same root, and growing without branches nearly straight from ten to fifteen feet in height. When in blossom it is exceedingly beautiful. In winter, while the circulation of the sap is suspended, it seems to be saturated with an unctuous substance that causes it to burn with a brilliant light like fat pine; at night, therefore, it serves as a torch." *APS*, 212–13.

12. Ibid., 214.

13. IT, 54–57a. Professor Jacob W. Bailey, Tidball recalled in his memoir "Getting Through West Point," "was a man beloved by all, but by none more than cadets who recognized him as an able instructor as well as a kind and considerate friend. He was erudite in every branch of his department, and his informal lectures were replete with original thought." JCTP, "Getting Through West Point," part 2, 75. An 1832 graduate of West Point, Bailey was the first person to hold the permanent professorship at West Point in chemistry, mineralogy, and geology, but he earned his scholarly reputation in botany,

winning international recognition for his studies of freshwater algae. Morrison, *The Best School*, 52–53.

14. *APS*, 213–14; Conrad, "Whipple Expedition in Arizona, 171.

15. IT, 58a.; Taft, *Artists and Illustrators*, 256–57, n. 17. Foreman selected this lithograph as one of the two illustrations for his book; it appears on page 209, with the same title. The lithograph in my possession, based on the same drawing, is entitled *Valley of Williams River*.

16. *APS*, 214; MD, 224–25

17. WJ, February 5, 1854; *APS*, 215; SD, February 6. Pitahaya is the name by which the *Cereus giganteus* is known among Mexicans and Indians on Rio Gila. *APS*, 215, n. 26.

18. *APS*, 216–17. In one reference work, the "trivial reason" is attributed to Whipple, who, the author surmised, named it because of its resemblance to a cannon. Barnes, *Arizona Place Names*, 202.

19. IT, 25. Möllhausen also sketched Artillery Peak. His drawing is in the Oklahoma Historical Society Archives, and it so closely resembles the woodcut that it is likely that it was the basis for the illustration rather than Tidball's sketch.

20. *APS*, 217; TD, February 7.

21. WJ, February 8, 1854.

22. TD, February 8; *TICC*, 175; SD, February 8.

23. *APS*, 218–20.

24. TD, February 10; Vol. 3 of the *Reports*, annotated by JCT, 106; *TICC*, 177; SD, February 10.

25. TD, February 12; WJ, February 12, 1854.

26. IT, 58–59; *TICC*, 177–78.

Chapter 8. The Mountain Spur Was a Confused Mass of Serrated Crests

1. *APS*, 221; TD, February 14.

2. Morrison Jr., ed., "Getting Through West Point," 305; Calef, "A Distinguished Horse Artilleryman," 113.

3. *APS*, 221–22; WJ, February 15, 1854.

4. *TICC*, 179; Conrad, "Whipple Expedition in Arizona," 173; WJ, February 16, 1854; SD, February 16; TD, February 17.

5. WJ, February 17, February 18, 1854.

6. TD, February 18; JCT, *Report of Journey Made by General W. T. Sherman*, 208.

7. *APS*, 224; IT, 52d–53. In the Oklahoma Historical Society Archives there are two sketches of this illustration. One is John Tidball's original drawing and one is a copy by John James Young, a copy artist who would influence how the public perceived the work of the Pacific railroad artists. "Young was a Prussian-born civilian draftsman employed by the Office of Exploration & Surveys to copy, rework, and complete sketches by the expedition artists so they could be reproduced as illustrations for published official government reports." Young did not copy the artists' drawings exactly but redrew and rearranged the figures to suit his own artistic tastes. A further iteration was the engraving, and the engraver also altered the scene redrawn by the copyist. All three renditions are

similar, but figures and other peripheral matter have been rearranged. This three-step process further complicates identifying the original artist, especially when two artists drew the same scene, as in the case of Tidball and Möllhausen. See Huseman, *Wild River, Timeless Canyons*, 24–25.

8. *RES*, part 4, 3:50, 51. There is no corroborative evidence that Tidball was responsible for the drawings that ended up as either of these woodcuts. There is a Möllhausen original in Potsdam of a scene entitled *Rock Formations near the Mouth of Bill Williams Fork* that closely resembles the woodcut *Lava Bluffs on the Hawilhamook*, and may well be the basis for the illustration rather than a drawing by Tidball. It is possible that both artists made sketches of the scenes, but it is impossible to ascertain with certainty which was used for the woodcuts; we have only Tidball's word for it that he is the artist.

Oddly, although the name "Hawilhamook" is twice used in the captions for Tidball's woodcuts, it does not appear anywhere in the text of Whipple's "Itinerary," nor in Grant Foreman's annotated version of the "Itinerary," nor, for that matter, in any of the standard references identifying Arizona place names, except in the appendix of Granger's *Arizona Names*, where, however, it is not explained or described by a corollary entry in the text of the book. On page 50, part 4, vol. 3 of the *Reports* there is a reference to "the Hawilhamook, or Bill Williams Fork," and it is explained, after a fashion, on page 16, part 3, vol. 3 of the *Reports*, "Report Upon The Indian Tribes." Plate 2 on that page is entitled "Yuma map of Rio Colorado, with the names and location of tribes within its valley." The text describes the map's origin. "The accompanying sketch of this country is from a tracing upon the ground by a Yuma (Cuchan) Indian, giving the names and positions of various tribes as indicated by him." Along with the names of the tribes, the names of the rivers are also given. The Rio Colorado is entitled "Hah Weal Asientic," and a tributary flowing into it from the east is referred to as "Hah-Weal-ha-mook." Kroeber translates this Indian word to mean "third river." Kroeber, *Mohave Indians*, 56.

9. SD, February 19; WJ, February 20, 1854; Conrad, "Whipple Expedition in Arizona," 173–74; *APS*, 226. Neither of the sketches by Tidball and Möllhausen of the confluence of the Bill Williams Fork and the Rio Colorado appears in the *Reports* identified as such, although there is a Möllhausen watercolor of the mouth of Bill Williams Fork in the Oklahoma Historical Society. On the other hand, Professor David Miller thinks the engraving entitled *Banks of the Hawilhamook* is a sketch of the confluence of Bill Williams River and the Colorado and may have been sketched by either Möllhausen or Tidball. "In this scene, we are looking south down the Colorado toward the Monument Mountains (and Parker Dam). Bill Williams River is flowing into the Colorado from the left. The artist's vantage point is on the north bank of Bill Williams River and the east bank of the Colorado. The site is just upstream from Parker Dam and is under the waters of Lake Havasu." Letter to author from David Miller, December 26, 2001.

10. IT, 59–60; TD, February 21.

11. IT, 60–61; *APS*, 227; *TICC*, 185. In his memoirs Tidball included two accomplished pencil sketches that he admitted failed to convey an adequate concept of "the magnitude and forbidding aspect of the mountains into which the Colorado hid itself from our view." One drawing shows the river receding between steep banks overlooked by serrated mountains; the other depicts the wagon train meandering through the rough country.

12. IT, 62–62a; TD, February 22; WJ, February 22, 1854; *APS*, 230. This is not to say that the diary entry is the last Tidball ever made; it is simply the last one in the four-by-six-inch leatherbound volume marked "No. 2," in the Special Collections of the University of Arizona library. We don't know where volumes one and three are.

13. IT, 62a–67.

14. MD, 2:242–43.

15. IT, 62a; *APS*, 232.

16. *APS*, 232–34.

17. SD, February 24; WJ, February 24, 1854.

18. IT, 67–68.

Chapter 9. Lieutenant Tidball Ordered the Soldiers to Fix Their Bayonets

1. IT, 39–46b

2. American Indian Publishers, *Dictionary of Indian Tribes*, 534; Swanton, *The Indian Tribes of North America*, 357; A. Wallace, "Across Arizona to the Big Colorado," 355. "In 1857 the Quechan-Mohave allies suffered a disastrous defeat at the hands of a combination of Pima and Maricopa warriors. Still smarting from their defeat, and apprehensive about the increasingly frequent intrusions of Whites into their country, Mohave warriors in 1858 attacked a wagon train bound for California. As a consequence, a United States military post, later to be named Fort Mohave, was established in the Mohave Valley." The tribe was still defiant, however, and "in 1859 a battle was fought in which the Mohave warriors were mowed down by the rifle fire of solders. This defeat ended the resistance of the Mohaves, and paved the way for their subsequent acculturation." Sturtevant, *Handbook of North American Indians*, 56–57;

3. MD, 2:253.

4. IT, 69–71.

5. Ibid., 71–73.

6. MD, 254–57.

7. IT, 73–76.

8. WJ, February 24, 1854; SD, February 25.

9. *APS*, 235–36. Samuel Peter Heintzelman, author of the duplicitous note that the Mojave chief so proudly showed to Whipple, graduated from West Point in 1826 and was a decorated veteran of the Mexican War. The post visited by Captain Francisco and commanded by Major Heintzelman was established on the Colorado River in September 1849 by none other than Lieutenant Cave Couts, the dragoon who so mercilessly disparaged Whipple; he called it Camp Calhoun. In 1850 Heintzelman arrived with three companies and changed the name to Camp Independence; in 1851 the troops moved to a low hill on the west bank of the river. When reoccupied on February 29, 1852, the installation became Fort Yuma. When the Southern Pacific completed its road east, connecting with other lines, the post became unnecessary, and in 1883 it was abandoned. A year later it was turned over to the Interior Department and eventually became Fort Yuma Indian School. Barnes, "Arizona Place Names," 498; Altshuler, *Starting With Defiance*, 67–72. In 1861, as a brigadier general of volunteers, Heintzelman commanded a

division at the first Battle of Bull Run, where he was wounded. He went on to become a major general of volunteers and a corps commander. Although never lacking for gallantry, his performance throughout the war was lackluster. He returned to the Southwest in August 1865 as commander of the Seventeenth Infantry; he retired in 1869 and died in 1880. Hubbell and Geary, *Biographical Dictionary*, 248.

10. WD, February 25, 1854; *APS*, 237.

11. IT, 77.

12. SD, February 27; MD, 259–60. Robert Taft reported that Tidball's camp scene drawing is credited to Campbell in some printings and is uncredited in others. Taft, *Artists and Illustrators*, 265, n. 17. Huseman speculates, "the lithograph probably depicts a view drawn by Campbell." Huseman, "Romanticism and the Scientific Aesthetic," 188. Taft and Huseman evidently are unaware that some lithographs of this scene are attributed to Tidball. The Oklahoma Historical Society has two lithographs of this scene in its archives, one credited to Tidball and one uncredited; the origins of both are shown as being derived "From Sketch taken by Lt. J. C. Tidball." Stoddard, "Amiel Weeks Whipple," 234. A lithograph and a photocopy of another lithograph in my possession are both credited to Tidball; a third one is uncredited.

13. *APS*, 239–40; *RES*, part 3, 3:23. A similar drawing of a Mojave dwelling appears in volume 2 of Möllhausen's diary, facing page 262, depicting the same dwelling, from a different aspect, with an Indian standing on the roof and two Indians in the background. In the foreground, however, in addition to the woman walking past with a basket on her head, two men are chasing a hoop with sticks. Possibly both Tidball and Möllhausen sketched the same house at about the same time.

14. IT, 80–86. Tidball's reference to "old slavery times" comes from his experience visiting plantations while he was briefly stationed in Augusta, Georgia, in 1849. There he learned that the value of a plantation was based on the number of slaves who worked it. "The value of a plantation was never estimated by the number of its acres but by the number of able-bodied Negroes worked on it. There were ten Negro plantations and fifty and even up to five hundred Negro plantations. The number of Negroes worked by a planter was furthermore an index of his standing and importance in the community in which he resided. The family of a ten Negro planter could not hold up its head on a level with the one of fifty Negroes, and stood no showing whatever with the one of five hundred." JCTP, "Augusta," 218–18a. In his use of the pejorative term "nigger," recently described as a "paradigmatic ethnic slur," Tidball was quoting common southern usage at the time. He disapproved of slavery and a few years later would go to war to abolish it.

15. *APS*, 240–41; *TICC*, 194.

16. IT, 87–89.

17. *APS*, 241–42; WJ, February 27, 1854.

18. No treaty was ever made with the Mojave Indians respecting their original territory; the reservations to which they were to be confined were created by act of Congress, in 1865. Under the Indian Claims Act, the Mojave tribe brought a claim against the United States government, seeking compensation for additional lands taken from them without compensation. The commission heard testimony from several ethnologists who testified as to which lands were tribal lands of the Mojaves. A complicating factor was the

definition of "ownership" of land, which to Europeans was a legalistic concept based on title. Justice Black made this astute observation in *Shoshone Indians v. United States*, 324 U.S. 335, 357 (1945): "Ownership meant no more to them than to roam the land as a great common, and to possess and enjoy it in the same way that they possessed and enjoyed sunlight and the west wind and the feel of spring in the air. Acquisitiveness, which develops a law of real property, is an accomplishment only of the 'civilized.'" That difficulty did not prevent the commission from finding in favor of the Mojave tribe and ordering the government to compensate the Indians for the value of the land wrongfully taken from them. Two of the prime pieces of evidence considered by the commission were the maps sketched by Indians and reproduced in Whipple's report. *RES*, part 3, 3:16. *Mohave Tribe of Indians, et al, v. United States of America*, Dockets Nos. 283, 295, decided March 19, 1959, reproduced in Kroeber, *Mohave Indians*.

Chapter 10. The Clothes of the Murdered Mexican Were Riddled with Arrows

1. *TICC*, 196–97; *MD*, 280–81.

2. MD, 281–82; Office of Explorations and Surveys, *Report Upon the Colorado River*, 69–70.

3. *APS*, 247–49; SD, March 1.

4. WJ, March 2, 1854.

5. IT, 91–92.

6. WJ, March 3, 1854; *APS*, 250.

7. WJ, March 5, 1854; *APS*, 251; IT, 93.

8. *TICC*, 202.

9. WJ, March 8, 1854; *APS*, 255; Vol. 3 of the *Reports*, annotated by JCT, 123.

10. IT, 93–94; *RES*, part 4, 3:53. In my biography of John Tidball, *No Disgrace to My Country*, I attributed four woodcuts and four lithographs to him. Since then his memoirs describing his adventures with the Whipple expedition have come to light. I now believe that he can be credited with seven woodcuts and four lithographs, and possibly one additional lithograph and one more woodcut. Möllhausen is, I believe, responsible for *Artillery Peak* and *Lava Bluffs on the Hawilhamook*, both sketched by both Möllhausen and Tidball; the similarity of the woodcuts and the Möllhausen drawings make that conclusion all but inescapable. The lithograph *San Francisco Mountain* remains in doubt; either Tidball or Möllhausen could have been responsible for it. The same is true of the woodcut *Mojave Dwelling*, which also was claimed by Tidball.

11. JCTP, "Getting Through West Point," 52, 83–84; "Genealogy," 66–67. In 1839, five years after he accepted the position of instructor of drawing at the academy, Weir prepared this "Outline of Instruction in Drawing": "(1) geographical signs; (2) topographical delineation of rocks and hills, wild and uncultivated ground; rivers, lakes and marshes; (3) formation of letters; (4) course of topography with brush, laying flat, broken and blended tints (symbol of various grounds, etc.), shading mountains, rocks, trees and other objects. (5) This completes course in topography. The course in freehand work began with outline drawings of human figure (anatomical) in three positions and outline

drawing from Flaxman and Retzch which concluded the 3rd Class course. In the 2nd Class, landscape is taken up under the following heads: (1) measurement; (2) form: simple and compound; (3) aerial perspective; (4) light, copying the same design; (5) different scales; (6) drawing on tinted paper; (7) use of brush (sepia); (8) coloring; (9) finished drawings from standard works." Weir, *Robert A. Weir, Artist,* 66–67.

12. IT, 95–96.

13. *APS,* 256–57; WJ, March 9, 1854.

14. *APS,* 259.

15. IT, 96–98.

16. Woodward, "Irrataba—'Chief of the Mohave,'" 53–68.

17. *TICC,* 204

18. *APS,* 262–63.

19. WJ, March 12, March 14, 1854.

20. *Report of the General of the Army to the Secretary of War,* 1883, 249; Creer, "The Explorations of Gunnison and Beckwith," 191–92; Mumey, "John Williams Gunnison," 32; Ball, *Army Regulars,* 158–59; Arrington and Alexander, "The U.S. Army Overlooks," 328.

21. Anderson, *Desert Saints,* 130–31; Miller, "Impact of the Gunnison Massacre." Professor Miller's account of the apprehension and trial of the Indians is both absorbing and comprehensive.

22. IT, 99–101. Lucius Licinius Lucullus was a Roman general and counsel. His wealth enabled him to live a life of luxury, and Lucullan feasts became legendary. *Wordsworth Dictionary of Biography,* 268.

23. *APS,* 267; WJ, March 15, 1854. Whipple overestimated the expansionist tendencies of the Latter-day Saints. San Bernardino was established in 1851 when Brigham Young decided to extend the scope of Mormon influence. Elders of the church purchased the Rancho San Bernardino, a tract of 37,999 acres, for $77,500. The community thrived, but in a few years the invasion of Utah by federal troops induced Young to abandon the settlement and direct its inhabitants to return to Utah. *APS,* 264, n. 12; Anderson, *Desert Saints,* 185.

24. *TICC,* 208–09; *APS,* 268–69; MD, 2:314.

Chapter 11. I Will Not Have to Go Back to That Miserable Place

1. IT, 101–2.

2. Ibid., 102–103a. Nora L. Tidball, the most accomplished artist of all John's daughters, signed the drawing. At the time he wrote his memoirs, she would have been about seventeen; she died nine years later.

3. *APS,* 272–73.

4. Ibid., 273–76. The Cucamonga Ranch is about five miles northeast of Ontario and twenty miles northwest of Riverside. Rancho de China is about five miles southeast of present-day Pomona.

5. IT, 103–8. Unlike his three guests, Lieutenant Christopher Lovell was not a West Pointer. Originally from South Carolina, he was commissioned a second lieutenant in the

Second Infantry in 1838. He served as a captain in the Mexican War and was brevetted for gallant and meritorious conduct in the battles of Contreras and Churubusco. It is not known whether he served in the Civil War, or if so, on which side. He died in 1868. Heitman, *Historical Register*, 643–44.

6. IT, 108–9; JCTP, "Ft. Leavenworth," 43–44. John Bankhead Magruder graduated from West Point in 1830 and won two brevets in the Mexican War. He resigned his commission April 20, 1861, was appointed major general, C.S.A., and fought well in the early Peninsula campaign, but in subsequent action during the Seven Days' battles was "cautious and bumbling" and spent the remainder of the war in the West. Following the war, he became an officer in Mexico under Maximilian. Burton was given command of the Artillery Reserve of the Army of the Potomac in January 1864 and commanded the artillery of a corps in the Army of the Potomac late in the war, the same position held by Tidball. He was brevetted brigadier general, for Petersburg. Boatner, *Civil War Dictionary*, 501.

7. IT, 109; Heitman, *Historical Register*, 396.

8. Fuller, *San Diego Originals*, 41–43;

9. *TICC*, 25.

10. Heitman, *Historical Register*, 368; IT, 109.

11. *APS*, 276–77.

12. Ibid., 277; *RES*, appendix B, 3:36.

13. MD, 2:339.

14. *APS*, 277–79.

15. IT, 110–11.

16. Ibid., 112–13.

17. Ibid., 113–14. The term *filibuster* is derived from the Dutch word *vrijbuiter*, meaning "freebooter," which was applied in the seventeenth century to English buccaneers; it denoted a private military invasion of a foreign country or colony with which the invader's own country is at peace. Filibustering operations peaked in frequency between 1848 and 1860 when the United States gained notoriety as the world's center of filibustering activity. This rash of filibustering grew largely out of the expansionist sentiment in the agrarian western and southern United States, encouraged by the prerogative of Manifest Destiny. Besides the acquisition of territory, the motives included personal ones by the expedition leaders, political or financial advantage from their supporters in the United States, and the lucrative expansion of slavery for the American South. Faragher, *American Heritage Encyclopedia of American History*, 306; *Funk and Wagnalls New World Encyclopedia*, "Filibustering Expeditions." William L. Walker was probably the most famous of all American filibusters. Born in Tennessee, he came to California in 1850. After attempting to annex the Mexican state of Sonora, he led a small band of adventurers to Nicaragua and joined a revolutionary faction there. He was elected president in 1856 but was ousted in 1857. He was arrested by a British naval officer in Honduras and turned over to Honduran authorities, by whom he was court-martialed, convicted, and shot. *Webster's New Biographical Dictionary*, "Walker, William." Count Gaston Raoun de Raousset-Bolubon was captured and executed by the Mexican army in Sonora in 1854. Ball, *Army Regulars*, 102.

18. IT, 114–15. John Ellis Wool was born in 1784. Although unsuccessful in his civil career, he excelled as a militia officer, and in 1812 was commissioned captain. He was cited for bravery in several battles in the War of 1812, and brevetted a lieutenant colonel. During the Mexican War, at Buena Vista, by then a brigadier general, he repulsed a much larger Mexican army that was under Santa Anna. Sent to the division of the Pacific from 1854 to 1857, Wool grappled with filibusters, vigilantes, and hostile Indians. He retired in 1863, a major general, and died in 1869. Hubbell and Geary, *Biographical Dictionary*, 602–3. For an interesting description of how the army attempted to cope with the outbreak of filibustering, and particularly General Wool's "bold charge" against the filibusters, see Ball, *Army Regulars*, 89–106.

19. IT, 120–21.

20. McCullough, *The Path Between the Seas*, 35–38. Years later, when he sat in the White House, President Grant ordered seven scientific expeditions to Central America between 1870 and 1875 to examine the practicality of constructing a transoceanic canal. Ibid., 26–27.

21. IT, 121–22.

22. WJ, April 25–26, 1854; Conrad, "The Whipple Expedition in Arizona," 177.

23. *TICC*, 217–18.

24. JCT, "Mary Hunt Davis," 11–12.

25. JCTP, "Genealogy," 88–89; JCT, "Mary Hunt Davis," 12–13. Major William Nicholson Grier, the "Buena Commandante" of whom Tidball was so fond, graduated from West Point in 1835 and was brevetted major for gallant and meritorious conduct in the Mexican War. He was brevetted colonel in 1862 for gallant and meritorious service at the Battle of Williamsburg, where he was wounded. He was brevetted brigadier general for war service and retired as a colonel in 1870. He died in 1885. Childs, ed. *Register of Graduates*, 260; Heitman, *Historical Register*, 478.

26. JCTP, "Genealogy," 88–90; IT, 138–39. John Lawrence Grattan graduated from West Point on July 1, 1853. His career as an army officer lasted one year and fifty days; he was killed at the age of twenty-four in a fight with the Sioux near Fort Laramie, Nebraska, on August 19, 1854, some considerable distance from Tidball's column. For a description of the Grattan massacre, see Ball, *Army Regulars*, 44–45; Childs, ed. *Register of Graduates*, 277; Heitman, *Historical Register*, 471. Alexander Dallas Bache, the great-grandson of Benjamin Franklin, graduated first in his West Point class of 1825 and spent the next year teaching mathematics and natural philosophy at the academy. During his career he played a central role in the organization and management of a number of scientific institutions, including the American Association for the Advancement of Science, the Smithsonian Institution, and the National Academy of Sciences. Slotten, *Patronage, Practice and the Culture of American Science*, 8–9, 99; Malone, *Dictionary of American Biography*, 1:461–62; John Tidball to William Tidball, June 20, 1857, JCTP.

27. RES, 1:22, 29, 31, 78.

28. Goetzmann, *Army Exploration*, 295–97.

29. Ibid., 297–98, 300.

30. Ibid., 302–3.

31. *TICC*, 226–32; *Harpers New Monthly Magazine*, 448–67.

32. Goetzmann, *Army Exploration*, chapter 8; U.S. Congress, *Congressional Globe*, 240.

The *Reports* have an interesting and involved bibliographical record that is set out in exquisite detail in Taft, *Artists and Illustrators*, 254, n. 13.

33. Goetzmann, *Army Exploration*, 304.

34. Goetzmann and Goetzmann, *West of the Imagination*, 108

35. Novak, *Nature and Culture*, 137.

Epilogue

1. Letter to the Secretary of War, June 30, 1855; *RES*, 3:viii.

2. Malone, *Dictionary of American Biography*, 20:66–67; Hubbell and Geary, *Biographical Dictionary*, 583–84; Stoddard, "Amiel Weeks Whipple," 228–29.

3. MD, vi–vii.

4. Malone, *Dictionary of American Biography*, 5:520–21; E. S. Wallace, *The Great Reconnaissance*, 202; Strode, *Jefferson Davis, Confederate President*, 1:11–12.

5. Evans, ed., *Confederate Military History*, 4:612–13; *Annual Reunion*, 1903, 48–50.

6. U.S. Adjutant General's Office, War Department, Case of John P. Sherburne; U.S. War Department, *The War of the Rebellion*, part 2, ser. I, 19:539, 581, 799–800; Heitman, *Historical Register*, 881; Welcher, *The Union Army*, 50–51.

7. IT, 210–11. Henry Rowe Schoolcraft was a prominent explorer, geologist, and ethnologist. His wide acquaintance with Indians led to his appointment as an Indian agent, and he married a quarter-blood Chippewa girl. For the remainder of his life he pursued the subject of the Indian and published many works, which were literary rather than scientific, as was characteristic of the unspecialized anthropological science of the period. Malone, *Dictionary of American Biography*, 16:456–57. Eastman graduated from West Point in 1829 and taught drawing there for several years before serving in the Florida Indian Wars. He worked on Schoolcraft's illustrations from 1853 to 1856 and then served in the office of quartermaster general in Washington. He was brevetted brigadier general for meritorious services during the war. After the war he engaged in painting Indian scenes and views of western forts for the Capitol; he died in 1875. Childs, ed., *Register of Graduates*, 255.

8. IT, 211–12. Thomas Ewbank was born in England and started a career in the trades as a tinsmith, plumber, wire worker, and brass founder. He emigrated to New York and became a manufacturer with marked success. He was appointed commissioner of patents by President Taylor in 1849 and held the office until 1852. Upon his return to private life, he again began traveling and became interested in ethnology. He died in 1870. Malone, *Dictionary of American Biography*, 6:227–28.

9. JCTP, "Genealogy," 130–32.

10. JCTP, "War Period," 20–24, 74, 121–28.

11. JCTP, "Fort Pickens," 206–13.

12. *Annual Reunion*, 1908, 36.

13. JCT, "Artillery Service in the War of the Rebellion," 472; Kirk, *Heavy Guns and Light*, 442–43; Grant, *Personal Memoirs*, 692–93.

14. *Annual Reunion*, 1908, 38; IT, 89–90a.

15. *Report of Journey by General W. T. Sherman in 1883*, 244.

16. *Annual Reunion*, 1908, 37.

Works Cited

Manuscript Sources

Fort Defiance, New Mexico, Returns, September 1851–April 1861. Adjutant General's Office, NA. RG M617.

Records of United States Army Continental Commands, 1821–1920. Letters Sent by the 9th Military Dept. on New Mexico, 1849–1890. Records of the Adjutant General's Office, NA. RG 393, M1072, Roll 1.

Second U.S. Artillery Regiment Returns, January 1851–December 1860. Records of the Adjutant General's Office, NA. RG M744, Roll 12.

Sherburne, John P., case of. Records of the Appointments, Commissions and Personnel Branch, 1775–1917. Records of the Adjutant General's Office, NA. RG 94.

Stanley, David S. "Diary of D. S. Stanley, United States, 2d Dragoons, of a March from Fort Smith, Arkansas to San Diego, California, made in 1853." Archives and Manuscript Division, Oklahoma Historical Society, Oklahoma City. A published version of Stanley's Diary, which ends at the western border of present-day Oklahoma, is Lona Shawver, ed., "Stanley Explores Oklahoma," *Chronicles of Oklahoma* 22 (Autumn 1944): 259–70.

Tidball, John Caldwell. Papers. Manuscript. United States Military Academy Archives, West Point, New York, including memoirs, letters and miscellaneous writings. The memoirs are referred to by chapter title, and miscellaneous writings are referred to by title.

——. Annotated vol. 3 of the *Reports*. Special Collections, The University of Arizona Library, Tucson.

——. "Itinerary." Manuscript, 228 pp. Beinecke Rare Book and Manuscript Library, Yale University, New Haven.

——. "John C. Tidball en route for California." Special Collections, The University of Arizona Library, Tucson. This is a four-by-six-inch leatherbound diary, marked "No. 2," written in pencil, covering the period from January 3 to February 22, 1854, containing several rough maps and sketches.

——. "Mary Hunt Davis." Manuscript, 15 pp., in possession of Gordon Blaker of Augusta, Georgia.

U.S. Military Academy Cadet Application Papers, 1805–1866. Records of the Adjutant General's Office. National Archives. RG 94, M688, Roll 178.

Whipple, Amiel W. Journal. Manuscript. Archives and Manuscripts Division, Oklahoma Historical Society, Oklahoma City. The time covered by the microfilmed material not only includes his journal of the 1853–1854 expedition, but also some earlier notes from 1849, as well as later entries, including his Civil War experiences. The last legible entry is October 18, 1862, but the title to the last segment states that it covers the period through March 4, 1863, two months before Whipple was mortally wounded at Chancellorsville. A published version of Whipple's journal, which ends at the western border of present-day Oklahoma, is Muriel H. Wright and George H. Shirk, "The Journal of Lieutenant A. W. Whipple," *Chronicles of Oklahoma* 27 (Autumn 1950): 235–83.

Books, Articles, and Films

Altshuler, Constance Wynn. *Starting With Defiance: Nineteenth Century Arizona Military Posts.* Tucson: The Arizona State Historical Society, 1983.

American Indian Publishers. *Dictionary of Indian Tribes of the Americas.* 6 vols. Newport Beach, Calif.: Author, 1980.

Anderson, Nels. *Desert Saints, The Mormon Frontier in Utah.* Chicago: University of Chicago Press, 1966.

Annual Reunion of the Association of the Graduates of the United States Military Academy. Saginaw, Mich.: Seeman & Peters, various years.

Arrington, Leonard J., and Thomas G. Alexander. "The U.S. Army Overlooks Salt Lake Valley: Fort Douglas, 1862–1965." *Utah Historical Quarterly* 33, no. 4 (fall 1965): 327–42.

Ball, Durwood. *Army Regulars on the Western Frontier: 1848–1861.* Norman: University of Oklahoma Press, 2001.

Barnes, Will C. *Arizona Place Names.* Tucson: University of Arizona Press, 1970.

——. "Arizona Place Names." *University of Arizona Bulletin,* General Bulletin No. 2, January 1, 1935.

Bergon, Frank, ed. *The Journals of Lewis and Clark.* New York: Penguin Books, 1989.

Boatner, Mark M., III. *The Civil War Dictionary.* New York: David McKay Company, 1998.

Burns, Ken. *The Civil War—A Film by Ken Burns.* Alexandria, Va.: PBS Home Video, 1990.

Calef, John. "A Distinguished Horse Artilleryman." *Journal of the Military Service Institution of the United States* 42 (July–Nov. 1908): 111–27.

Chaffin, Tom. *Pathfinder: John Charles Frémont and the Course of American Empire.* New York: Hill and Wang, 2002.

Chaput, Donald. *Francois X. Aubry: Trader, Trailmaker and Voyageur in the Southwest, 1846–1854.* Glendale, Calif.: The Arthur H. Clark Company, 1975.

Childs, Jr., Paul W., ed. *Register of Graduates and Former Cadets of the United States Military Academy.* West Point, New York: Association of Graduates, 1990.

Coffman, Edward M. *The Old Army.* New York: Oxford University Press, 1986.

Conrad, David E. "The Whipple Expedition in Arizona, 1853–1854." *Arizona and the West* 11 (Summer 1969): 147–78.

——. "The Whipple Expedition on the Great Plains." *Great Plains Journal* 2 (1963): 42–66.

Creer, Leland. "The Explorations of Gunnison and Beckwith in Colorado and Utah, 1885." *The Colorado Magazine* 6, no. 5 (September 1929): 180–92.

Dawdy, Doris Ostrander. *Artists of the American West: A Biographical Dictionary.* Vol. 1. Chicago: The Swallow Press, 1974.

De Mallie, Raymond J., ed. *Lakota Society.* Lincoln: University of Nebraska Press, 1982.

Dippie, Brian W. "Government Patronage: Catlin, Stanley and Eastman." *Montana: The Magazine of Western History* 44 (Autumn 1994): 49.

Engstrand, Iris H. W., and Mary F. Ward. "Rancho Guajome: An Architectural Legacy Preserved." *Journal of San Diego History* 41 (Fall 1995): 250–83.

Evans, Clement, A., ed. *Confederate Military History: A Library of Confederate States History in Seventeen Volumes.* 1899. Reprinted and Extended. Wilmington, N.C.: Broadfoot Publishing Company, 1987–1989.

Faragher, John Mack. *American Heritage Encyclopedia of American History.* New York: Henry Holt and Company, 1998.

Foreman, Grant, ed. *A Pathfinder in the Southwest.* Norman: University of Oklahoma Press, 1941. This work reproduces Whipple's "Itinerary," which is the chronological record of the expedition as found in the *Reports of Explorations and Surveys,* vol. 3, cited below. For convenience, Foreman's book is used to reference the "Itinerary" and is cited rather than the official *Reports,* except in instances where the location of drawings in the *Reports* is required.

Fuller, Theodore W. *San Diego Originals.* Pleasant Hill: California Profiles Publications, 1987.

Funk and Wagnalls New World Encyclopedia. On INFOPEDIA. CD-ROM, Softkey Multimedia.

Gilbert, Bil. *Westering Man: Life of Joseph Walker.* New York: Atheneum, 1983.

Garraty, John A., and Mark C. Carnes, eds. *American National Biography.* New York: Oxford University Press, 1999.

Garraty, John A., and Jerome Sternstein. *Encyclopedia of American Biography.* New York: Harper Collins Publishers, 1996.

Goetzmann, William H. *Army Exploration in the American West, 1803–1863.* New Haven, Conn.: Yale University Press, 1959.

——. *Exploration and Empire.* New York: Alfred A. Knopf, 1966.

Goetzmann, William H., and William N. Goetzmann. *The West of the Imagination.* New York: W. W. Norton & Company, 1986.

Gordon, Mary McDougall, ed. *Through Indian Country to California: John P. Sherburne's Diary of the Whipple Expedition, 1853, 1854.* Stanford, Calif.: Stanford University Press, 1988.

Granger, Byrd Howell. *Arizona Names (X Marks the Place).* Tucson: The Falconer Publishing Company, 1983.

Grant, Ulysses S. *Personal Memoirs.* 1885. Reprint. New York: The Library of America, 1960.

Harpers New Monthly Magazine 17 (September 1858).

Heitman, Francis B. *Historical Register and Dictionary of the United States Army.* Vol. 1. Urbana: University of Illinois Press, 1965.

Hubbell, John T., and James W. Geary, eds. *Biographical Dictionary of the Union.* Westport, Conn.: Greenwood Press, 1995.

Huseman, Ben W. *Wild River, Timeless Canyons: Balduin Möllhausen's Watercolors of the Colorado.* Tucson: University of Arizona Press, 1995.

Kearney, T. H., and R. H. Peebles. *Arizona Flora.* Berkeley: University of California Press, 1960.

Kirk, Hyland C. *Heavy Guns and Light: A History of the Fourth New York Heavy Artillery.* New York: C. T. Dillingham, 1890.

Kroeber, A. L. *Mohave Indians.* New York: Garland Publishing, 1974.

Malone, Dumas, ed. *Dictionary of American Biography.* 22 vols. New York: Charles Scribner's Sons, 1928–1958.

McCullouch, David. *The Path Between the Seas.* New York: Simon and Schuster, 1977.

McKanna, Clare V. Jr. " 'An Old Town Gunfight': The Homicide Trial of Cave Johnson Couts, 1866," *Journal of San Diego History* 44 (Fall 1998): 258–73.

McMullin, Thomas, and Walker, David. *Biographical Directory of American Territorial Governors.* Westport, Conn.: Meckler Publishing, 1984.

Miller, David H. "A Prussian on the Plains: Balduin Möllhausen's Impressions." *Great Plains Journal* 12 (Spring 1973): 175–93.

Möllhausen, Heinrich Balduin. *Diary of a Journey from the Mississippi to the Coasts of the Pacific.* 2 vols. Introduction by Peter A. Frizell. New York: Johnson Reprint Corporation, 1969.

Morris, John Miller. *El Llano Estacado: Exploration and Imagination on the High Plains of Texas and New Mexico.* Texas State Historical Association, 1997.

Morrison, Jr., James L. *"The Best School": West Point, 1833–1866.* Kent, Ohio: The Kent State University Press, 1998.

——, ed. "Getting Through West Point: The Cadet Memoirs of John C. Tidball, Class of 1848." *Civil War History* 26 (December 1980): 304–25.

Mumey, Nolie. "John Williams Gunnison: Centenary of His Survey and Tragic Death (1853–1953)." *Colorado Magazine* 31 (January 1954): 19–32.

Nevins, Allan. *Ordeal of the Union,* Vol. 1, *Fruits of Manifest Destiny, 1847–1852.* New York: Charles Scribner's Sons, 1947.

——. *Ordeal of the Union,* Vol. 2, *A House Dividing, 1852–1857.* New York: Charles Scribner's Sons, 1947.

Nicandri, David L. *Gustav Sohon's Views of the 1855 Stevens Treaty Councils.* Tacoma: Washington State Historical Society, 1986.

Norris, L. David, James C. Milligan, and Odie B. Faulk. *William H. Emory: Soldier-Scientist.* Tucson: University of Arizona Press, 1998.

Novak, Barbara. *Nature and Culture: American Landscape and Painting, 1825–1875.* New York: Oxford University Press, 1980.

Ortiz, Alfonso, ed. *Handbook of North American Indians,* Vol. 10, *Southwest.* Washington D.C.: Smithsonian Institution, 1983.

Quaife, Milo Milton, ed. *The Diary of James K. Polk.* Chicago: A. C. McClurg & Co., 1910.

Richards, Kent D. *Isaac I. Stevens: Young Man in a Hurry.* Provo, Utah: Brigham Young University Press, 1979.

Scharf, Thomas C. "Amiel Whipple and the Boundary Survey in Southern California [1849]." *Journal of San Diego History* 19 (1973): 18–31.

Slotten, Hugh Richard. *Patronage, Practice and the Culture of American Science: Alexander Dallas Bache and the U.S. Coast Survey.* Cambridge University Press: 1994.

Stanley, David S. *Personal Memoirs of Major-General D. S. Stanley.* Cambridge: Harvard University Press, 1917.

Stegmaier, Mark J., and David H. Miller. *James F. Milligan: His Journal of Frémont's Fifth Expedition, 1853–1854; His Adventurous Life on Land and Sea.* Glendale, Calif.: The Arthur Clark Company, 1988.

Stoddard, Francis R. "Amiel Weeks Whipple," *Chronicles of Oklahoma* 27 (Autumn 1950): 225–34.

Strode, Hudson. *Jefferson Davis, Confederate President.* 3 Vols. New York: Harcourt Brace and Company, 1964.

Sturtevant, William, C., ed. *Handbook of North American Indians.* Vol. 10, edited by Alfonso Ortiz. Washington, D.C.: Smithsonian Institution, 1983.

Swanton, John R. "The Indian Tribes of North America." *Smithsonian Institution Bureau of American Ethnology Bulletin 145.* Washington, D.C.: USGPO, 1952.

Taft, Robert. *Artists and Illustrators of the Old West.* Princeton, N.J.: Princeton University Press, 1953.

Tate, Michael L. *The Frontier Army in the Settlement of the West.* Norman: University of Oklahoma Press, 1999.

Thompson, Gerald. *The Army and the Navajo.* Tucson: The University of Arizona Press, 1976.

Tidball, Eugene C. "In the Footsteps of Lewis and Clark: The Northern Route of the 1853 Pacific Railroad Survey." *Military History of the West* 28, no. 2 (Fall 1998): 125–60.

——. *No Disgrace to My Country: The Life of John C. Tidball.* Kent, Ohio: Kent State University Press, 2002.

Tidball, John C. "The Artillery Service in the War of the Rebellion, 1861–1865." *The Journal of the Military Service Institution of the United States* 13 (May 1892): 466–90.

Utley, Robert. *The Lance and the Shield: The Life and Times of Sitting Bull.* New York: Ballantine Books, 1993.

Webster's New Biographical Dictionary. On INFOPEDIA. CD-ROM, Softkey Multimedia, Inc.

Waldman, Carl. *Who Was Who in Native American History: Indians and Non-Indians from Early Contacts Through 1900.* New York: Facts on File, 1990.

Walker, James R. *Lakota Society.* Edited by Raymond J. DeMallie. Lincoln: University of Nebraska Press, 1982.

Wallace, Andrew. "Across Arizona to the Big Colorado: The Sitgreaves Expedition of 1851." *Arizona and the West* 26 (1984): 325–64.

Wallace, Edward S. *The Great Reconnaissance.* Boston: Little Brown and Company, 1955.

Weir, Irene. *Robert A. Weir, Artist.* New York: House of Field, Doubleday, 1947.

Welcher, Frank J. *The Union Army; 1861–1865: Organization and Operations,* Vol. I, *The Eastern Theater.* Bloomington: Indiana University Press, 1989.

Woodward, Arthur. "Irrataba—'Chief of the Mohave.'" *Plateau,* 25 (January 1953): 53–68.

The Wordsworth Dictionary of Biography. Hertfordshire, U.K.: Helicon Publishing, 1994.

Wright, Muriel H., and George H. Shirk. "The Journal of Lieutenant A. W. Whipple." *Chronicles of Oklahoma* 27 (Autumn 1950): 235–83.

Government Publications

Coast Survey. *Report of the Superintendent of the Coast Survey during the Year 1855.* 34th Cong., 1st sess., 1856. S. Doc. 22, serial 826.

Office of Explorations and Surveys. *Report upon the Colorado River of the West Explored in 1857 and 1858 by Lieutenant Joseph C. Ives.* 36th Cong., 1st sess., 1861. S. Doc. 90, serial 1058.

Pacific Railroad Reports. In *Reports of Explorations and Surveys to Ascertain the Most Practicable and Economical Route for a Railroad from the Mississippi River to the Pacific Ocean.*

Pierce, Franklin. *Message from the President of the United States to the Two Houses of Congress.* 33d Cong., 1st sess., Dec 6, 1853. H Doc. 1, serial 710.

"Report on the Botany of the Expedition." In *Reports of Explorations and Surveys to Ascertain the Most Practicable and Economical Route for a Railroad from the Mississippi River to the Pacific Ocean.* Vol. 4. 33d Cong., 2d sess., 1856. S. Doc. 78, serial 761, and H. Doc. 91, serial 794.

"Report on the Topographical Features and Character of the Country." In *Reports of Explorations and Surveys to Ascertain the Most Practicable and Economical Route for a Railroad from the Mississippi River to the Pacific Ocean.* Part 2, vol. 3, 33d Cong., 2d sess., 1856. S. Doc 78, serial 760, and H. Doc. 91, serial 793.

Reports of Explorations and Surveys to Ascertain the Most Practicable and Economical Route for a Railroad from the Mississippi River to the Pacific Ocean, 1853–54. Vol. 1, 33d Cong., 2d sess., 1855. H. Doc. 91, serial 791.

Reports of Explorations and Surveys to Ascertain the Most Practicable and Economical Route for a Railroad from the Mississippi River to the Pacific Ocean. Vol. 3, 33d Cong., 2d sess., 1856. S. Doc. 78, serial 760, and H. Doc. 91, serial 793.

Reports of Explorations and Surveys to Ascertain the Most Practicable and Economical Route for a Railroad from the Mississippi River to the Pacific Ocean. Vol. 4, 33d Cong., 2d sess., 1856. S. Doc. 78.

Reports of Explorations and Surveys to Ascertain the Most Practicable and Economical Route for a Railroad from the Mississippi River to the Pacific Ocean. Book 1, Vol. 12, 36th Cong., 1st sess., 1860. H. Doc. 56, serial 1054.

Tidball, John C. *Report of Journey Made by General W. T. Sherman in the Northwest and Middle Parts of the United States, 1883.* In *Report of the General of the Army to the Secretary of War,* 48th Cong., 1st sess., 1883. H. Doc. 1, part 2, serial 2182.

U.S. Congress. *Congressional Globe,* 35th Cong., 2d sess. (January 6, 1859).
U.S. Department of War. *Report of the Secretary of War.* 31st Cong., 2d sess., 1851. S. Doc. 26, serial 589.
———. *Report of the Secretary of War.* 32d Cong., 2d sess., 1852. S. Doc. 1, serial 659.
———. *Report of the Secretary of War.* 33d Cong., 1st sess., 1853. H. Doc. 1, serial 711.
———. *The War of the Rebellion: A Compilation of the Official Records of the Union and Confederate Armies.* 128 vols., with supplements. Washington. D.C.: GPO, 1880–1901.

Unpublished Sources

Huseman, Ben Wayne. "Romanticism and the Scientific Aesthetic: Balduin Möllhausen's Artistic Development and the Images of the Whipple Expedition." M.A. thesis, University of Texas at Austin, 1992.
Mangiante, Rosal. "History of Fort Defiance, 1851–1900." M.A. thesis, University of Arizona, 1950.
Miller, David H. "The Impact of the Gunnison Massacre on Mormon-Federal Relations: Colonel Edward Jenner Steptoe's Command in Utah Territory, 1954–1855." M.A. Thesis, University of Utah, 1968.
Tidball, Barbara. (comp.). "The Tidball Family History in the United States," typescript, 484 pp., in possession of the author, 1986.
Wallace, Andrew. "Where Was New Year's Spring?" Paper presented at the 1993 Annual Arizona Historical Convention in Nogales, Arizona.

Figure Credits

Arizona Historical Society/Tucson

Amiel Weeks Whipple. AHS no. 28835
Balduin Möllhausen. AHS no. 53041
Fort Defiance, 1860. AHS no. 62068

Beinecke Rare Book and Manuscript Library, Yale University

Dr. Bigelow's Moment of Triumph
The Mule of Total Depravity
Irrataba

Library of Congress

Officers of Battery A, Second Artillery. Photograph by James F. Gibson

Pacific Railroad Reports at the Arizona Historical Society/Tucson

San Francisco Mountain
Black Forest, Pichaco, and Mountains North of Aztec Pass
View of Aztec Pass
Bivouac, Jan. 26
Bivouac, Jan. 28
Cereus Giganteus, on Bill Williams Fork
Valley of Bill Williams Fork
Artillery Peak
Cañon of Bill Williams Fork
Camp Scene in the Mojave Valley of the Rio Colorado

Mojave Dwelling
Valley of the Mojave

**United States Military Archives. United States Military Academy,
West Point, New York**

John C. Tidball

Index

vations on travel by, 32, 43–44, 93–94, 106–7, 157, 177–78, 188n. 19; opinions of, 24; report illustrations by, 108, 136, 138, 145, 147, 191nn. 18, 19, 199n. 19, 202n. 13, 203n. 10; on the route of the expedition, 36, 44, 113; Tidball's illustrations attributed to, 86–87, 96, 117–18, 136, 194n. 9, 197n. 3, 200n. 8, 203n. 10; as a topographer and naturalist, 19, 108, 124

Moqui (Hopi), 47

Mormons, 153–56, 158, 159, 183, 204n. 23

Mormon Trail, *34,* 144, 153

Mount Taylor, 48

Mullan, Lt. John, 33, 84, 85

Münchhausen, Baron Karl Friedrich Hieronymus, 194n. 3

Nacogdoches (Tex.), 4

Navajos, 5, 28, 44, 48, 50, 51–52, 54, 83, 86, 193n. 14

Nebraska Territory, 16

Needles (Calif.), 124

New Mexico Territory, 13, 67; military presence in, 28–29, *34,* 40, 44, 189n. 27, 192n. 14; 35th Parallel survey expedition in, *34–35,* 42–44, 45–50

New Year's Spring, 34, 78, 88, 195n. 2, 197n. 15

New York Heavy Artillery, 183

North, sectionalism and, 4, 8, 58, 60, 61

Northwest Passage, 3

ocotillo. *See* cactus

Office of Explorations and Surveys, 9, 16, 199n. 7

Office of Indian Affairs, 18

Office of Pacific Railroad Explorations and Surveys, 19, 21

Oglethorpe Barracks (Savannah, Ga.), 26

Ojo del Oso Pass, 64

Oklahoma, 30. *See also* Indian Territory

Old Cap, 130

109th Meridian, 50

Pacific railroad, 4, 7, 16, 183–84. *See also* transcontinental railroad

Pacific railroad surveys, xi, 7–8, 83, 84, 173–74; artists and, 79–80, 82–87, 196n. 7, 199n. 7

Paiutes, 45, 48, 83, 146, 149, 151, 153–55

Panama, 167–68

Parke, Lt. John G., 6, 9–10, 193n. 2

Parke, Thomas H., 65, 72, 73

Peale, Titian, 81

Pecos River, 17

Pennington, Lt. Alexander C. M., *182*

Perry, Stephen, 33

Phoenix, John, 162

Pierce, Pres. Franklin, 7, 39

Pike, Lt. Zebulon, 3

Pimas, 9

pitahaya, 199n. 17

Polk, Pres. James K., 10, 26, 187n. 17, 189n. 23

Pope, Capt. John, 9–10

Prudhomme, Leon V., 160

Pueblo Indians, 51

Purtes, Mary, 105

Quapaws, 36

railroads, xi, 15–16, 24, 160–61, 168, 195n. 9, 201n. 9

Raousset–Bolubon, Count Gaston Raoun de, 166, 205n. 17

Red River, 9, 38

Reports of Explorations and Surveys: artists' contributions to, 80, 86–87, 145, 174–75, 191n. 19; lithographs in, 68–70, *69,* 96, *97,* 105, *106,* 136, *137,* 194n. 9; preparation of illustrations for, 198n. 4, 199–200n. 7; publication of, xi, 169, 173–74; Tidball's comments on, 78–79, 95, 146, 176, 195n. 11; Tidball's illustrations in, 94, 96,

Index / 223

About the Author

Eugene C. Tidball is a graduate of the University of Montana School of Law. His writing has recently been published in numerous journals, including *Montana: The Magazine of Western History*, *The Journal of Arizona History*, *Colorado History*, *Military History of the West*, and *Civil War History*. His biography of John C. Tidball, *No Disgrace to My Country*, was a finalist for the Army Historical Foundation's 2002 Distinguished Writing Award in the Biography/Autobiography category. John C. Tidball's uncle, James Tidball, is the author's great-great-grandfather. In the arcane language of genealogy, this means that the author and John Tidball are first cousins, three times removed. Tidball lives in the mountains west of Boulder, Colorado, with his wife and dog.